Praise for David Fagen: Turncoat Hero

"If you have never heard of David Fagen as American "turncoat hero," grab this fabulous account of his exploits as a "Buffalo Soldier" who joined the Filipino guerrillas resisting U.S. bloody pacification of the Philippines in the beginning of the twentieth century. It is filled with new discoveries nuanced by the multiple perspectives of diverse observers, witnesses, and survivors. But this is not just one man's story. Hoffman uses a versatile protagonist as vantage point to sketch the panorama of the ceaseless struggle of Filipinos, African-Americans, and ordinary citizens against racial, class, and colonial bondage. Hoffman frames Fagen's exemplary life in the contemporary context of the global war against religious extremism and the terrorizing drug wars worldwide. He thus reminds us of the lessons of the Philippine-American War (1899-1903), about the value of cross-cultural solidarity, secular-democratic humanism, and the critical questioning of official versions of history. A timely, brave achievement, and a necessary guidebook in understanding the fraught U.S.-Philippine relations today!"
-**Dr. E. San Juan, Jr.,** professorial lecturer, Polytechnic University of the Philippines, Manila; author, *U.S.Imperialism and Revolution in the Philippines*; *Beyond Postcolonial Theory*, and other works.

"*David Fagen: Turncoat Hero* is a book that transcends the life of its main character. It is a story of imperialism, racism, and resistance. But it is equally a compelling story of the conflict within Black America as to our relationship to the very system itself. Despite knowing how the story would conclude, I kept hoping for a different ending, a sure sign that this book captured my imagination."
-**Bill Fletcher, Jr.,** Author, labor union activist, former senior staff person of the AFL-CIO, former president of Trans-Africa Forum, a Senior Scholar at the Institute for Policy Studies, and editorial board member of BlackCommentator.com.

"To understand history, one needs to understand the values that historic characters bring to the decision-making process (their values are different than ours because they lived in different times and circumstances). One needs to have a very clear, articulate understanding of their own values in order to evaluate choices made in the past. That is exactly what the Fagen book does."
-**Larry L. Nelson,** former chief administrator of Fort Meigs State Memorial in Perrysburg, Ohio, and an assistant professor of history at Bowling Green State University, author and editor of five books and writer of several articles on topics relating to Ohio history and military history, and a former site manager of Fort Meigs State Memorial.

DAVID FAGEN
Turncoat Hero

PHILLIP W. HOFFMAN

AMERICAN HISTORY PRESS
STAUNTON VIRGINIA

Copyright © 2017 Phillip W. Hoffman

All rights reserved. No part of this book may be transmitted in any form by any means electronic, mechanical or otherwise using devices now existing or yet to be invented without prior written permission from the publisher and copyright holder.

Staunton, Virginia
(888) 521-1789
Visit us on the Internet at:
www.Americanhistorypress.com

First Printing September 2017
Cover design by Louise A. Donahoe

To schedule an event with the author, or to inquire about bulk discount sales, please contact American History Press.

Library of Congress Cataloging-in-Publication Data

Names: Hoffman, Phillip W., 1936- author.
Title: David Fagen : turncoat hero / Phillip W. Hoffman.
Description: Staunton, Virginia : American History Press, 2017. | Includes bibliographical references and index.
Identifiers: LCCN 2017033019 (print) | LCCN 2017033048 (ebook) | ISBN 9781939995261 (eBook) | ISBN 9781939995254 (pbk. : alk. paper)
Subjects: LCSH: Fagen, David, 1875-1901. | Philippines--History--Philippine American War, 1899-1902--Collaborationists. |
Philippines--History--Philippine American War, 1899-1902--Participation, African American. | Philippines--History--Philippine American War, 1899-1902--Biography. | United States. Army. Infantry Regiment, 24th--Biography. | African American soldiers--Biography. |
Soldiers--United States--Biography. | Traitors--United States--Biography.
Classification: LCC DS682 (ebook) | LCC DS682 .H64 2017 (print) | DDC 959.9/031 [B] --dc23
LC record available at https://lccn.loc.gov/2017033019

Manufactured in the United States of America on acid-free paper.
This book exceeds all ANSO standards for archival quality.

This book is dedicated with admiration and affection to author-lecturer Anthony L. Powell, Jr., America's foremost authority on the history of the Buffalo Soldiers. Tony's knowledge of Fagen and the 24th Infantry Regiment (USCT), his advice, his wondrous Buffalo Soldier photo collection, and his constant, cheerful encouragement have been invaluable.

This book is equally dedicated to Luana, the black nurse whom I loved when I was six, and whom I have never forgotten.

TABLE OF CONTENTS

Prologue   iv

1. Jim Crow Tampa   1
2. Deadly Racism Divides US Troops   54
3. Voyage of the Damned   50
4. Quit Yourselves Like Men and Fight   75
5. The Double-Cross   98
6. We Don't Need No White Officers   111
7. The Nigger War   130
8. Victims   154
9. Payback and Audacity   167
10. Fagen's Fate   203

Epilogue   218
Acknowledgements   232
Bibliography   235
Index   238
About the Author   249

PROLOGUE

TWO STORIES WILL UNFOLD in the following pages. One relates the adventures of David Fagen, an African-American soldier who was born in Tampa, Florida in 1878. Twenty years later, seeking to escape from the terrors of the Jim Crow South, he joined the 24th Infantry Regiment, USCT (United States Colored Troops), and enlisted as a Buffalo Soldier. Five days later Fagen found himself onboard a troop transport that was destined to carry him to the shores of Santiago, Cuba, and the opening battle of the Spanish-American War.

More than a third of the population of Santiago was black. Unfortunately for them, three-fourths of the American troops who would come ashore to fight the Spaniards were white. Accordingly, Fagen and his fellow Buffalo Soldiers were afforded the opportunity to witness the latest variety of exported American racism. And this was only the beginning.

In 1899, Fagen's regiment shipped out for the Philippine Islands, to fight in what most of the American soldiers who were already there were calling *The Nigger War*. Six months later, having made up his mind to renounce his participation in white racism and U.S. imperialism, Fagen rode off to join the army of his country's enemies. A well-trained American combat veteran, Fagen's knowledge of U.S. infantry tactics helped the Filipino freedom fighters resist and stay alive. Appreciative of his help, they rewarded him with a lieutenant's commission.

For the first time in his life, twenty-one-year-old Fagen was living in a world where he was no longer despised for being black. The Filipinos were fast becoming his people and they would engage in the war together.

The second story tells how, desiring recognition as a major player in a world where the English, French, Dutch, Spanish, Portuguese and Belgians ruled colonies in countries they had conquered, the United States turned

PROLOGUE

to imperialism. By 1896, the growing strength of the Cuban rebels who were fighting for their independence from Spain had caught America's attention. The Spaniards were losing, and one of the issues American leaders considered was the fact that a very large segment of Cuba's citizens were black. Haiti was a black country and the U.S. did not welcome the idea of another colored government in the Western Hemisphere.

As things turned out, Washington, D.C.'s decision to put an end to Spanish colonialism in Cuba was propelled by a combination of racism and the predatory desires of Big Business.

Immediately following the American victory in Cuba, in a stunning double-cross of their former allies, the U.S. made a promise to Spain to bar any representatives of the Cuban Revolutionary Army from attending the formal surrender ceremony in Santiago City. The action was a terrible shock to the Cuban freedom fighters whose heroic and strategic fighting before and after the invasion had been instrumental in achieving a final victory.

With Cuba now firmly in its grasp, America's next adventure in voracious imperialism began when its Pacific navy squadron was ordered to attack the Spanish fleet anchored in Manila Bay. In one audacious stroke Commodore George Dewey slipped his ships inside the bay late one night before the enemy vessels could build-up steam. The entire Spanish navy was sent to the bottom.

Ashore, the beleaguered Spanish army forces had already been confined to a few strongholds by the Philippine Army of Independence, whose numbers had dramatically increased with each success. One by one the besieged Spanish fortresses had been falling and now, without any ships with which to restore their supplies, the outcome was assured.

After a brief period of pretending to ally and support the Filipino struggle for independence, during which time American forces slipped thousands of troops ashore in Manila, the U.S. accepted the Spanish surrender. The U.S. Army then turned on their former allies and ordered the Philippine Army of Liberation to lay down their arms and swear loyalty to Old Glory.

Thirsting for freedom and independence after having suffered under one colonial power for three centuries, the Filipinos weren't about to bow down to another. Only war would decide the issue.

I hope these two connected stories—that of Fagen and that of the Americans and Filipinos during the Philippine-American War—prove as interesting and exciting to you as they were to me.

What caused me to chase Fagen's story was my interest in understanding why soldiers desert and join their former enemies.

Soldiers desert during wartime for various reasons: fear, thirst or hunger, exhaustion, distrust of their superiors, or rejection by their comrades-in-arms. Sometimes they quit because they no longer see any point to the conflict. Much to the chagrin of rabid nationalists, patriotism has little if any bearing on a deserter's decisions.

Defection is another matter. Most often, when a traitor takes up arms against his former comrades, his action is the result of a lengthy, stressful and soul-searching personal battle, an ethical dilemma. He or she switches sides because they conclude that it's the the correct and just thing to do. The dangers of such a decision are overwhelming. Once made, there is no going back. The opposite of self-righteous "my-country-right-or-wrong" patriots, turncoats who defect because they believe it's *the right thing to do* meet every definition of a hero. Despite overwhelming odds, they are determined to fight and die for what they truly believe.

To be frank, as a writer and historian I'm addicted to finding out more about people who defect, believing their actions are morally justified. Count Claus Schenk Graf von Stauffenberg, the decorated German officer who tried to assassinate Hitler during World War II, comes to mind. No question that von Stauffenberg and his co-conspirators believed that murdering Hitler was the right thing to do for Germany and the world. Unfortunately, the plot failed and von Stauffenberg paid the ultimate price.

Twenty years of my life were spent researching the true story of the life of one of America's earliest turncoats, the seemingly notorious Simon Girty. A notable frontiersman, Girty defected in the middle of the Revolutionary War to fight with Indian allies of the King of England against his former countrymen. For over two centuries, Girty's name was high on the list of infamous American traitors and renegade outlaws. He was vilified academically, militarily and congressionally, and accused of being both a

PROLOGUE

traitor to his nation and to his race. The thing was, Girty's real loyalty was neither to the American rebel cause nor to King George, but rather to the Indian nations of the Ohio Valley, including those who had adopted and raised him.

Both Simon Girty and the subject of this book, David Fagen, defected from the American military and ended up fighting their former comrades because of a moral conviction which prompted them to do what they thought was ethically and morally correct.

Girty defected because he understood the true goals of America's rebel leaders regarding the frontier—as soon as the King had been defeated it was their intention to destroy the Native Americans across the Ohio River and "civilize" their lands by overrunning them.

To the Native Americans living in the Ohio Valley, Simon Girty was a hero. And to the Filipino freedom fighters devoting their lives to Philippine independence, so was David Fagen.

Like Girty's true story, Fagen's is also one we ought to know.

Phillip W. Hoffman
Pace, Florida
September 2017

PLEASE NOTE: *Portions of this book consist of quoted original material. In an effort to retain authenticity and accuracy, the quotes have not been altered or corrected for spelling or grammar.*

◄ Chapter One ►

JIM CROW TAMPA

Downtown Tampa, Early Evening, 6 June 1898

MAYBE SHE FIGURED the drunken white soldiers wouldn't harass her if she was carrying her two-year-old child, but she was wrong.

A mob of Ohio Volunteers surrounded the black woman on a main street located in the Fort Brooke garrison area, near Ybor City, where two Ohio regiments were encamped. The street was rife with saloons and whorehouses and the men had been "recreating." The soldiers man-handled her and made lewd remarks.

One of the soldiers pulled her child from her arms and, holding both its feet in one hand, suspended the infant upside down while walking out in the roadway. There was a wooden roof shingle lying in the street and he picked it up with his one free hand. He stopped halfway across the road and turned back to face his pals. Then he whacked the child's bottom with the shingle. The child screamed, its mother did likewise, and the soldiers laughed.

According to the *Tampa Tribune* of Wednesday, June 8, 1898:

> ...The child was then held at arm's length, by the feet with head down, and the man holding it called to another to shoot at it. The man with the pistol might have been a good shot and had no intention of hitting the child, but the escape was a close one. The bullet from his revolver passed through the child's night dress, grazing its arm.
>
> Satisfied, the soldiers returned the wailing child to its mother. A man who saw the whole affair said yesterday, that the men

implicated wore the uniforms of the Ohio Volunteers.[1]

At the time of the incident, there were approximately 3,000 African-American, or "Buffalo" soldiers encamped in Tampa. After being refused service at most Tampa businesses, saloons and whorehouses, these frustrated and angry men chose to remain at their camps rather than provoke confrontations. News of the outrageous molestation of the black mother and child spread fast and detonated whatever reserve had prevented the men of the 24th and 25th Infantry Regiments U.S.C.T. (U.S. Colored Troops) from expressing their anger. The greatest race riot that young Tampa and its five-man police force had ever experienced was about to begin.

It's common knowledge that black Africans were first brought to the New World as slaves, but few people know why. The importation of African captives to the New World began early in the 16th century, when Spanish colonists in the Caribbean realized that the thousands of local natives they had planned to do all the hard work on their plantations were dying from both cruelty and from the diseases the Europeans and their animals had introduced.

Long before the Spaniards invaded, the Indians of the Caribbean had become chronically infected with *Plasmodium vivax* malaria, which in turn had left them vulnerable to a myriad of newly introduced European diseases. The black West Africans that the Spaniards subsequently brought to the western hemisphere had a genetic immunity to *vivax* malaria, linked to the sickle cell trait. Their captors, of course, could not possibly have comprehended the underlying science of their new strategy; nevertheless, it was this gene that protected the newly-arrived black slaves from endemic malaria. West Africans were far more suitable as slaves than the Native Americans. To the Spanish, enslaving and then working Africans was a logical, profit-driven business decision.[2]

David Fagen's parents had been born into slavery. Although David was born a freedman as a result of the conclusion of the Civil War, he was anything but equal in the eyes of the whites who dominated turn-of-the-century Florida.

W.E.B. Du Bois, the great black American author and activist, described his feelings as a child in the 1860s when he discovered that he was different:

> ...It is in the early days of rollicking boyhood that the revelation first bursts upon one, all in a day, as it were. I remember well when the shadow swept across me. I was a little thing, away up in the hills of New England, where the dark Housatonic winds between Hoosac and Taghkanic to the sea. [Great Barrington, Massachusetts] In a wee wooden schoolhouse, something put it into the boys' and girls' heads to buy gorgeous visiting cards—ten cents a package—and exchange. The exchange was merry, till one girl, a tall newcomer, refused my card—refused it peremptorily, with a glance. Then it dawned upon me with a certain suddenness that I was different from the others; or like mayhap, in heart and life and longing, but shut out from their world by a vast veil. I had thereafter no desire to tear down that veil, to creep through; I held all beyond it in common contempt, and lived above it in a region of blue sky and great wandering shadows. That sky was bluest when I could beat my mates at examination time, or beat them in a foot race, or even beat their stringy heads.
> - W.E.B. Du Bois *The Souls of Black Folk* [3]

As shocking as his sudden awareness of what being "different" meant for young W.E.B. Du Bois, Great Barrington, Massachusetts is literally and figuratively a long, long way from the Scrub—the black shanty town ghetto in Tampa, Florida where David Fagen, the sixth and last child of Sam and Sylvia Fagen, was born in 1878. And while they shared the same skin color, coming into this world as a black male in Tampa in the last quarter of the nineteenth century presented challenges to David Fagen that were considerably more difficult than anything the young Du Bois had faced.[4] As an adult, Du Bois became one of America's great black authors and lecturers. He was an articulate, tireless and fearless foe of racism, and a fighter who spent the majority of his adult life striking back with powerful and moving words.

Poor and uneducated, David Fagen fought against racism with bullets.

The Scrub. (*Courtesy Tampa Bay History Center*)

The Scrub

Tampa in 1880 was a lonely outpost of a city situated adjacent to the finest harbor on the Gulf Coast, and was home to 720 people, of whom 274 were black.[5] Located on the edge of Tampa, the 39-acre neighborhood called the Scrub—after the scrub palmetto that grew in wild profusion there—was a crowded mishmash of tiny wooden shacks and shanties. Crisscrossed by unpaved roads and alleys, it lacked running water and sewers, and was the home of some of the poorest inhabitants of the region. Initially inhabited by Cubans, West Indian refugees and freed black slaves during the early 1800s, the prevalent language of the Scrub was a spicy jargon of English, Spanish and ancient African dialects. By the time of David Fagen's birth, the area had become a congested slum, and an important reservoir of cheap, black laborers essential to the builders, developers and other growing businesses of early Tampa.

Sam and Sylvia Fagen, Tampa, October, 1878

Thirty-two years old and in his prime, David's father Samuel had been

Boy with Scrub Palmetto, plant from which the town derived its name. (*Courtesy Tampa Bay History Center*)

born in North Carolina in 1846 to parents who were probably natives of Virginia. Sam was a wily salvager, scavenger-trader, repairman, fisherman, and sometimes-laborer. By the standards of most of the African Americans then living in Florida, he apparently knew a lot more than just how to "get by." Sam was acutely aware of the role assigned to his kind under Jim Crow rules, and he was good enough at it to own a horse, feed and clothe his large family, and to aspire to owning his own home someday.[6]

Prior to thirty-six-year-old Sylvia's current marriage to Sam, she had been briefly married to (or lived with) a man whose surname was Douglas. Sylvia's nine-year-old son Jim and her eight-year-old boy George were the result of that earlier arrangement. The Federal Census of 1870 lists her as a black, twenty-eight-year-old farm laborer from Georgia, and, like Sam, she had undoubtedly been born a slave. In May of 1872 she had married Sam Fagen, in Hillsborough County, Florida, and in time had given birth to Charles, Louisa, Alice, Joseph, William and finally David. Altogether she now had eight youngsters to mother, and Sam had a total of ten bellies to feed.[7]

Samuel Fagen was nineteen years old when the Civil War ended in 1865, and it appears that he migrated to Florida shortly thereafter. These were trying times for former slaves, as the following story attests:

> My paternal grandfather …he was, I think, 17 when the war was over. He lived in Hoke County [North Carolina] between Laurinburg and Raeford and Fayetteville and Red Springs and Aberdeen. He said that the Yankees came through and just swept anything they wanted to, because they had won. He said that they [the slave owners] called him and said, "Dave, I want you to keep the horses." It's a place we call Lumber River; it's not a river, but there's water and a bridge there and everything. Said, "I want you to keep them down here." And all the white people in there, the white men, brought their best horses—because the Yankees, as you know, were riding through, just taking them—and gave them to Dave. Said, "Dave, you keep them quiet now." He had them down at Lumber River, this place you can go to, you wouldn't see the horses. It's sand all around. It could have been a beach if you had somebody to do it, you know. Because we look at it now when we go to Laurinburg, say, "Dave was down there with the horses." He had a gang of horses, all the best that these people had, because the Yankees would ride through and just take them.
>
> My grandfather was listening. He could hear them coming, hear the Yankees coming, because they was making a lot of noise. They had won and they were taking things. He said he just waited. He had on a white shirt. So he took it off and he was down there with the horses. He heard them hit the bridge, a long bridge over Lumber River. He took off, took his white shirt, and he stopped them right there. He said, "Come over here and get all these horses." They went down there, and every man took one, and he rode off with them. He knew he had to go or [the Confederates] would have killed him.
>
> - Ila Jacuth Blue, in *Remembering Jim Crow*[8]

To Sam and the thousands of his fellow "freedmen" in the South who suddenly found themselves on their own without shelter, food, clothing or work, the true freedom promised at the end of the Civil War quickly faded into distant memory. In 1866, Florida's legislature was composed of delegates who had spent their lives as members of the dominant white class in a society whose labor system was based on racial chattel slavery. Within this political framework the Black Codes that established segregation were swiftly enacted.

The men who created these codes believed "that blacks were so mentally inferior and incompetent to order their own affairs that subjection to the superior white race was their natural condition." Post Civil War segregation in the South was conceived of and promoted by rich white farmers and businessmen. It was means to divide poor white and black farmers who might otherwise unite on the basis of their common class interests to overthrow the political and economic hegemony of the South's elite. In order to lend definition to a separate, inferior class of citizenship for blacks, laws were created that governed crime and punishment, vagrancy, apprenticeship, marriage, taxation, and labor contracts. These new laws became the basis of the Black Codes that would endure long after reconstruction.[9]

Deemed outrageous by Washington, D.C. and the North in general, the 1866 Florida Black Codes resulted in a Federal backlash that ushered in martial law and the "carpetbagger" era, all of which failed in one way or another to bring genuine freedom to former slaves like the Fagens. Although most of the new laws were eliminated from the official criminal justice system, the unofficial codes of segregation were nonetheless enforced by white mobs or night-riding bands of hooded horsemen. Blacks were threatened, and if the threats went unheeded, victims were ambushed, beaten, tortured, lynched or shot. The burgeoning violence was not, however, strictly limited to blacks; it also included white Republicans who had advocated for equal justice since the end of the Civil War. "Dozens of white Republicans and Negroes were assassinated throughout the Florida black belt from Jackson County on the Apalachicola River to Columbia County on the Suwannee and southward to Gainesville. In Jackson County alone between 1868 and 1871 more than 150 persons were killed."[10]

At the time of David Fagen's birth, poll taxes and the use of separate ballot boxes for every name on a ballot (necessitating the ability to read in order to properly cast one's vote) were among the many grim realities the Fagens of Tampa faced. In 1873, Florida legislators had enacted a "civil rights law calling for equal accommodations in public places," a law permitting, but not requiring, integrated schools. Within months of its enactment it was essentially nullified by a Leon County jurist. When several Negroes complained that they had been denied access to a skating rink in Tallahassee, the judge ruled that private owners or commercial establishments had the right to refuse service to anyone they chose.[11]

In their book *Remembering Jim Crow*, editors William Chafe, Raymond Gavins and Robert Korstad wrote:

> ...life in the Jim Crow South was a process of navigating treacherous waters. Just as any stretch of ocean might offer smooth sailing on any given day, individual white southerners might be friendly and even helpful at times. However, they might also be unaccountably hostile and prejudiced. Thus blacks had to remain ever vigilant in case storms of white fury should suddenly begin to blow.[12]

Essentially following the guidelines of the original Florida Black Codes of 1866, the rules that Samuel Fagen and family had no choice but to obey served up a death penalty (by law or mob) for such diverse crimes as inciting insurrection, for molesting or raping a white female, or for administering poison. Burglary or malicious trespass brought severe criminal punishments, including long imprisonment and/or excessive fines. Unauthorized use of a horse, whether in the employ of an owner or not, was a criminal offense, and Negroes were prohibited from carrying firearms, knives or swords without first obtaining a license issued by a judge. All persons were subject to arrest who could not demonstrate they were gainfully employed, and while Negroes could testify in court cases that involved blacks, only white men could serve on juries. Violators faced long sentences that in most cases were served by the prisoner being leased out for hard labor. The system shoveled steady profits to state and municipal authorities as well as to the middlemen who specialized in supplying cheap labor.

Q: What were race relations like during those days in Phillips County?
A: Well, they were all right as long as you didn't try to attend any of the whites' functions or their schools or anything else. You were supposed to be considered a good person if you tend to your own business and you "Yes, sir" and "No sir." But if you tried to attend any of their functions or socialize with them or anything, you might come up killed or anything, whipped, caught and whipped, and this, that, and the other.[13]
-Willie Ann Lucas in *Remembering Jim Crow*

Like all African Americans living in the South, Sam and Sylvia Fagen were denied the courtesy titles of "Mr." or "Mrs." and were required to enter white-owned homes through the back door. Most white businesses also had a side or back door, or a special serving window for blacks. The 1880 Federal Census lists Sylvia Fagen's occupation as "Keeping House," which was a very desirable situation. To the women of the Scrub, staying at home was much preferred to having to work as a house servant for some white family across town. By staying home she could keep her youngest children by her side, limit their exposure to traumatic racial "incidents," and, at the same time, it helped her to avoid other problems, including sexual compromise.

...A white woman told me one time—we were talking about a situation—she say, "What if your husband built a house right adjacent in the back of your house, and he slept with another woman and was having children by her right in your yard? What would you do? I said, "I wouldn't stay there. I would leave." She said, "Well, I didn't go anywhere because when he asked for my hand in marriage, he asked my father could I be controlled. My father told him "yes" because my father was guilty of the same thing." She said, "I stayed there and while this woman worked in the field, I had to tend to the children." Now I know what I'm talking about like that because this man is going to do what he want to. You don't know what he's doing until the flowers start to blooming, that's what they say. ...this woman that's got these children, she's going to dress better than anybody in the community, and she got money all the time, and her children are taken care of. He does it undercover, but everybody know what's going on.

It's like I say, what is slavery? Yes, they abolished the chains, they abolished this here, abolished that, but you still a slave—you understand me?—in so many words because that greenback dollar can make you a slave. When you don't have anything and you trying to make it, you're still a slave.- Ann Pointer in *Remembering Jim Crow*[14]

According to Tampa's *Sunland Tribune*, in the year David was born his father Samuel made news by attempting to catch an alligator by hand. Another story in the same paper in 1881 stated that Fagen had been jailed for stealing oats for his horse. But perhaps the best of all the stories about Sam Fagen was the one written by local historian D. B. McKay and published in *Pioneer Florida* in 1959:

Sam Fagin [sic] was a shiftless old Negro who was never known to work, but had about 20 children. I mention him because I recall a funny story about him. When the late Clarke Knight had just graduated from law school he walked into the police station one morning looking for business. He saw old Sam in a cell and asked him why. Sam said he was accused of stealing chickens. Clarke volunteered to represent him. The next morning when Sam was arraigned before Judge Harry Peoples the judge glared at him and evidently unnerved him. Told to plead to the charge, Sam whispered, 'Jedge, when you looks at me lak dat it seems lak you looks right through me. I ain't gwine lie to you, Jedge—I's guilty.' Clarke was on his feet instantly to protest: "Judge Peoples. You frightened this poor old man so badly with your fierce expression that he doesn't know what he is saying. I am his lawyer, and I tell you he is not guilty." Whereupon the honorable court delivered himself of this gem: "Sam Fagin, stand up! I'll have you know that I came from South Ca'lina, and I was taught to always take the word of a white in preference to the word of a Negro. You say you are guilty—your lawyer says you are not guilty. I prefer to believe your lawyer. Case dismissed."[15]

The Sam Fagen-stolen-chickens-trial story, written in the fading days of segregation, reeks of good old patronizing, "down-home," light-hearted Southern humor. But for Fagen, the incident may have been deadly serious. Under "Pig Laws," originally created in Mississippi to provide a steady stream of black prisoner laborers, conviction of the theft of all farm animals—including poultry—brought a lengthy sentence. In addition to producing desirable profits for the enforcers, the arrangement virtually reproduced the conditions of slavery which had supposedly been abolished when the Confederate States lost the Civil War. Favorably viewed throughout the South, the "Pig Laws" were quickly adopted by several southern states, including Florida.[16]

Leased convict laborers serving sentences during the last quarter of the nineteenth century may actually have looked back at their former lives as slaves with some fondness. As a slave, a man was valuable property to his master, and it made good sense to keep him fed and healthy since you were profiting from his labor. Convict leasing was a whole different story. The railroaders, turpentine makers, lumber companies, mining firms and other businesses who eagerly exploited leased convicts had no investment to protect and little if any reason to care about their living conditions. Incidents involving the deaths of leased convicts were seldom if ever investigated. If a man got killed or starved to death you could replace him relatively quickly with a new order sent to one of the big leasers. In his book *Worse than Slavery*, historian David M. Oshinsky quotes from former Florida convict camp captain J. C. Powell's *The American Siberia*:

...But his most vivid memory of convict life was his very first one: the sight of twenty-seven half-dead prisoners staggering from a freight train in the north Florida town of Live Oak in the fall of 1876. The men had been leased to the St. Johns, Lake Eustis and Gulf railroad company, which was adding a line through the tropical marshes and palmetto jungles of the inland wilderness.

'There was no provision made for either shelter or supplies,' Powell recalled. 'Rude huts were built of whatever material came to hand ...The commissary department dwindled into nothing. I do not mean that there was some food, but that there was no food at all. In this extremity, the convicts were driven to live as the wild beasts, except that they were only allowed the briefest intervals from labor to scour the woods for food.'

The ranks began to thin. Starvation, exposure, scurvy, dysentery, pneumonia, malaria—all took their toll. To maintain crumbling discipline, prisoners were tortured for minor infractions of the rules. Some were whipped to death; others, strung up by their thumbs, were left with hands 'resembling the paws of certain apes.' By the time the job ended, the land alongside the tracks was dotted with graves. Forty-five of the seventy-two convicts did not return. And the survivors—the young men who reached Live Oak on that fall day in 1876—were vermin-covered, mostly naked, and wasted with disease. In Powell's words, 'The sun never shone upon a more abject picture of misery and dilapidation.'[17]

According to census records, Sylvia Douglas Fagen died between 1880-1885. The cause of her death is unknown, but tuberculosis or malaria are likely suspects. Care for the younger Fagen children, including David, now became the responsibility of Louisa, aided by her younger sister Alice. There were two or three small black schools operating in the Scrub. It is unknown if any of the Fagen children attended. A few black churches offered rudimentary schooling to children, but the majority of the people of the Scrub were illiterate. As a disillusioned black schoolteacher from Mississippi said: "You educate your children—then whatcha' gonna' do? You got any jobs for 'em? You got any business for 'em to go into?"[18] By now, Jim Douglas, the eldest of Sylvia's boys, was fourteen and probably working at anything he could to help provide for the family. Articles in the local papers make it clear that the Scrub, with its bars, prostitution, gambling and crime, was considered by Tampa's white elite as a mean, filthy and dangerous place—and one to be avoided at all cost, especially after dark. But to the Fagens and all the other people who lived there, the Scrub was where people were your color, the words were your kind of words, the music was your music, the noise was your noise, the smells were your smells, the food was your food, and all the churches and shops were yours, too. Outside the Scrub was the man's world, with all its rules, requirements and concomitant threats. Inside the Scrub you could be you.

As he grew up, David learned to love the Scrub in the same way he at first had only known and loved the inside of his home. The people there knew more than just how to get by; they also knew how to have fun. Their music made that a certainty. The guerilla leader that young David later became had a reputation among the Filipinos as a man who reveled in their feasts, fiestas, the crowds, the drinking, the music, dancing, family fun and togetherness—traits that young Fagen was first exposed to in the Scrub. In 1883, phosphate was discovered in the Bone Valley region southeast of Tampa. A year later, Henry B. Plant's new South Florida Railroad reached Tampa and connected the city to the country's growing railway system.

In 1885, the Tampa Board of Trade tried to charm Vincente Martinez Ybor and Ignacio Haya, two highly successful Spanish cigar makers whose factories in Key West were suffering labor problems, to relocate their business to Tampa. Everything they needed was there: a fine port for the ships that would bring in Cuban tobacco, the new railroad line that would carry their products to the entire country, subsidized land upon which to build their factories, and the housing necessary for hundreds of highly skilled Spanish and Cuban workers. Ybor and Haya seized the opportunity. Ybor City had been born, and as Tampa's cigar industry rapidly expanded, it pressed right up against the Scrub. Powered by the cigar business, the phosphate industry and the naval stores and turpentine business, Tampa's population and importance suddenly exploded. In the decade from 1870 to 1890 the city grew from 720 residents to over 5,000 (of which some 1,500 were black).

Ybor City's cigar workers (mostly Cuban) who came to Tampa "brought with them both their cigar making skills and their traditions of labor militancy, which found expression in radical ideologies and trade unionism.… In Tampa they had to contend not only with factory owners but also with local power brokers, who soon found the cigar industry a mixed blessing. Although the rapid expansion of cigar manufacturing increased the power and wealth of Tampa's leading businessmen and professionals, it also created conditions which threatened the hegemony of the ruling elite. To counter the legal activities of cigar workers, prominent Tampans relied on their vigilante tradition to protect their interests, which they identified with those of the cigar factory owners."[19]

While Tampa's leaders tolerated unionism, they were deathly afraid that strikes and labor disputes might drive Ybor and Haya away, as had happened first in Miami and then Key West. Their chosen solution was vigilantism aimed at union organizers. In Tampa in the last quarter of the nineteenth century, more lynching victims were killed because of their activities as union organizers than because of the color of their skin.

Labor disputes sparked by the cigar industry soon spread to the turpentine and phosphate mining businesses which used blacks for the most back-breaking and labor-intensive jobs. Both businesses supplemented their employee rolls by leasing convicts—and there can be no doubt this practice also had its desired dampening effect on troublesome workers. In November of 1892, the great Cuban revolutionary José Martí visited Ybor City. Fagen was fourteen at the time, and although it is unknown whether he ever saw Martí, the excitement generated among the Cuban workers by the presence of Cuba's leading voice for independence must have affected him. A perceptive black teenager living in the Scrub in the 1890s surely understood the appeal and the advantages for oppressed people to join together in pursuit of common goals. Fagen's world thus exposed him to an early and potent awareness of revolutionary and labor struggle.

In his well-researched article Seeking David Fagen, Frank Schubert, former historian in the Office of the U.S. Chairman of the Joint Chiefs of Staff wrote about the phosphate industry where Fagen finally found steady work:

> ...This industry, which had its start in the waters near Tampa in 1883 during the dredging of the Hillsborough River channel, followed a standard pattern, with mines using blacks for common labor and whites as foremen and mechanics. Black laborers earned one dollar per day, usually for ten hours of work, breaking off

phosphate rock with crow bars, picks, and oyster tongs while standing in rivers abuzz with mosquitoes, and tossing the rock into small boats, to be dried and crushed for use in fertilizer, baking powder, matches, and cleaning and water softening compounds. Blacks provided as much as 95 percent of the workforce, and when there were not enough workers, mines used convict gangs on a contract basis at forty cents per man per day. Ninety percent or more of these prisoners were black as well. Overall, phosphate mining in the 1880s and 1890s was a brutal, demanding grind of long hours, hard work, and low pay, "requiring strong men with the stamina to perform back-breaking work under Florida's burning sun."

Phosphate mining by hand, Polk County, c. 1900. (*Courtesy Tampa Bay History Center*)

It takes little imagination to understand why the phosphate industry was a center of worker radicalism. Like the Black laborers' efforts to increase wages and improve conditions in the turpentine and timber camps, phosphate mines were violent places that suffered concerted resistance from the operators. In 1899, an effort to stop escalating racial violence against black phosphate workers in Dunnellon resulted in the formation of an

"Anti-Lynch and Mob" club. In October of that year, members of the club fought a pitched battle with local law enforcement officers in which two club members were killed and the organization effectively broken.[20]

By 1898, twenty-year-old David Fagen was 5' 10" tall and weighed about 140 pounds. Physically, his face was long and narrow with pointed features. He worked for Hull's Phosphate Company and was lean, wiry, and heavily muscled from long days of standing in mosquito-infested creeks or rivers, breaking phosphate rock from the riverbanks with a sledge hammer or crowbar. He also had a curved, linear scar on his chin; whether it was the result of an accident or a brawl is unknown. He was earning a dollar a day, but just across the stream or down the river were black men not unlike him, sweating under the hot son under the watchful eyes of their shotgun-wielding white guards. What the convicts were working for was nothing more than a bowl of bean soup twice a day. What Fagen realized by then was that good people through no real fault of their own were often bullied, bossed, cheated and used by the powerful, and that not only did it feel right to strike back against such oppression, but sometimes it was the only way to survive. Fagen knew about these things the way only a boy who had grown up on the mean streets of the Scrub would know them.

A year earlier, perhaps driven by a desire to be an adult, or maybe because he was sexually infatuated, Fagen had entered a close relationship with a young woman named Maggie Washington. They were married on October 23, 1897, and records indicate that the couple lived briefly at 813 Harrison Street in the Scrub. The history of their short relationship suggests that it was the unfortunate result of one of Fagen's rash decisions.[21]

With no education or special skills, Fagen's future in Tampa seemed bleak. During the same time period, the United States had decided to make war on the Spanish in Cuba. With the advent of the Spanish-American War, Tampa—with its railheads, docks and huge harbor—was selected as the point of assembly and embarkation for America's soldiers. Among the several thousands of troops bivouacking on the heights not far from the docks were four black regiments of veteran soldiers. They had come from western outposts where they had fought for more than two decades. They had slaughtered, beaten and finally policed Sioux, Arapaho, Cheyenne, Nez Perce, Pima, Navaho and Apaches, Paiutes, Kiowas, Comanches, Mandans

JIM CROW TAMPA

Buffalo Soldiers of 9th Cavalry arrive in Tampa, 1898.
(*Courtesy of Tampa Bay History Center*)

Military encampments, 9th US Infantry, Tampa, 1898. (*US National Archives*)

17

and Shoshones, many of whom were now imprisoned on reservations. These veterans—popularized as the "Buffalo Soldiers"—were members of the 9th and 10th Cavalry regiments, and the 24th and 25th Infantry Regiments of the U.S.C.T. (United States Colored Troops). These men were the most mature, best trained, best equipped and most battle-experienced soldiers in the regular U.S. Army, and as Tampa was about to discover, they were not about to be intimidated by Jim Crow rules. Off-duty, they strolled in small groups through Tampa's downtown streets wearing their side arms.

On May 5, 1898, a feature story in that day's Tampa Morning Tribune proclaimed: "The colored infantry men stationed in Tampa and vicinity have made themselves very offensive to the people of the city. The men insist upon being treated the same as white men are treated, and the citizens will not make any distinction between the colored troops and the colored civilians." [22]

During his whole life David Fagen had never seen a black man carry a gun in public. There should be little doubt that he watched what was happening around him with an intense scrutiny. What may have come clear to him right then was that wherever these black soldiers came from, it was better than where he was from. That realization may have been quickly followed by a thought that had been troubling him for a long time: *The Scrub was a trap*.

Notes

1. Quote from *Tampa Tribune*, "Inhuman Brutes," page 1, Wednesday June 8, 1898.
2. Edward Van Zile Scott, The Unwept, *Black American Soldiers and the Spanish American War*, Black Belt Press, Montgomery, Alabama, 1996, note 9, p. 223.
3. Quote from W.E.B. Du Bois, *The Souls of Black Folk*, Atlanta, Ga. 1903 from reprint, Simon and Shuster, NY, 2009, pp. 6-7.
4. The exact date of David Fagen's birth is unclear. The Federal Census for 1880 lists him being one year old, or having been born in 1879, while the Florida Census for 1885 claims he was seven and was therefore born in 1878. His official U.S. Army enlistment records (available from the National Archives, Washington D.C.) show that on the day of his first enlistment on June 4,

1898, he was 22 years and 7 months of age. The official records for his re-enlistment on February 9, 1889 states he was 23 years and 4 months of age. Both of Fagen's enlistments indicate he was born in October or November of 1875 but, considering his overwhelming desire to use the U.S. Army as a ticket to leave Jim Crow-era Tampa, and deducing that his chances were better if he presented himself a little older than a teenager, there is a strong likelihood he lied about his age at the recruiting office. Frank Schubert, former historian in the Office of the U.S. Chairman of the Joint Chiefs of Staff, wrote two important articles on Fagen, and in his *Seeking David Fagen: The Search for a Black Rebel's Florida Roots,* Tampa Bay History, 2008, vol. 22 pp. 19-34, Mr. Schubert came to the same conclusion about the age of Fagen at the time of his initial enlistment. We will use the birth date of 1878 throughout this book.

5. Federal Census of 1880; also see: Robert P. Ingalls *Urban Vigilantes in the New South,* 1993, University Press of Florida, Gainesville, first paperback edition, 1993, pp. 26-27.
6. See Federal Census 1880, Florida Census 1885, City Directory 1886, as cited by Frank Schubert, in *Seeking David Fagen,* Tampa Bay History vol. 22, 2008, pp. 19-34. See also: https://familysearch.org/pal:/MM9.1.1/FW3L-VWP retrieved from that website in 2011. Note: There are several spelling variations of the Fagen surname, including: Fagan, Fagon, Faggins, Faggines, Fagans, Fagens, Fagin, and Fagean.
7. Federal Census of 1870, City of Tampa, Hillsborough County, Florida, p. 40, line 24, Sylvia Douglas, black, age 28, farm laborer, born in Georgia.
8. From *Remembering Jim Crow,* Edited by William H. Chaffee, Raymond Gavins, Robert Korstad, The New Press, New York, NY, paperback edition, 2008, p. 60-61.
9. The quotes "men who had spent their lives" and "blacks were mentally inferior" are both from *Custom, Law, and History: The Enduring Influence of Florida's "Black Code"* Jarrell H Shofner, in Florida Historical Quarterly, vol. LV, No. 5, p. 278.
10. Ibid., p. 285.
11. Ibid., p. 286.
12. From *Remembering Jim Crow,* p. 2.
13. Ibid., p. 30.
14. Ibid., pp. 52-53.

15. D. B. McKay, *Pioneer Florida,* Tampa: Southern Publishing, 1959, 1:238, quote taken from Schubert, *Seeking David Fagen,* Op. Cit. p. 21.
16. See David M. Oshinsky, *Worse than Slavery,* Free Press Paperbacks edition, 1997, N.Y. p. 40.
17. Quote "But his most vivid memory..." Ibid. pp. 55-56. The text includes quotes taken from J. C. Powell, *The American Siberia, or Fourteen Years' Experience in a Southern Convict Camp* (Philadelphia, H.J. Smith & Co., 1891).
18. "As a disillusioned black..." quote taken from Schubert, *Seeking David Fagen,* p. 27.
19. Quote from Robert P. Ingalls, *Urban Vigilantes in the New South,* 1988, University of Tennessee Press, first paperback edition, University Press of Florida, Gainesville, 1993, p. 31.
20. Frank Schubert, *Seeking David Fagen: The Search for a Black Rebel's Florida Roots,* Tampa Bay History, 2008, vol. 22, pp. 24-25 For the quote within the quote "requiring strong men with the stamina ..." Schubert cites: Leon F. Litwack, *Trouble in Mind: Black Southerners in the Age of Jim Crow* (New York: Knopf, 1998, p. 343.
21. David's height, weight and scar are mentioned in his enlistment records, RG 94, Records of the Adjutant General's Office, Entry 91, Series II Enlistment Papers (1894-1912), for David Fagen, copies sent me by Paul Harrison, Archives I, Reverence Section, Research Services, National Archives and Records Administration, Washington, D.C. For Fagen's marriage to Maggie Washington, see: Schubert, *Seeking David Fagen,* p. 27.
22. Quote from: Frank Schubert, *Seeking David Fagen: The Search for a Black Rebel's Florida Roots,* Tampa Bay History, 2008 vol. 22, p. 26.

◀Chapter Two▶

DEADLY RACISM DIVIDES U.S. TROOPS

ACCORDING TO THE NATIONAL PRESS, of the 50,000 troops then assembling at Tampa, some 4,000 were African American members of four regiments of United States Colored Troops shipped in from the far west. It was these men who had captured David Fagen's attention.

Black or white, in the spirit of 1776, the soldiers coming to Tampa were dedicated to fighting and defeating the Spanish army in Cuba. They believed their mission was to liberate the poor, oppressed people of Cuba from Spanish rule, thus being instrumental in making it possible for them to experience true freedom and independence.

Amidst parades, flag-waving and marching bands, scores of volunteer soldiers at rail stations across the country boarded trains bound for Tampa.

MARCHING TO CUBA

We're going down to Cuba, boys, to battle for the right
We're going to show those Spaniards that we Yankee boys can fight
And when they see us coming they'll scatter left and right,
When we march into Cuba.

(Chorus)

Hurrah ! Hurrah ! Hurrah!
We'll sound the jubilee.
Hurrah ! Boys, Cuba shall be free,
And we'll sing the chorus from Mt. Gretna to the sea,
While we are marching to Cuba.

'Twas in Manila, boys, our ships the foe did meet.
We didn't need a hurricane to wreck,

> To wreck the Spanish fleet,
> But just one Dewey morning, and our victory was complete,
> As we were marching to Cuba.
>
> (Chorus)
>
> In Santiago harbor Sampson had them bottled tight.
> Hobson put the cork in, and we think he did it right,
> And when they find they can't get out, they'll have to stand and fight,
> When we march into Cuba.
>
> (Chorus)
>
> With Dewey, Schley, and Sampson, we need not have a fear,
> For they will guard the harbors while we attack the rear.
> We'll plant our flag on Morro and give one mighty cheer,
> When we march into Cuba.[1]

The national fervor had been fueled by the mysterious explosion and sinking of the battleship USS *Maine* in Havana Harbor. She had been sent to Cuba as an implied threat to Spanish authorities, warning them to neither molest nor interfere with American businesses and citizens in Cuba.

The presence of the *Maine* was unnecessary. In deep trouble trying to fend off Cuban guerrillas and retain control of the country, the last thing the Spaniards wanted was to provoke the United States. Accordingly, on January 25, 1898, the Spanish harbor commander graciously welcomed the American *Maine*, displaying all the traditional naval salutes and courtesies due the arrival of a friendly and important foreign ship. The *Maine* was led to a buoy in the bay, and was soon floating peacefully at its berth.

At 9:40 p.m. on February 15, while most of the *Maine*'s crew were sleeping or resting in the enlisted quarters in the forward part of the ship, some five tons of powder charges for the six- and ten-inch guns abruptly ignited, and the forward third of the ship was ripped apart

DEADLY RACISM DIVIDES U.S. TROOPS

Battleship *Maine* entering Havana Harbor. (*US National Archives*)

Wreck of the battleship *Maine*. (*US National Archives*)

by explosions. Two successive detonations occurred, the concussions of which broke windows on Havana's waterfront, a mile away. Now thoroughly engulfed in flames, what was left of the stricken vessel rapidly sank to the bottom of the bay, thirty feet below. Two hundred sixty-seven sailors had been blown apart by the explosions, and six of the many wounded would later succumb to their injuries. The *Maine*'s captain, Charles Sigbee, and most of the ship's officers survived because they were in the back portion of the ship when it detonated. The Spanish cruiser *Alfonso XII* and the American liner *City of Washington* were anchored close enough to the *Maine* to be struck by flying debris. Crews from both these vessels quickly lowered boats and raced to save the ship's survivors.

A subsequent U.S. Naval investigation was unable to determine whether the explosion was the result of a mine colliding with the ship's hull, or if it was caused by the spontaneous combustion of coal dust in a fuel bunker, which, in turn, had ignited several tons of gunpowder stored in adjacent magazines. There was no evidence whatsoever of Spanish involvement in the disaster.

The American press—goaded on by a government who wanted broad public support for making war on Spain—penned the following phrase which quickly became the nation's rallying cry: "Remember the *Maine* and to hell with Spain!"

Hidden beneath all the stirring patriotic hullabaloo and flag waving was the real driving force behind the hysterics: America was now producing more than she could consume—in oil, raw resources, food, iron and steel, farm machinery, and in manufactured goods of all types. Driven by the threat of choked warehouses and consequent falling prices, business leaders and their agents were urgently pressing the government to open new overseas markets, and Cuba looked ripe for the taking.

Three years earlier, when the Cubans began their latest revolution against Spanish rule, America's business leaders considered the war's effects on commerce because, in fact, there already was substantial economic interest in the island. "It is reasonably estimated," President Grover Cleveland stated, "that at least $30,000,000 to $50,000,000 of

American capital are invested in the plantations and in railroad, mining and other enterprises on the island. The volume of trade between the United States and Cuba rose in 1893 to about $103,000,000."[2]

While popular American support centered on bringing freedom to the people of Cuba, the U.S. government's focus was on power and profit. Neither Grover Cleveland nor William McKinley (who succeeded him as president) ever officially recognized the Cuban insurgents as belligerents: "To have done so would have enabled the United States to give aid to the rebels without sending an army. But there may have been fear that the rebels would win on their own and keep the United States out."[3] Adding to the commercial concerns were racial issues: "A Cuban victory might lead to a white and a black republic, since Cuba had a mixture of the two races, and the black republic might be dominant."[4]

In an article in *The Saturday Review*, twenty-five-year-old Winston Churchill wrote: "A grave danger represents itself. Two-fifths of the insurgents in the field are negroes. These men…would, in the event of success, demand a predominant share in the government of the country…the result being, after years of fighting, another black republic."[5]

The discussions in Washington, D.C. included conversations concerning what to do with Cuba once it was taken from Spain. If Cuba was destined to become an American territory or even a state, it would be difficult if not impossible to prevent unlimited numbers of black Cubans from moving to the American homeland. Work began at once to come up with a better way to handle the situation.

According to historian Howard Zinn, "Russell Sage, the banker, said that if war came, there is no question where the rich men stand."[6]

Secretary of State John Hay wrote to Teddy Roosevelt that the coming fight against the Spanish in Cuba was to be a "splendid little war." Simultaneously, as United States policies were being formulated, contractors for military ships, equipment, stores, projectiles, munitions and other supplies were swarming through Washington D.C. like foraging ants.

Meanwhile, almost immediately after their arrival from the far west, the Buffalo Soldiers were engaged in their own little war.

The chaplain of the 9th Cavalry told the editor of the *Cleveland Gazette*:

May 13, 1898
Hon. H. C. Smith
Editor, Gazette
Dear Sir:

Yesterday, May 12, the Ninth was ordered to be ready to embark at a moment's notice for Cuba. ...We are here waiting for the order to march. Possibly before you shall have been in receipt of this communication, the Ninth, with the Twenty-fourth and Twenty-fifth infantries and eight batteries of artillery will be in Cuba. These men are anxious to go. The country will then hear and know of the bravery of these sable sons of Ham.

The American Negro is always ready and willing to take up arms, to fight and to lay down his life in defense of his country's flag and honor. All the way from northwest Nebraska this regiment was greeted with cheers and hurrahs. At places where we stopped the people assembled by the thousands. While the Ninth Cavalry band would play some national air the people would raise their hats, men, women and children would wave their handkerchiefs, and the heavens would resound with their hearty cheers. The white hand shaking the black hand, the hearty "goodbyes," "God bless you," and other expressions aroused the patriotism of our boys...These demonstrations so enthusiastically given, greeted us all the way until we reached Nashville. At this point we arrived about 12:30 a.m. There were about 6,000 colored people there to greet us (very few white people) but not a man was allowed by the railroad officials to approach the cars. From there until we reached Chattanooga there was not a cheer given us, the people living in gross ignorance, rags and dirt. Both white and colored seemed amazed; they looked at us in wonder. Don't think they have intelligence enough to know that Andrew Jackson is dead. Had we been greeted like this all the way...there would have been many desertions before we reached this point.

The prejudice against the Negro soldier and the Negro was great, but it was of heavenly origin to what it is in this part of Florida, and I suppose that what is true here is true in other parts of the state. Here, the Negro is not allowed to purchase over the same counter in some stores that the white man purchases over. The southerners have made their laws and the Negroes know and obey them. They never stop to ask a white man a question. He (Negro) never thinks of disobeying. You talk about freedom, liberty etc. Why sir, the Negro of this country is freeman and yet a slave. Talk about fighting and freeing poor Cuba and of Spain's brutality; of Cuba's murdered thousands and starving reconcentrados. Is America any better than Spain? Has she not subjects in her very midst who are murdered daily without a trial of judge or jury? Has she not subjects in her own borders whose children are half-fed and half-clothed, because their father's skin is black.... Forgetting that he is ostracized, his race considered dumb as driven cattle, yet, as loyal and true men, he answers the call to arms and with blinding tears in his eyes and sobs he goes forth....

The four Negro regiments are going to help free Cuba, and they will return to their homes, some then mustered out and begin again to fight the battle of American prejudice....

Yours truly
Geo. W. Prioleau
Chaplain, Ninth Cavalry [7]

Immediately following the arrival of the first black soldiers in Tampa, the city's white citizens began to complain. As black historian Willard B. Gatewood, Jr. wrote in his article *Negro Troops in Florida, 1898*: "Undoubtedly earlier reports from Key West that the Negro infantrymen had forced the release of one of their fellows from a local jail enhanced the existing antipathy toward black soldiers...." Almost daily, from the time they arrived until they departed for Cuba, the local press gave front-page coverage to every incident involving Negro troops. Sensational accounts of "rackets" and "riots" by "these black ruffians in uniform" appeared regularly in dailies throughout the entire South.

Negro troops resented what they interpreted as deliberate attempts to malign them and to cast aspersions upon the distinguished record that they had compiled during the Indian Wars in the West. In a letter addressed to a friend, a black infantryman declared: "Prejudice reigns supreme here against the colored troops. Every little thing that is done here is chronicled as Negro brazenness, outlawry, etc. An ordinary drunk brings forth scare headlines in the dailies. Some of our boys were refused a drink at one of the crackers' saloons … and they politely closed him up. That was put down as a 'nigger riot' and the commanding general was appealed to in the interest of the 'respectable white citizens.' From the beginning the Negro troops in the Tampa area made it clear that they had no intention of submitting to the discriminatory treatment accorded black civilians."[8]

Three black soldiers. (*Courtesy Anthony Powell, Jr.*)

DEADLY RACISM DIVIDES U.S. TROOPS

Within a few days of their arrival in Lakeland, Florida, troops of the 10th Cavalry demonstrably refused to accept local racial customs. "Angered by the refusal of the proprietor of Forbes Drug Store to serve one of their comrades at the soda fountain, a large group of armed black soldiers returned to the store and to a barbershop next door. When the white barber yelled obscenities at a Negro trooper who requested a shave, they 'shot-up the barbershop.'"[9]

The altercation quickly escalated out into the street, where a crowd had gathered. Threatened and outnumbered, the frightened soldiers began to fire indiscriminately. A white shopkeeper named Joab (Abe) Collins, who had been hurling insults at them, was struck and killed by a stray bullet. A few moments later, several white officers of the 10th Cavalry arrived and took control of the situation. Following an investigation, two black cavalrymen, James Johnson and John Young, were turned over to local authorities for trial.

David Fagen had made up his mind by mid-May. Joining the army had now become his most important and immediate goal. He set out learning the requirements and discovered that a recruit under the age of twenty-one had to bring his parents to the recruiting office to give permission for their son's enlistment. Other prerequisites demanded that the enlistee be single, and that he must be able to read. Fagen had already decided to lie about his age and marriage, and to seek additional help from two of the most respected men from the Scrub. The literacy requirement worried him the most; he had no idea how he would get around it.

Lt. Colonel Frederick Funston – Iola, Kansas

While Fagen dealt with the challenges of enlisting and escaping from the Scrub, the white officer who would eventually become his most dedicated enemy was at home in Iola, Kansas, trying to recover his health after serving two years with rebel insurgents in the mountains and jungles of northern Cuba. Frederick Funston was suffering from both malaria and malnutrition.[10]

Funston's Cuban adventure had begun in 1896 during a visit to New York City. There he attended the Cuban Fair in Madison Square

Lieutenant Colonel Frederick Funston.
(*Library of Congress*)

Garden—a fund-raising exhibit in support of Cuban revolutionaries. Already sympathetic to the Cuban cause, Funston drew further inspiration from a dynamic and eloquent speech delivered by Civil War hero General Daniel E. Sickles. The next morning, he sought out Cuban diplomats and agents, and expressed his desire to join the rebel army. As he had had no prior military experience, the Cubans rejected his request. Nevertheless, Funston doggedly pursued his objective and eventually learned that the Cubans needed help with the training, use and maintenance of their new Hotchkiss 12-pounder rapid firing cannons. Funston immediately traveled to the New York offices of arms dealers Hartley and Graham, and persuaded the firm to teach him everything about setting up, sighting, firing and maintaining the Hotchkiss 12-pounder.

Returning to the Cuban agents, he convinced them that he had the useful skills that they needed. They took him in, and, along with a few other American volunteers, he was smuggled by boat to a tiny inlet on Southern Cuba's north shore, in Camaguey Province. He was quickly escorted to General Rafael Cabrera, who, after interviewing him, granted Funston a temporary commission as captain of artillery and placed him in charge of two Hotchkiss guns. Funston proved himself a natural leader, and his gun crews performed brilliantly through several battles. After the Battle of Guaimaro on 17-28 October, 1896, Funston was promoted to major, and following a number of other battles—which he himself was surprised to have survived—he was promoted to lieutenant colonel.

This brave young American, who had fought so valiantly with the Cuban revolutionaries, was educated, well read, and had several official expeditions as a field botanist under his belt. In addition to mountain climbing and extensive hiking through Montana and Wyoming, Funston had also served as a key member of scientific explorations to Death Valley and Yosemite. He had also experienced a two-year excursion through the Yukon wilderness collecting flora specimens for the United States Department of Agriculture. He was, in short, a veteran outdoorsman and adventurer. Funston was also a talented writer who had worked as a crime reporter and journalist for two city newspapers, and he had sold some vivid accounts of his outdoor experiences to popular magazines.

His appearance belied his history. At five-foot-four inches in height, and weighing just over one hundred pounds, the aggressive nature of the round-faced young man with the serious eyes was wonderfully masked. Anyone who mistakenly assumed that he was weak or soft was in for a rough surprise.

Funston's six-foot-two, two-hundred-pound Irish immigrant father was a pugnacious farmer-legislator who had served as a Union Army artillery officer during the Civil War. After the war, he campaigned and won election as a state legislator, and after several terms became a state senator. Loquacious and quick to offer his opinions on any subject, Edward Hogue Funston had an obstreperous reputation.

His eldest son was also opinionated, but preferred to air his viewpoints through writing rather than rhetoric. In fact, young Frederick disliked both politics and politicians. One character trait he apparently did inherit from his larger-than-life father was a fast temper and an icy willingness to use his fists to resolve altercations with opponents of any size whenever challenged.[11]

Despite his pugnacity, during his grade school years in Kansas, young Frederick was a lively, popular boy, a prankster whom classmates later remembered as a happy kid with a ready smile. Oddly, although his parents maintained a superbly stocked home library and young Funston was an avid reader of classic works—including Roman and Greek military histories and novels—his early grades were no better than average.

After graduating from a high school to which he rode a horse five miles to and from each day, Funston applied to West Point. Denied entrance due to his mediocre grades, he spent a year teaching at a rural school and then attended the University of Kansas at Lawrence. Becoming bored with academics, he left college in 1887 to work three months with rail engineers for the Atchison, Topeka and Santa Fe Railroad. By 1888, now on his own, Funston took a job as a conductor and train bouncer on the A.T. & SF line, working mostly on runs between eastern Kansas and Albuquerque, New Mexico.

On one trip, Funston approached a tall cowboy and asked him for his ticket. The cowboy drew a revolver from his belt holster, and shaking it in his raised hand in lieu of producing his ticket, quipped: "I ride on this."

Funston nodded. "That's good," he replied quietly. "That's good," he repeated. Then he wheeled and walked off towards the next car.

Sometime later, Funston reappeared and approaching the cowboy from behind, he levered a cartridge into the rifle he was pointing at the man, who had not yet noticed him. The man's head swiveled and his face paled and froze when he saw the muzzle of Funston's rifle.

"I came back to punch that ticket," the little conductor said softly.

Surprised, the hapless cowboy nodded and, moving slowly and carefully, dug out his ticket from a shirt pocket and meekly offered it to his opponent. Lesson learned.[12]

Funston:

> Temporarily broken in health, I had returned to the United States from Cuba early in 1898, and was at my old home in Kansas, enjoying the companionship of my family and friends, and doing my best to obliterate the memory of lean days in the "bush" by a generous patronage of everything in the nature of real food.
>
> The *Maine* had already been blown up, and the country was full of the ramblings of the approaching war with Spain. To the

last I doubted whether it would really come to a clash, having in mind several cases within my own recollection when we had apparently come to the verge of war, but in which the matters in dispute had been settled without recourse to arms. But the clamor of the yellow section of the press and the deliverances of politicians playing to the galleries so enflamed public sentiment that the hand of the administration was forced, and we were in for a sharp and short little war....

When the President issued to the governors of the various States his call for volunteers, Kansas was asked to furnish three regiments of infantry of about one thousand men each. Under a subsequent call there was organized a two-battalion colored regiment, and three hundred recruits were provided for each of the three existing regiments. Immediately upon the issue of the first call, Governor Leedy sent me a telegram requesting that I come to Topeka at once – Upon reporting, I was informed that he had determined to ignore the National Guard organization of the State, building three new regiments from the ground-up. Members of the National Guard could enter these organizations as individuals. I was to be named as a colonel of one of the three regiments.

I protested against the expediency of a policy which I thought might keep out of the service a number of officers and men who had had at least the rudiments of military training, and further stated that while I had seen much campaigning and no little fighting, my service had been in a force in which drill or other training was a practically unknown quantity. I felt that the instruction of a regiment made up largely of absolutely raw material should be under the direction of one who knew at least something of infantry drill. But the governor told me bluntly that he had not sent for me to hear my views, as he had some of his own. If I did not take the regiment he would give it to Mr. So and So. I knew that I could not be a worse colonel than the man named, and accepted.[13]

-Frederick Funston, in *Memories of Two Wars*

General William Shafter. (*US National Archives*)

Soon after accepting command of the 20th Kansas Volunteers, Funston traveled to Tampa for debriefing by staff officers of sixty-three-year-old Major General William R. Shafter, commander of V-Corps (the army with which he was to invade Cuba). Funston arrived in late May, and after a short introduction to the general—a massive, three hundred pound, gout-ridden man—Shafter turned him over to a staff officer. Funston quickly sensed that the regular officers were skeptical of how he had obtained his high Cuban rank without any military training whatever, and why he deserved his appointment to command the 20th Kansas Volunteers. Even so, they thoroughly questioned him about local conditions:

> ...I doubt if any of the information obtained from me was ever of any value, except that as to general conditions, as I was not familiar with the country in the immediate vicinity of the city of Santiago, the scene of the only campaign. Had it been otherwise, I am of the opinion that the data as to roads, rivers, and the

practicable crossing-places thereof, as well as other information on local conditions, which had been given in such detail, would not have been utilized. General Shafter seemed to regard me with suspicion, while General Miles, who had meantime arrived, was very courteous, but neither officer seemed to care to talk with me as to conditions on the island, and I had too much self-respect to give unasked-for information.[14]

As if the gods of war had decided to help David Fagen join the army, orders came down from the War Department that all regular regiments were to be comprised of three battalions of four companies each. In order to comply with these orders, the four United States Colored Troop outfits in Tampa were required to immediately set up recruiting operations. Their near-impossible objective was the urgent recruitment of some 750 new enlistees each. There can be little doubt that non-commissioned officers (NCOs) were sent into town to find, meet and persuade young black men to join their country's clarion call to duty. Meanwhile, by mid-May, the navy was scrambling to assemble dozens of ships and thousands of men together in the stifling heat and humidity of Tampa Harbor for the proposed invasion.[15]

Considering the importance young Fagen must have afforded to escaping from his life in the Scrub, there should be little doubt that he was as anxious to learn all that was required for him to enlist in the U.S. Army, as the recruiting sergeants were to provide him answers to all his questions.

> …A soldier cannot be made in a month, as a man must have experience and the class of recruits that we have been receiving of late are not up to the standard; many of whom are mere boys 17 and 18 years of age. They cannot stand the hardship of the soldier's life, yet some of the recruits are an honor. They have only been here a few weeks and their whole heart, purpose and ambition is to be a soldier. These are the boys who have not spent their time idly; they have come from good families and have spent the best time of their life at school. I

still maintain that if our best people will encourage their sons to enlist in the army, they will be, when the war is over, an honor to themselves and the race. We must have intelligence, as brute force and ignorance are not the requisites upon which our great men won success.

Quite a number of people are of the opinion anyone can enlist in the army. This is a mistake, and I was told by a non-commissioned officer who was upon the recruiting service not long ago, that he was surprised at the number of young men who applied to enlist but were refused on account of their inability to read. They have had the opportunity but would not accept.

The 10th Reg. of Cavalry are in need of 300 recruits and you can see by that that the regiment is far from being recruited up to full war strength. We have about 200 recruits who are being drilled very hard every day, and it is surprising how they stand up under the warm weather. There are but few cases of sickness among the men and we have not had one death while the white troops are having a great deal of sickness and death.
- John E. Lewis, Tenth Cavalry, Lakeland, Florida, to the editor of the *Illinois Record*, June 5, 1898 [16]

On 4 June, Fagen appeared before the 24th Infantry Regiment recruiters, accompanied by two respected residents who could attest to his character. David was prepared with answers to all the questions he expected to be asked, but for one: if he was forced to prove he could read, there was no way for him to avoid rejection. The physical condition of enlistment applicants played a major role in recruiters' decisions, and Fagen's heavily-muscled physique, molded by heavy labor, was uniquely impressive.

The officers and NCOs who dealt with Fagen included the unit's Assistant Surgeon, 1st Lt. L. J. Kirkpatrick, who certified: "I have carefully examined the above-named man agreeably to the General Regulations of the Army, and that, in my opinion, he is free from all bodily defects and mental infirmity which would, in any way, disqualify him from performing the duties of a soldier." Kirkpatrick also wrote down Fagen's identifying features on the enlistment papers, citing a "square scar ¼" on right cheek, and an "oval scar ½" by ¼" on his left cheek."[17]

The acting adjutant of the 24th Infantry, and the officer-in-charge during Fagen's recruiting interview, was 1st Lieutenant Charles E. Tayman. Two of the black regiment's sergeants, Anthony A. Marrow and John Calloway, were also present. Marrow was a former schoolteacher from North Carolina who was nearing the end of his first enlistment with H Company of the 24th, and Calloway was a former printer from Richmond, Virginia, who had risen quickly to the rank of sergeant major.[18]

Nineteen-year-old Fagen swore that he was twenty-two years and seven months of age, single, and that he was employed as a laborer by Hull's Phosphate Company. After hearing him attest that he was born and raised in Florida and was a U.S. citizen, neither of Fagen's pair of witnesses indicated that they disagreed with his statements.

The two men Fagen had brought with him were William Hicks and Samuel Bryant. According to historian Frank Schubert: "William Hicks remains obscure, but Samuel Bryant was a pillar of the black community. His mother, Dorcas Bryant, was a prominent early entrepreneur who made her money the hard way, as a laundress and landowner. Samuel Bryant owned the Nebraska Avenue Carpenter Shop, was active in the Republican Party during Reconstruction, and built Mt. Sinai African Methodist Episcopal Zion Church on land donated by his mother."[19]

David probably answered the question of his literacy by saying something like: "Yessir, some," and 1st Lt. Tayman evidently didn't care to press the issue. But then, just prior to being sworn in, one of the white officers handed him a pen and pointed to the line on the enlistment contract where he was to sign his name. The moment Fagen had dreaded most had arrived, and all he could do was stand there with the pen in his hand in excruciating silence. Most likely it was 1st Lt. Tayman who came to his rescue by motioning for him to make an X on the signature line. As soon as Fagen had done so, Marrow and Calloway quickly signed as witnesses to Fagen's mark. Fagen was in.

Less than an hour later, Fagen and other raw recruits were marched to a supply tent where they were issued uniforms, boots and gear. The sergeants placed in charge of the new enlistees had orders to do all they could to make soldiers out of these men during the precious few days they had left before shipping out to Cuba. That night was Fagen's first experience in a crowded tent lying on a canvas cot in his underwear listening to H-Company's bugler sound *Taps*. Although the day's dizzying events had left him exhausted, he no doubt had plenty to think about.

Why his father or any of David's brothers or sisters had not come to see him join the army remains unanswered. It may well have occurred to him that in his zeal to abandon his life in the Scrub, he was also abandoning his family. Other thoughts, and perhaps fears, dealt with having become a soldier who was about to go to a far away land to kill or be killed. The new recruit had plenty to ponder as he adjusted to the sounds and smells of military life. Outside, there were armed sentries stationed near the tents of the new enrollees. Once they were in, the army was taking no chances that any of these new soldiers would change their minds.

The outlook of the new men was different from that of the veteran soldiers of the regiment. The racial hatred that the black regulars had encountered from Tampa's residents had been supplanted by the virulent animosity of gangs of undisciplined white troops. Many of them were raw volunteers from Mississippi, Georgia, Alabama, and other Jim Crow states, who roamed Tampa's downtown each night, getting drunk and looking for trouble. The black Buffalo Soldiers from the far west were more than ready to accommodate them.

The Buffalo Soldiers were veterans who looked forward to the business of fighting, and until they could tangle with the Spanish army the abusive white cracker soldiers would be a good stand-in. The pressures caused by the scorching racial conflict were inexorable, and the anticipated explosion occurred during the night of 6 June 1898.

As historian Willard B. Gatewood , Jr. wrote:

> ...Apparently the riot was triggered by a group of intoxicated white volunteers from Ohio who "decided to have some fun" with a two-year-old Negro boy. The child was snatched from his mother by a white soldier who entertained his comrades by holding him in one hand and spanking him with the other. Then, held at

arm's length with his head down, the child served as a target for several soldiers to demonstrate their marksmanship. Presumably, the winner was the soldier who sent a bullet through the sleeve of the boy's shirt. Having had their "fun," the soldiers returned the dazed child to his hysterical mother. Already angered by an accumulation of "outrages," the black troops of the Twenty-fourth and Twenty-fifth Infantry regiments viewed the behavior of the Ohio volunteers as anything but sporting. In fact, the incident set them off on a wild destructive rampage. They stormed into the streets firing their pistols indiscriminately, wrecking saloons and cafes which had refused to serve them, and forcing their way into white brothels. Apparently, they clashed not only with white civilians but also with white soldiers. The reaction of the Tampa Morning Tribune to reports that black soldiers had "outraged" white prostitutes was ironic in view of its disregard for the legal rights of Negroes. "While these women are of the lowest type," the Tribune editorialized, "the law gives them protection."

The provost guards and the Tampa police tried in vain to restrain the rioters. Finally, troops from the Second Georgia Volunteer Infantry, a white regiment, were assigned the job of restoring order. The relish with which the Georgia soldiers performed the task was equaled only by their deadly efficiency. Near daybreak on the morning of June 7, the riot was quieted. The Tampa paper which published the highlights of the disturbance came to regret the publicity given the affair, apparently out of fear that it would reflect adversely upon the city. The newspaper later denied that there had been any riot and classified as "sheer rot" reports that the streets of Tampa "ran red with negro blood." Yet, twenty-seven black troops and several white Georgia volunteers from Tampa, all with serious wounds, were transferred to Fort McPherson near Atlanta, corroborating rumors of a bloody race riot.[20]

Outraged by national newspapers carrying blaring headlines about bloody race riots on the streets of Tampa, there can be little doubt that the city's authorities confronted General William Shafter and his staff at his headquarters on the morning of 7 June. There they demanded that immediate steps be taken to gain control of his troops and prevent any further incidents that would "blacken" Tampa's fair name.

Before their arrival, Shafter had already issued orders restricting the enlisted personnel of his four Buffalo Soldier regiments to their encampments. Whether Shafter's decision was prompted by his needs to satisfy Tampa's civil authorities, or to preserve as many of his most important and experienced fighting men is unknown. There can be no doubt, however, where Shafter stood in relation to the racial strife that was taking place, since he had a special fondness for all the Buffalo Soldiers. As a young Lt. Colonel, Shafter had been appointed as second in command when the 24th Infantry Regiment was originally formed in 1869. In the following years, he had led various outfits of Buffalo Soldiers in the Indian Wars, the U.S. Army's only theatre of combat operations following the Civil War.

Shafter knew that his men were about to go up against professional, combat-savvy Spanish soldiers led by intelligent, well-trained officers. While he was being plagued with massive organizational, supply and equipment problems, the Spanish were putting the final touches on entrenched defensive positions, including reinforced stone blockhouses at key high-ground positions above Santiago. They were also much more familiar with the terrain, since they had gained both operational and actual combat experience from fighting Cuban insurgents.

The general also knew that the Spaniards' weaponry was superior to his own. The enemy was equipped with the superb M1893 Mauser bolt-action repeating rifle, and both the Spaniard's artillery pieces as well as their rifles utilized smokeless gun powder. Shafter's own artillery pieces were of smaller caliber and could be out-ranged by the Spanish guns. Completely unfamiliar with the poorly mapped jungle terrain over which he was to command his troops, Shafter was facing a much more serious problem—the navy had been unable to acquire even half of the transport ships that he needed for the actual invasion.

Shafter was hanging everything on the aggressiveness and experience of his four best regiments—the Buffalo Soldiers. The other units of his rapidly diminishing invasion force were mostly volunteer outfits which had received

DEADLY RACISM DIVIDES U.S. TROOPS

Artillery company moving to Tampa Harbor to board ship bound for Cuban invasion.
(*US National Archives*)

Troop transports being boarded at Tampa Harbor. (*Courtesy Tampa Bay History Center*)

a total of only two or three months' training. It was impossible for Shafter to evaluate their combat potential.

Pressed by the War Department to speed up the attack, Shafter decided that except for their officers, all his cavalry regiments would have to leave their horses ashore in Tampa and fight as infantry in Cuba. On 9 June, he ordered the loading of transports at Tampa's docks to begin early in the morning the next day.

Writing as company historian in 1923, Captain William G. Muller, adjutant of the 24th Regiment, stated that orders came down on the morning of June 7 because of the bloody riot the night before. No one was to leave camp and on the ninth at early morn, the regiment proceeded by rail to Port Tampa whence they were embarked on the transport *City of Washington* (No. 16).[21]

The enlisted men of H-Company, 24th Infantry Regiment, were confined well below decks. They knew they were on their way to Cuba, but had no idea when or where they were to invade. There has been some speculation by a few historians who wrote about Fagen that neither he nor any of the new enlistees would have been put aboard the invasion transports. They reasoned that army policy would surely not allow raw recruits to be thrown directly into combat. Accordingly, they wrote that Fagen and all the other raw recruits were held back in Tampa and shipped to Cuba after the initial fighting was over.

But in 1898, keeping raw recruits from combat was, in fact, not the army's policy:

> …Two famous Civil War generals wrote pertinent comments about the value of mixing new recruits with seasoned regular soldiers. General of the Army William T. Sherman wrote: "I believe that five hundred new men added to an old and experienced regiment were more valuable than a thousand men in the form of a new regiment, for the former, by association with good, experienced captains, lieutenants, and non-commissioned officers, soon became veterans, whereas the latter were generally unavailable for a year." General Grant echoed this: 'The citizen

soldiers were associated with so many disciplined men and professionally educated officers that, when they went into engagements, it was with a confidence they would not have felt otherwise. They became soldiers themselves almost at once.'[22]

In addition, on 5 June, 1898, General Nelson A. Miles telegraphed the War Department from Tampa:

> This expedition has been delayed through no fault of any one connected with it. It contains the principal part of the army [the "regular" army] which for intelligence and efficiency is not exceeded by any body of troops on earth. It contains fourteen of the best-conditioned regiments of volunteers, the last of which arrived this morning. Yet these have never been under fire. Between thirty and forty per cent are undrilled, and in one regiment over three hundred men had never fired a gun. This enterprise is so important that I desire to go with this army corps or to immediately organize another and go with it to join this and capture position 2 [Puerto Rico].[23]

New recruits certainly did fight at the battles of Caney and San Juan Hill, as attested to by the following letter from Trooper Presley Holliday of Troop B, 10th Cavalry, to the editor of *The New Age*:

> ...as long as we stood to the front and fought, unfortunately some of our men (and these were all recruits with less than six months' service) felt so much out of place that when the firing lulled, often showed their desire to be with their commands.
> ...I remember an incident of a recruit of my troop, with less than two months' service, who had come up to our position during the evening of the 1st....[24]

In his 1904 book *The Colored Regulars in the United States Army*, Chaplain T. G. Steward, D.D., of the 25th U.S. Infantry, quotes a statement from Captain B. H. Leavell, commander of Company A, 24th Infantry Regiment as follows:

This regiment (24th) had won great credit in its advance upon the enemy, but it was to win still greater in the field of humanity. Capt. Leavel [sic], who commanded Company A, said: "It would be hard to particularize in reporting upon the men of the company. All—non-commissioned officers, privates, even newly joined recruits—showed a desire to do their duty, yea, more than their duty, which would have done credit to seasoned veterans. Too much cannot be said of their courage, willingness and endurance."[25]

Capt. Leavell's praise for the men he commanded in the battle makes it absolutely clear that "newly joined recruits" were not only present, but performed with valor in the bloody fight for San Juan Hill. Leavell's statement completely invalidates speculative assertions that new recruits like Fagen did not ship from Tampa with the initial invasion fleet.

The 24th Infantry Regiment had just embarked aboard the Ward Liner City of Washington when rumors began to spread that Spanish gunboats were approaching Tampa. This caused the men to rapidly disembark, after which the ship steamed off to the outer harbor. Later, the rumors proved to be untrue, and the men of the 24th were re-boarded, after which their ship sailed to the outer harbor and anchored under the blazing sun. The City of Washington was to remain there until 14 June, at which time the invasion convoy was to be formed to sail for Cuba.

After having been loaded with men and animals (officers' horses, wagon horses and mules) eight of the troop transports remained berthed at Tampa's docks. Men and animals suffered near-suffocation in the oven-like heat, and a growing stench of vomit and excrement fouled the stifling air. There were no fans, and since the ships were not underway, no fresh air could find its way down ventilator shafts. Whether a soldier was aboard a ship tied to the dock or anchored out in the bay, the conditions were identical. On 14 June, after the convoy finally got underway and set out for Cuba, the foul air improved somewhat. Still, life on board was still anything but pleasant. The following account, written years later by a sergeant major of the 25th Infantry Regiment, describes the ordeal:

The regiment went aboard the Government transport, No. 14—

Conch—June 7, 1898. On the same vessel were the 14th U.S. Infantry, a battalion of the 2d Massachusetts Volunteers and Brigade Headquarters, aggregating about 1,300 soldiers, exclusive of the officers. This was the beginning of real hardship. The transport had either been a common freighter or a cattle ship. Whatever had been its employment before being converted into a transport, I am sure of one thing, it was neither fit for man nor beast when soldiers were transported in it to Cuba. The actual carrying capacity of the vessel as a transport was, in my opinion, about 900 soldiers, exclusive of the officers, who, as a rule, surround themselves with every possible comfort, even in actual warfare. A good many times, as on this occasion, the desire and demand of the officers for comfort worked serious hardships for the enlisted men. The lower decks had been filled with bunks. Alas! The very thought of these things of torture makes me shudder even now. They were arranged in rows, lengthwise the dimensions of a man's bunk was 6 feet long, 2 feet wide and 2 feet high, and they were arranged in tiers of four, with a four inch board on either side to keep one from rolling out. The Government had furnished no bedding at all. Our bedding consisted of one blanket as mattress and haversack for pillow. The 25th Infantry was assigned to the bottom deck, where there was no light, except the small port holes when the gang-plank was closed. So dark was it that candles were burned all day. There was no air except what came down the canvass air shafts when they were turned to the breeze. The heat of that place was almost unendurable. Still our Brigade Commander issued orders that no one would be allowed to sleep on the main deck. That order was the only one to my knowledge during the whole campaign that was not obeyed by the colored soldiers. It is an unreported fact that a portion of the deck upon which the 25th Infantry took passage to Cuba was flooded with water during the entire journey.

Finally the 14th of June came. While bells were ringing, whistles blowing and bands playing cheering strains of music, the transports formed "in fleet in column of twos," and under convoy of some of the best war craft of our navy, and while the thousands on shore waved us godspeed, moved slowly down the bay on its mission to avenge the death of the heroes of our gallant *Maine* and to free suffering Cuba.

The transports were scarcely out of sight of land when an order was issued by our Brigade Commander directing that the two regiments on board should not intermingle, and actually drawing the "color line" by assigning the white regiment to the port and the 25th Infantry to the starboard side of the vessel. The men of the two regiments were on the best of terms, both having served together during mining troubles in Montana. Still greater was the surprise of everyone when another order was issued from the same source directing that the white regiment should make coffee first, all the time, and detailing a guard to see that the order was carried out. All of these things were done seemingly to humiliate us and without a word of protest from our officers. We suffered without complaint. God only knows how it was we lived through those fourteen days on that miserable vessel. We lived through those days and were fortunate enough not [to] have a burial at sea.[2]

Frank W. Pullen, Jr.
Ex-Sergeant-Major 25th U.S. Infantry
Enfield, S.C. March 23, 1899

Another black trooper wrote:

We were huddled together below two other regiments and under the water line, in the dirtiest, closest, most sickening place imaginable. For about 15 days we were on the water in this dirty hole, but being soldiers we were compelled to accept this without a murmur. We ate corn beef and canned tomatoes with our hard bread until we were anything but half way pleased. In the fifth or sixth day out to sea the water furnished us became muddy or dirty and well flavored with salt, and remained so during the rest of the journey. Then, the ship's cooks, knowing well our condition, made it convenient to themselves to sell us a glass of clean ice water and a small piece of bread and tainted meat for the sum of seventy-five cents, or, one dollar, as the case might be.[27]

DEADLY RACISM DIVIDES U.S. TROOPS

Surely, veteran soldiers, most likely sergeants, would have taken the new recruits under their wing and attempted to provide them basic military instruction at this point. This might have included basic familiarization with the new .30-40 caliber Krag-Jorgensen rifles the regiment had just been issued, replacing the old, single-shot M1873 "trapdoor" Springfields that had served the men of the 24th for more than twenty years. The new rifles brought two major improvements: first, they fired a cartridge loaded with smokeless powder, and second, they were a bolt-action repeater that carried five rounds in a box magazine that could be quickly loaded via a hinged door on one side of the rifle's action. The old single-shot Springfield issued a cloud of white smoke each time it was fired, which then had to be allowed to dissipate before the soldier could see to aim another shot. This also allowed his enemy to calculate his location. A man with one of the new Krags could fire several rounds in the same amount of time as single bullet could be fired from the now-obsolete Springfield. Having acquired but a limited number of the new rifles by the time of the Cuban conflict, the army had decided to issue them initially to the regular army units. The National Guard and volunteer regiments would have to fight with the old smoke-belching Springfields.

Although the limited space in the crowded aisles between rows of bunks in the hold of the transport would have precluded any marching or drilling, it is likely that Fagan and his fellow raw recruits would have been taught how to hold, sight, dry-fire, field strip, clean and re-assemble their new rifles. It is also likely that an NCO or two would have taken it upon themselves to teach the new men as much as they could about soldiering, and to assign each recruit to a veteran soldier whom they were to stay close to and obey when they entered combat.

As the convoy approached Cuba, the thought may well have crossed Private David Fagen's mind that by joining the army he had invited dangers far deadlier than those he had faced in the Scrub.

Notes

1. Song quoted from: http://www.wyomingtalesandtrails.com/russellbells.html.
2. Quote from Howard Zinn, A People's History of the United States,

HarperCollins Publishers, NY 1999, reprint, paperback, Harper Perennial Modern Classics, NY, 2005, pp. 302-303.

3. Ibid., pp. 303.
4. Ibid., p. 303.
5. Ibid. Quote from *Saturday Review* taken from Howard Zinn, *A People's History of the United States*, p. 303. Note: By "another black republic," Churchill was referring to Haiti.
6. Ibid. p. 305.
7. Quote, George W. Prioleau, Ninth Cavalry to H.C. Smith, Editor, *Cleveland Gazette*, in Willard B. Gatewood, Jr., *Smoked Yankees and the Struggle for Empire*, University of Arkansas Press, Fayetteville, 1987, pp. 27-29.
8. Quote from Willard B. Gatewood, Jr., "Negro Troops in Florida," 1898, in *Florida Historical Quarterly*, vol. xlix No. 1, July 1970, pp. 3-4.
9. Quote, Ibid. p. 4.
10. Frederick Funston, *Memories of Two Wars: Cuban and Philippine Experiences*, New York, Scribner's Sons, 1911, paperback reprint, University of Nebraska, 2009.
11. Thomas W. Crouch, "Frederick Funston of Kansas: His Formative Years, 1867-1891," in *The Kansas Historical Quarterly*, Summer, 1974, vol 40, pp. 177-211.
12. Ibid.
13. Funston, *Memories of Two Wars*, pp. 150-151.
14. Funston quote: Ibid, pp. 156-7.
15. Gatewood, Negro Troops in Florida, pp. 2-3
16. Quote: John E. Lewis, 10th Cavalry, Lakeland, Florida, to Editor, *Illinois Record*, June 5, 1898, from: Gatewood, *Smoked Yankees*, pp.30-33.
17. Official Enlistment Records from National Archives, Washington D.C. copies provided to me by Paul Harrison, Archives I Reference Section, Research Services, Washington, DC, letter Harrison to Hoffman, September 27, 2011. The documents furnished by Mr. Harrison were found in Record Group 94: Records of the Adjutant General's Office, Entry 91: Series II Enlistment Papers, (1894-1912) for "a David Fagan/Fagen. Company H, 24th U.S. Infantry." Included are two Registers of Enlistment, as well as other Enlistment Papers and his Registers of Enlistment.
18. Frank Schubert, "Seeking David Fagen: The Search for a Black Rebel's Florida

Roots," in *Tampa Bay Historical Quarterly*, Vol. 22 (2008), p. 27.
19. Ibid. p. 24
20. Gatewood, Negro Troops in Florida, pp. 7-8
21. Quote: Captain William G. Muller, Adjutant, *The Twenty Fourth Infantry Past and Present*, U.S. Army Regimental Record, first published 1923, paperback reprint, Old Army Press, Ft. Collins, Colorado, 1972, p. 14 [Note: The pages of this reprint are unnumbered. The page I cite is counted from the first page of historical copy following the lists of former commanders, citations, etc.).
22. Quote, Edward Van Zile Scott, *The Unwept, Black American Soldiers and the Spanish-American War*, Black Belt Press, Montgomery, Alabama (1996) Note 8, pp. 222-3.
23. Telegram, Gen. Miles to War Department, from: Richard H. Titherington, *A History of the Spanish-American War of 1898*, D. Appleton & Co., N.Y. 1900, paperback reprint: BiblioLife, LLC, Charleston, S.C. 2010, p. 208.
24. Quotes from Holliday to Editor, *New York Age*, in: Gatewood, Smoked Yankees, pp. 95-96.
25. Quote, Chaplain T.G. Steward, *The Colored Regulars in the United States Army*, A.M.E. Book Concern, Philadelphia, 1904, reprint, Forgotten Books, Classic Reprint Series, January 2012 p. 221, see: www.forgottenbooks.org
26. Quote, Frank W. Fullen., Jr. in: Edward A. Johnson, *History of Negro Soldiers in the Spanish-American War, and other Items of Interest*, March 23, 1899, Raleigh, N. C. reprint, Electronic Paperback Edition, Filiquarian Publishing, LLC, pp. 16-17.
27. Quote, Ibid. p. 116-117.

◀Chapter Three▶

VOYAGE OF THE DAMNED

SHEPHERDED BY FIVE WARSHIPS, the thirty-one-ship convoy which was carrying Fagen to war slipped away from Tampa Bay over calm seas. Just after sunset, the officer in charge of the 24th Infantry Regiment's band decided it was the perfect time for stirring music. Delighted to escape the hellhole of the *City of Washington*'s fetid hold, the musicians hurriedly made their way to the upper deck with their instruments. The ship's deck lights were turned on and the band assembled just forward of the bridge. A few moments later, exulting in the light breeze, they struck up the *Star-Spangled Banner*.

It was one of those windless nights when sound carries for miles across the surface of a becalmed sea. In a minute or two, responding to the music, one after another the deck lights on the other transports came on. Soon other regimental bands were blaring out patriotic and martial tunes. The ambiance of the convoy changed from that of a menacing fleet of warships carrying some 17,000 invasion troops, to that of a flotilla of pleasure liners sailing on a light-hearted summer cruise.

As the faster ships drew forward, the perimeter of the convoy lengthened, and soon the fleet stretched for twenty-five miles across the horizon. Every few hours General Shafter halted the Ward Liner *Seguranca*, his flagship, to allow the fleet to advance to his position and be counted. It soon became apparent that the *City of Washington* and the *Yucatan* (with Teddy Roosevelt and his fellow Rough Riders on board) were the slowest ships in the convoy. Shafter repeatedly ordered the gunboat *Bancroft* and the armed yacht *Wasp* to speed back, locate the laggards and herd them once again into the main fleet.

By eight p.m. the 24th Infantry band members were ready to play for the entire voyage if they could remain on the upper deck.

Standing at the railing just outside the bridge of the *Seguranca,* Captain Alfred W. Paget of the Royal Navy, stared at the merry convoy in utter disbelief. Paget was one of two foreign attachés assigned as observers, and he had already noted that the troopships were carrying only enough lifeboats to serve their crews. The young captain was also very much aware that the fleet could be attacked at any moment by speedy Spanish torpedo boats (later, these little fighting ships would be called "destroyers"). In his report, Paget noted, "Had any of these made an attack on the fleet spread over an enormous area, each ship a blaze of lights and with the bands playing at times, a smart Spanish officer could not have failed to inflict a very serious loss."[1]

General Shafter believed the only Spanish fighting ships that posed any danger to the invasion fleet were now confined within Santiago Bay, blockaded by a vastly superior American fleet under the command of Rear Admiral William T. Sampson.

The trapped Spanish squadron consisted of five cruisers and two light destroyers, all commanded by fifty-nine-year-old Admiral Pascual Cervera. The Admiral knew that waiting for him just outside the 350-foot-wide mouth of Santiago Bay were five U.S. battleships, two heavy cruisers, two armed yachts, a gunboat, a collier (a ship designed to carry coal for the warships) and a steel tugboat. Sampson's fleet was deployed so that each of the battleships and cruisers could train their heavy guns on the narrow mouth of Santiago Harbor.

Cervera's hapless situation was further aggravated by the fact that one of his biggest cruisers had not had her guns mounted and consequently, was of no use other than as a target. Another of his heavy cruisers was undergoing repairs and was essentially immobile. At anchor, sheltered inside Santiago Bay, the Spanish ships were covered by a number of shore batteries located in key positions in the hills above the bay, and there were two armed forts guarding its entrance. Unless the Americans sailed away, Cervera knew that if he was ordered to make a run for it, their heavily-gunned warships would quickly obliterate his little fleet. It wouldn't be a fight, it would be a massacre, and Admiral Cervera did not want to be remembered as the naval officer responsible for the deaths of so many brave Spanish sailors.

In letters to the Minister of Marine in Madrid, to General Blanco at

Havana, and to General Linares at Santiago, Cervera informed his superiors that his fleet had no chance at all if ordered to vacate the bay. To challenge the superior enemy force that was waiting for him would be pointless. The American ships were like a pride of lions awaiting an orphaned wildebeest.

Forty miles to the east of Santiago Bay, a few hundred U.S. Marines had landed near Guantanamo, and after considerable fighting they and the Cuban insurgent forces sent to aid them were now in possession of the place, assuring that its big harbor was available if needed.

Things were not going well for the Spanish navy. Just fifteen days earlier, Admiral George Dewey's American Squadron had slipped into Manila Bay at dawn and had sunk virtually all the Spanish warships in the Philippine Islands. Thus far, the Spanish navy had been greatly outmatched.

David Fagen—17 June—Aboard the *City of Washington*

Because he had worked for at least a year harvesting phosphate rock under Tampa's glaring sun, David Fagen was in far better shape to endure the fetid, oven-like conditions of the transport's hold than his fellow soldiers. Even so, the stench from the mixture of human and animal feces and vomit was so awful that everyone was more than eager to get ashore, whether the enemy was waiting there for them or not. Unable to avoid the constant noise from the throbbing of the ship's steam engine, most of Fagen's comrades would have given anything to have been freed from their iron prison. Had they been told that they would have to endure their tortuous captivity for two full weeks, the probability of mutiny or suicide may well have become a reality.

Just after dawn on the morning of 19 June, fifty-nine-year-old General Calixto Garcia, Frederick Funston's former patron, commander, and benefactor during the time when Funston had fought with the Cubans as an artillery officer, was seated aboard a whaleboat rowed by four American sailors over big, rolling swells. Behind the whaleboat was the beach of the coastal town of Aserrederos, and a mile or so off its bow was the menacing silhouette of the armed cruiser U.S.S. *New York*, where Admiral William T. Sampson awaited the Cuban leader.

Born into a Spanish military family in Cuba in 1839, Major General

General Calixto Garcia and staff, in camp at Aserrederos, Santiago, Cuba.
(*US National Archives*)

Calixto Ramon Garcia de Ineguez was a tall, big-boned, ramrod straight Creole with an ugly, sunken scar in the center of his forehead. Balding, with a large, flowing white mustache, Garcia had been battling against Spanish rule in Cuba for over thirty years. In September 1874, when he was thirty-five years old, a vastly superior force of Spanish troops cornered Garcia and some twenty of his comrades, and the outcome was obvious. Rather than being taken alive, Garcia uttered a short prayer, placed the muzzle of his pistol inside his mouth, and pulled the trigger. Instead of destroying his brain as he had intended, the heavy .45 caliber bullet bounced off some bone and exited through the center of his forehead. Much to his chagrin, when he regained consciousness, his head was bandaged and he was confined in Spanish shackles.

After being shipped to Spain, Garcia was imprisoned near Madrid for four long years. His eventual release was a consequence of a short-lived peace treaty enacted between Cuban revolutionaries and the Spaniards. Within months he had made his way back to Cuba. If anything, the time he spent rotting in the Spanish prison had served to solidify his opposition. He next played a major role in yet another doomed revolt, this one ending in 1880 with Garcia once again a prisoner of the Spanish. This time he was exiled to Madrid with his family, where they lived under house arrest under the full-time observation of the Guardia Civil. Garcia remained there for fifteen years. Then, just after the current Cuban revolution broke out in 1894, he escaped, and by 1896 the general was once again back fighting Spaniards in his home country.[2]

Seventeen days earlier, at the coastal town of Banes, located directly north of Santiago but on the Atlantic side of the island, an American naval lieutenant had delivered Garcia a message from the Commander-in-Chief of the U.S. Army, General Nelson A. Miles. Miles informed the Cuban that America soon meant to invade and capture the City of Santiago, and the United States was requesting his aid and support.

In response, Garcia rushed thousands of insurgents to the three chief Spanish military posts in the province, with orders to block Spanish attempts to reinforce Santiago once the American invasion was under way. In addition, Garcia had sent several brigades of troops to help the American marines who had landed at Guantanamo. Supplied with rifles, ammunition and other stores by the U.S. Navy at Banes Harbor, Garcia and 4,000 Cuban volunteers set out for Aserrederos, some twenty-one miles west of Santiago Bay. Despite being short of provisions and fresh water, Garcia and his guerrilla army had crossed the island, climbing over the Sierra Maestra (Cuba's largest mountain range) in the process, and, after marching for nine days had that very morning arrived at their destination.

Garcia recognized that a successful American invasion and the capture of the City of Santiago—Cuba's oldest city and its former capital—plus the destruction of the Spanish fleet now trapped in Santiago Bay, would mean the end of Spanish control over Cuba. With no way to re-supply their troops from Spain, the enemy was doomed. As a result, Garcia was aware that his forthcoming meeting with Admiral Sampson would be one of the most important events of his life. As a representative of the Cuban people and as a leader who had spent most of his adult life fighting for Cuba's liberty, Calixto Garcia wanted very much to make a favorable impression. But at the moment he was seasick, and the only battle he was fighting was the one he was losing against the urge to vomit.[3]

On the bridge of his flagship, Rear Admiral Sampson was one of the few American officers who did not underestimate the importance of General Garcia and the Cuban insurgents. While the coastal maps at his disposal were more than satisfactory, American inland maps for this region of Cuba provided little detail and were utterly useless to an invading army. Sampson knew that what the United States desperately needed was the native Cubans' knowledge of the terrain. Although he had the Spanish fleet bottled up in Santiago Harbor, even if he sank their whole damned navy it would all be meaningless if the invasion failed. The invasion was the main event, and as things stood at that moment the odds for an American victory were nil.

Initially, General Shafter's invasion force was to have no less than 50,000 troops. Later that number had been reduced to 31,000. Now, due to the shortage of transports, the real invasion strength had dropped below 17,000 troops. If they could be sure of the strength of the Spanish army around Santiago—their dispositions, their condition, their armaments, and their likely tactics—they would have a chance. Even so, the outcome would be dicey. The most optimistic estimates claimed that the Spanish had a minimum of 25,000 regulars available, many of them manning strong defensive positions that they had had years to perfect. Add to those factors the dangers of the infamous Cuban fevers and diseases that were exacerbated by the tropical heat and humidity, and you had a recipe for disaster. In the end, sinking the Spanish fleet would be the easy part.

After General Garcia had been ushered into his presence on the bridge, Sampson realized at once that the man was seasick. Even so, the Cuban's salute was quick and precise. Following introductions, Garcia asked in an urgent, embarrassing tone, to be taken to where he could be sick again. After returning, the pallid general withdrew several hand-drawn maps from his map case. He placed them over those that had already been stacked on the navigation table, and the real meeting commenced.

Although their discussion was interrupted by bouts of seasickness, Admiral Sampson was bolstered by his visitor. Within a few moments, he realized that Garcia and the Cubans knew all about the terrain and the Spanish forces that they would mutually face. Speaking convincingly, Garcia believed his men would be able to successfully block Spanish attempts at reinforcing Santiago City, and they would also be able to provide guides to the Americans—men who lived in the area and who knew every road, trail and path in the province. He then pointed out that his troops were in dire need of food, medical supplies and additional armaments, and he was relying upon these being supplied by the Americans.

Sampson agreed at once to supply the Cubans from his stores. Despite Garcia's recurring nausea, the old soldier's enthusiasm and optimism was infectious. By the end of their meeting Sampson was convinced that Garcia and his collection of gallant insurgents could make victory more than possible—in fact, they made it likely.

Placing one of his big hands on the map of Santiago Harbor, Garcia wanted to know the range of Sampson's heaviest guns. Sampson told him and the Cuban smiled. Garcia then pointed out that every approach to Santiago City as well as the city itself were within range of Sampson's fleet.

Aware that his guest was uncomfortable and likely had no appetite, Sampson hurried the ending of their conference. He informed Garcia that either the next day or the day after, General Shafter would arrive with the invasion fleet and he would most certainly want to meet with him. Garcia welcomed the meeting, but wryly insisted that this time it should take place at his headquarters at Aserrederos, on solid ground.

Sampson grinned and returned Garcia's salute. The general followed a Marine escort out of the bridge to stairs that led down to where his whaleboat was rising and falling with the swells. Still queasy, Garcia accepted the reality that there was no way for him to avoid another tortuous voyage back to his headquarters.

Admiral Sampson was in a good mood. He had indeed been favorably impressed by the Cuban general who had made him feel considerably better about the coming conflict. Writing about his impression of Garcia, Sampson said: "[He was] a man of most frank and engaging manners, and most soldierly appearance."[4]

As soon as the bottom of the whaleboat grounded over wet sand a few hundred feet from the high tide line, Garcia jumped down and was reassured by the solid feeling of *terra firma* beneath his feet. He nodded his thanks to the whaleboat crew who were already shoving their boat back into deeper water, turned and made his way up the beach. In an hour his appetite had returned, and like Admiral Sampson he too savored the moment. After a hearty lunch and his customary siesta, he summoned his generals and together they began to create the invasion plan Garcia would present to General Shafter.

Following the Battle of Santiago, in Garcia's official war report addressed to his superior, Major General Maximo Gomez, Commander-in-Chief of the Cuban armies, Garcia referred to his meetings with Sampson and Shafter as follows:

> My purpose at that place [Aserrederos] was to conference with U.S. Navy Admiral Sampson who had called the meeting to discuss the best way to attack Santiago. This conference took place on the U.S. Admiralty vessel New York.
>
> To clarify this matter, I ordered my troops to march on Santiago de Cuba; and went to the meeting called by the Chief of the U.S. Navy force. I began following orders and instructions of the Chiefs of the U.S. Armed Forces as soon as they began to attempt entry into areas under my command.
>
> On June 20 at 2 pm Brigadier General Demetrio Castillo, Commander of the Ramon de Las Yaguas Brigade landed at Aserradero. General Castillo had arrived from Sigua on a U.S. vessel. His purpose was to await my orders.
>
> Soon after, Major General William R. Shafter, Commander of the Fifth Corps of the U.S. Army came ashore to talk with me. General Shafter was in charge of the U.S. forces that were being readied to attack Santiago. After a long conference and having accepted my plan for landing his troops and advancing successfully on Cuba, the American general returned to the ship.[5]

A young lieutenant on General Shafter's staff wrote the following comments about the departure of the general from General Garcia's tent at the conclusion of their meeting:

> While the interview was going on, the troops were being assembled

to do honor to the General on his departure. Several companies were drawn up in front of the tent to present arms as he came out, and a regiment escorted him to the beach down the winding path, which was now lined on both sides by Cuban soldiers standing about a yard apart and presenting arms. The scene made a strong impression on all in the party, there seemed to be such an earnestness and fixedness of purpose displayed that all felt these soldiers to be a power. About fifty per cent were blacks, and the rest mulattoes, with a small number of whites. They were very poorly clad, many without shirts or shoes, but every man had his gun and a belt full of ammunition. [6]

As Sampson, Shafter and their staffs were meeting with Garcia and his principal officers, the soldiers of the invading army, packed tightly on the transports anchored offshore, roasted and gasped the hot, rancid air.

The Battle of Santiago began at dawn on 22 June, when a number of Sampson's warships (not including those still blockading Santiago Harbor) began to pound the shoreline with their big guns, aiming at targets from

Sunken Spanish warship beached just outside entrance to Santiago Harbor. Moro Castle on hill in background as American troopship approaches.
(US National Archives)

just west of Santiago Bay all the way to the port of Daiquiri. Sailing in a long line to facilitate massive broadsides, they fired at Spanish positions, blockhouses and forts, commercial buildings, villages, and even heavily forested ridges above the beaches. The barrage went on for a little over two hours.

For David Fagen, H Company, and all the other troops waiting in the holds of the transport ships, there was no mistaking the meaning of the thundering booming as salvo after salvo of shells flew landward. Two urges were now driving the troops: the first was to escape their iron ovens, and the second was the growing desire to get the battle started that they had come to fight. Anticipating the coming debarkation, the troops readied their uniforms, ammo belts, packs, blanket rolls and other gear. None of them knew when or where they were to be sent ashore, but everyone wanted to be prepared, and this at least gave them something to focus on. Given their situation, the waiting seemed interminable, and their gear was packed, unpacked, and then packed again.

The 24th Infantry Regiment had not been issued new uniforms, and they were wearing the same heavy clothing they had used while serving at Fort Douglas, Utah. Like the rest of his comrades, Fagen was sweating profusely. Among the many rumors and statements being passed around was one about the sea being their first and deadliest enemy. The sergeants warned that if they somehow fell overboard trying to climb in or out of the landing boats while wearing their gear, with their rifles slung cross-shoulder to leave their arms free for climbing, they would immediately plunge to the bottom, drowning on the way down.

Instead of joining up with the transports that were going to be landing their troops at Daiquiri, the *City of Washington* joined a smaller fleet of transports that sailed west about a mile beyond the entrance to Santiago Bay, and then started circling just off the coastal village of Cabanas. Closer to the shoreline, fast-moving U.S. warships began to shell the town.

Eventually, increasing their frustration, the men of the 24th Infantry were ordered to stand down. They were not going to disembark that day; at the moment, they were part of a *faux* invasion designed to confuse the Spanish.

Amidst curses and angry murmurs, the troops began to remove their gear, including their shirts, trousers and boots. Their disappointment was palpable. There was nothing else to do but lie in their bunks and sweat. They were very much aware that other troops, most of who were white, were being landed in the real invasion. Above them, their white officers were waiting in small cabins on the upper deck with doors and portholes open, or standing at the rail watching the distant naval show. To say that Fagen and his comrades were disgruntled would be an understatement. Some of the sergeants were considering their options if discipline broke down completely.

Soon after the naval bombardment of little Cabanas began, the outskirts came under attack by about a thousand Cuban fighters under General Agustin Cebreco. Playing their role in the false invasion subterfuge, the Cubans fired their rifles at Spaniards who had not yet withdrawn. Later that afternoon, in a deadly serious action, General Cebreco's troops hurried to block the roads that Spanish reinforcements would use to aid Santiago City.

The main American invasion began at 10:00 a.m., some fourteen miles Northwest of Santiago Bay, at the small hamlet of Daiquiri.[7]

Determined to protect their ships and their lives from mines or Spanish artillery, the civilian skippers who commanded the chartered transports kept their vessels two miles from shore. They pointedly ignored frantic signals from the nearby U.S. warships ordering them to move in closer. [8]

The navy had some fifty whaleboats available for ferrying troops to shore. Towed in strings of three or four by steam launches, some of the landing boats sailed out to the nearest transport with no regard for the invasion plan. Other boats searched for hours for their assigned ships. As a result, logistic and supply troops were the first to be put ashore, while some six hundred crack invasion troops remained aboard their transports until late in the afternoon. Chaos ruled.

The shoreline at Daiquiri was still being pounded by the warships. Buildings, rail stations, and even clumps of coconut trees were torn apart in the bombardment. Pushing retreating Spanish troops ahead of them, exactly as planned, a thousand Cuban troops under the command of Brigadier General Demetrio Castillo raced in and took possession of the little harbor. The Cubans hurriedly raised their flag, and as soon as it was spotted the U.S. naval barrage ceased. Thanks to Garcia's forces, the disorganized and confused Americans could now land unopposed.

American landings at Daiquiri, Cuba, June 22, 1898. (*US National Archives*)

There were two small piers in Daiquiri's harbor, one of which was a steel installation topped by a set of rails to allow ore cars to load ships. The metal pier was built and owned by an American mining company whose iron ore mine was a few miles inland. Built to service steamships, the coaling pier was far too high above the swells to offload troops from whaleboats. A second pier, this one a smaller wooden structure that the Spanish had attempted to burn, was chosen as an alternative. Because the swells were quite high, the landings at the short wooden pier were dangerous and chaotic. Each boat snugged up against the slippery pilings, her lines manned by sailors standing on the dock. The troopers nearest the pier waited for the top of a swell and then tossed their rifles or packs onto it. At the apex of the next swell, the soldiers themselves leapt to the dock.

While one whaleboat was being offloaded a dozen others drifted nearby, awaiting their turn. The process was taking too much time, and by mid-day the boats began disgorging their passengers directly onto the beach, just beyond the surf line. One boat soon capsized and two soldiers drowned; they were the first and only casualties of the landing. The beach operations continued, with offloaded soldiers holding their rifles overhead and wading towards the beach, reveling in the cool freshness of the water. Once they were up on the shoreline, most of the men quickly stripped off their sweat-soaked shirts; some of them even removed their trousers and went naked except for their hats. A few men washed their shirts in the surf while others, as though at a beach party, cavorted in the waves. Others began offloading equipment and supplies from grounded whaleboats. A few soldiers simply sat in chest-high water as if in meditation, and let the surf wash in and recede. Having been fed inadequate and rotten food during the voyage from Tampa, a number of men were already combing the jungle above the beach, collecting coconuts, mangoes and other wild fruits. Keeping their distance, the Cuban fighters watched in astonishment.

Dear Mother:

When we got to Cuba, we did not go on land for two days and remained two miles from shore, believing the harbor to be full of mines.

The first day Sampson got all his gunboats together and fired shots all around the landing, tearing everything all around there all to pieces. The following day we all landed and went about a mile before we struck camp. That night about 7 o'clock the Captain asked the 1st Sergeant to send C.D. Kelly to him. I reported to the Captain, who asked me if I was afraid of the Spaniards, and I replied that I was not afraid of anything, whereupon the Captain ordered me to take my gun and belt and report to him. I soon returned and he said, 'Kirby, I want you to go to the dock and watch the grub, and if anyone comes around there kill him.'

Where I was stationed it was very dark, but about half past 12 o'clock two Spaniards approached. I saw them and kept very quiet until they were very close to me, and although a little afraid myself, I commanded them to halt. They did not stop, and in a loud tone of voice I repeated it twice again, but they kept on coming, so I stepped behind a rock, took aim and killed one of them. The other shot at me, but missed, the bullet striking a rock, glanced and hit me on the shoulder, not doing any damage. I then shot at him, but did not kill him, although he fell to the ground. Going to him, I asked him how he was feeling and he said 'pretty bad,' whereupon I took the butt end of my gun and knocked him in the head. He groaned and moved.

When morning came, I reported to the Captain and told him what had happened. He asked me if it was I shooting and upon telling him, yes, he said: 'Kirby, you are a brave man; you can go to your troop and rest up.' I said, 'Very well, Captain,' and went out. That night about 8 o'clock we broke camp to go to the fighting line, and we walked all night...."

C.D. Kirby, Troop I, Ninth Cavalry [9]

During the landing at Daiquiri, no provisions had been made to offload officer's horses or the wagon and pack mules. One by one the animals were simply pushed over the sides of the transports and left to swim for shore on their own. Unfortunately, once in the water, many of these animals had no idea where the shore was, and a number of them were swimming towards the open ocean.

Of all the stock to be transported to shore at Daiquiri, two horses received extra special treatment, for they were the personal mounts of Lieutenant Colonel Theodore Roosevelt, second in command of the already famous 1st Volunteer Cavalry, also known as the "Rough Riders." While the former Assistant Secretary of the Navy watched from a railing above the main deck, his mare, Rain-in-the-Face, enfolded in a jury-rigged sling, was hoisted up onto the deck and then swung out over the water by the ship's boom. The merchant seamen assigned to this duty knew exactly who they were serving and the need for extreme care. Observing the swells closely to estimate the right moment, the boom operator lowered the helpless horse into the sea. At that moment the sling release snagged, and before the mare could be freed she disappeared under a huge swell. When the water receded the horse reappeared, hanging lifeless from her sling. A string of profane curses issued from Roosevelt, so loud they could be heard from stem to stern on the *Yucatan*. Realizing there was nothing else they could do, a crewman yanked again on the trigger line and Rain-in-the-Face sank slowly beneath the surface. At this point Roosevelt's other horse, Texas, was hoisted up to the deck. Badly shaken by the earlier calamity and Roosevelt's resulting outrage, this time the boom operator let the horse dangle over the water for several minutes. Unable to contain himself, Roosevelt's angry voice boomed: "Stop that God-damned animal torture!"

A moment later the sling released properly. Texas swam off and, as the story goes, was one of the animals who decided to swim back to Tampa. Fortunately, someone on the beach grasped the situation, and a bugler began to repeatedly trumpet cavalry calls. Hearing these familiar sounds, most of the officers' horses turned for shore, followed by many of the wayward mules.[10]

> We landed in Cuba June 22, 1898 and our past hardships were soon forgotten. It was enough to stir the heart of any lover of liberty to witness that portion of Gomez's ragged army, under command of General Castillo, lined up to welcome us to their beautiful island, and to guide and guard our way to the Spanish strongholds. To call it a ragged army is by no means a misnomer. The greater portion of those poor fellows were both coatless and shoeless, many of them being almost nude. They were by no means careful about their uniform. The thing everyone seemed careful about was his munitions of war, for each man had his gun, ammunition and machete. Be it remembered that this portion of the Cuban army was almost entirely composed of black Cubans ....
>
> Frank W. Pullen, Jr. Ex-Sergeant Major
> 25th U.S. Infantry (USCT) March 23, 1899

By sundown, some six thousand American troops were ashore at Daiquiri. Early the next morning, General Henry W. Lawton's division followed Cuban troops eleven miles westward to Siboney. General Shafter

Situational map of American, Cuban, and Spanish positions before the Battle of Santiago. (*US National Archives*)

had selected this city for his main supply base, and ten thousand more American soldiers were scheduled to be landed in the next three days. Pursued by Cuban fighters under General Castillo, the Spaniards who had vacated Daiquiri were in full retreat. Lawton sent a report to Shafter stating that "the town was in his hands, and he had also captured one locomotive and nearly one hundred cars loaded with coal."[11]

Moving inward early in the morning on 23 June, forward elements of a Cuban brigade led by General Castillo sought contact with Spaniards who had abandoned Siboney. Climbing over a footpath that wound upwards through dense jungle forestation, the Cubans reached a place where the trail joined the Camino Real highway, just at the base of a three-hundred-foot-high hill named after the *guacima* (hog-nut) trees that grew nearby—Las Guasimas. Unknown to the Cubans, the hilltop that they looked up at was now the redoubt of some 1,000 Spanish troops who, behind numerous barbed-wire entanglements, were manning trenches and a stone blockhouse that had firing loops (thin vertical holes) piercing its massive walls.

Hit suddenly by a volley of rifle fire, the Cubans at the point of their column dove down for cover, to no avail. Against the volume of fire they were taking from above, the vegetation they were hiding under was worthless. The bullets from Spanish Mausers peppered the area around them, and in a moment one man was dead and another nine were wounded. Outnumbered and vulnerable, the Cubans hastily withdrew, carrying their wounded with them. They were forced to leave their dead comrade at the head of the footpath.

General Joseph Wheeler, Confederate hero of the Civil War.
(*US National Archives*)

That evening, in his headquarters tent at the American encampment located in a valley just above Siboney, sixty-one-year-old General Joseph "Fighting Joe" Wheeler considered his next move. He was at Siboney only because General Shafter thought the inclusion of a former Confederate cavalry hero would help to show the country that the soldiers of the north and south were once again united. Seeking to earn his keep, and in pursuit of glory, "Fighting Joe" was determined to be the first to lead American troops into battle and victory in Cuba, and General Castillo, who stood beside him, had just revealed the location of the Spanish positions at Las Guasimas. Turning to Brigadier General S.B.M. Young, Wheeler began formulating battle plans for the next morning.

Before leaving Wheeler's headquarters tent, General Castillo offered to support the Americans with 800 of his men early in the morning, so that they could attack the Spaniards together. How General Wheeler regarded Castillo's offer is unknown, but it is not likely that he welcomed sharing his anticipated glory.

Cuban revolutionary soldiers in camp near Daiquiri, Cuba. *(US National Archives)*

At this point the majority of the Americans regarded the Cuban soldiers as mobs of undisciplined, untrained, half-naked black natives, poorly armed and clearly underfed. The Americans had already learned to cache their blanket rolls, haversacks or other equipment to march over rough, rugged terrain in the almost unbearable heat. However, when they returned to retrieve their belongings, they found that the Cuban fighters had already been there and had helped themselves to almost everything.

Since the majority of the civilians they encountered were black, in rags and half-starved, the white American soldiers showed them no compassion. The Buffalo Soldiers saw things differently. In their eyes, the Cubans were the obvious victims of terrible Spanish oppression and their men were fighting for their freedom. But because of their disorganized appearance and their lack of training and discipline, neither the Buffalo Soldiers nor the white troops thought much of the Cubans' fighting abilities, and were reluctant to rely upon them as combat allies.

One thing the American and Spanish forces shared were the latest European concepts of proper war conduct, including the "civilized" treatment of captured enemy forces. When the Battle of Santiago concluded, wounded soldiers from both sides were treated at Spanish and American hospital wards.

Ignoring European niceties of combat, the Cubans showed little if any mercy to the Spaniards who fell into their hands.

> The barracks where the 8th Illinois is quartered is an old Spanish prison and there are all kinds of evidence of cruelty and butchery—beheading blocks all covered with human hair and dried blood, and pieces of rope still hanging from the old round rafters, where many a poor unfortunate Cuban has been hung. Old bloody blankets were carried out of the hospital department of that old crib of a barracks where Cubans had been butchered, and the blankets burned by American soldiers. Some of these sights are terrible.
>
> W. B. Roberts
> Capt. Co F
> 23rd Kansas Regiment (USCT) [12]

None of the American troops now on Cuban soil could fully understand the depth of the anger of the Cubans who had endured savage treatment for decades under Spanish rule. The inhumanities included torture, starvation, rape, hangings and the forced confinement of entire populations in "concentration camps," the object of which was to deny insurgent fighters food, armaments, money or other supplies.

From the start, the Cuban revolutionaries were amazed by the Norte Americanos, who wore handsome new uniforms, fine hats, new boots and who carried ponchos, blanket rolls, haversacks, bayonets, knives, pistols and rifles. The Americans had machine guns, dynamite cannons, fast-firing Hotchkiss mountain guns, and were serviced by seemingly endless

Cuban refugees at Siboney, July 1898. (*US National Archives*)

lines of mule-drawn wagons bringing them ammunition, food, water and other supplies. They even had mule-drawn ambulances to carry away their wounded. Even so, at this point in time, when none of the Americans had yet faced the Spaniards, neither the Cuban officers nor their ragged fighters had any idea how well the invaders would fight, and they were anxious to find out.

Brigadier General Young's plan of attack was to advance a squadron of the 1st Cavalry and another of the 10th Cavalry (Colored)—four hundred sixty-four men in all—along with a battery of two Hotchkiss guns, about four miles up the Camino Real highway, while his other five hundred troops (the Rough Riders), led by Colonel Leonard Wood, were to climb up on the same jungle path that Castillo's men had taken the day before. The plan called for the two brigades to join together where the footpath crossed the main road and then proceed to assault the Spanish position. At half-past five the Americans began their march without Castillo and his Cuban fighters.[13]

Two hours later, on the same trail that the Cubans had used the day before, advance elements of the 1st Cavalry Volunteers (Rough Riders) climbed forward as stealthily as possible through trees and dense underbrush.

On point were Captain Allyn Capron and Sergeant Hamilton Fish—two of the biggest men in the regiment. A little behind them, mounted on his horse and flanked by three aides, was Colonel Wood. Behind Wood rode Teddy Roosevelt on his mount Texas, and walking beside him were his two favorite reporters, Richard Harding Davis of the *New York Herald* and Edward Marshall of the *New York Journal*.[14]

Off to their right and a half mile to the east, General Young and the two cavalry outfits were marching up the Camino Real.

Flushed with visions of patriotism, gallantry, bravery and heroism, Roosevelt and his cowboy volunteers' march to glory met reality head on a little after 7:30 a.m., when their Cuban scout came upon the abandoned and mutilated body of the Cuban trooper who had been killed there the day before. Vultures and land crabs had been at the fly-ridden body, which smelled terrible and whose eyes were now vacant sockets.

Roosevelt at this moment was sitting on the ground beside reporter Edward Marshall, discussing "a lunch they had once had with William Randolph Hearst at the Astor House."[15]

Suddenly, the violent sound of rifle and machine guns filled the air, and bullets struck the trees and ground around them. This was instantly followed by more sounds of gunfire coming from uphill. One of the bullets, a 7mm X 57 fully-jacketed Mauser projectile traveling at close to two thousand feet per second, burst into and out of Sergeant Hamilton Fish's head, exiting just ahead of a large spray of his blood and brain matter. With equal effectiveness, another Mauser bullet pierced Captain Allyn Capron's heart. No one hugging the ground at that moment was thinking about patriotism or glory, or a fine lunch at Astor House.

Roosevelt and his comrades were hopelessly pinned down by incessant, accurate fire from above and to their right. No response was possible since the Spaniards were using smokeless powder, and the Rough Riders had difficulty targeting them with their new Krag rifles. Hugging the ground beneath underbrush that did not in the least impede the Spanish bullets, the Rough Riders were in a very bad situation indeed.

At the first sound of firing, General Young put his two Hotchkiss guns into action and deployed troops left and right. Pressure from the 1st and 10th Cavalry soon forced the Spaniards shooting down on the right side of the Rough Riders to abandon their trench. With the pressure relieved, Roosevelt and his men started advancing up the hill, and an hour-and-a-half later the Americans pushed the Spanish off the top of Las Guasimas. The cost was sixteen men killed in action and fifty-two wounded. The Spaniards listed ten men killed and eight wounded, but these figures are disputed. Spanish troop strength at Las Guasimas is estimated to have been between 1,000 and 1,500 men.

Here is the version of the Las Guasimas fight that Fagen and the rest of the 24th Infantry heard after they had landed at Siboney, as revealed by Corporal John R. Conn, H Company, 24th Infantry, in a letter addressed to his sister on August 24, 1898:

> The first column, the Rough Riders, was the first to strike the enemy in ambush about 500 yards east of the junction of the two roads mentioned, receiving a volley that would have routed anybody but an American. The first regulars, hearing the music as they called it, hurried forward to join in the dance, and awoke a hornet's nest of Spaniards on the left, north of the party engaging the Rough Riders, and had more music than they could furnish dancers for. But, to the credit of the uniform and the flag, there is no account of either column giving an inch. They advanced sufficiently to come into line, and holding their ground until the much abused and poorly appreciated sons of Ham burst through the underbrush, delivered several volleys and yelling as only colored throats can yell, advanced on a run. Their position being still further to the north and opposite the left flank of the Spaniards, they (the Spaniards) broke and ran.... When the battle closed June 24 there were nineteen or twenty killed, but only one of them was colored.
>
> The first thing that greeted us when we came ashore was an exaggerated account of the day before. The killed and wounded, as rumor had it, was something like 200, and in evidence was a column of litters coming down the hill. I counted ten or twelve and they were still coming, and I think I was scared a little....[16]

The Splendid Little War had begun without David Fagen or the 24th Infantry, who were still sweating it out two miles off Siboney aboard the *City of Washington*. Orders for Fagen's unit to disembark arrived on the evening of 24 June. By then, having learned the hard way not to trust the civilian skippers, a navy captain had been assigned to board each transport, take command, and maneuver the ship to within a few hundred yards of shore. Under the glare of the ship's searchlights, the landings began early in the early morning on 25 June. What follows is an extract from the description of the event as written by one of the soldiers:

> It was one of the most weird and remarkable scenes of the war, probably of any war. An army was being landed on an enemy's coast at the dead of night, but with somewhat more of cheers and shrieks and laughter than rise from the bathers in the surf at Coney Island on a hot Sunday. It was a pandemonium of noises. The men still to be landed from the 'prison hulks,' as they called the transports, were singing in chorus; the men already on shore were dancing naked around the campfires on the beach… On either side rose black, overhanging ridges; in the lowland between were white tents and burning fires, and from the ocean came the blazing, dazzling eyes of the searchlights.[17]

Wading ashore with his new rifle held well above the water, David Fagen was intoxicated by the coolness of the water, the sweet fresh air, and the starry sky overhead. Around him, his comrades were whooping and laughing as they splashed their way towards shore. Ahead of him, glowing bonfires on the beach were multiplying. He could see the silhouetted forms of men jumping and dancing against the flames, and from behind him he could hear men singing. The way things were on the beach indicated that there must be fresh water and maybe something good to eat up there. Fagen's pace quickened.

No war worries tonight. Fagen was fast becoming a soldier, and like all the men of H-Company, 24th Infantry Regiment (USCT), this night was theirs and they would deal with tomorrow, tomorrow.

Notes

1. Quote "Had any of these" in: Edmund Morris *The Rise of Theodore Roosevelt*, (1979), Random House Trade Paperbacks edition (2010) p. 663.
2. From a biography of Calixto Garcia, on the website: http://spanamwar.com/Garciabio.htm.
3. See Richard H. Titherington, *A History of the Spanish-American War of 1898*, NY, 1900, reprint paperback, BiblioLife, Charleston, S. C. 2010, pp. 217-219.
4. Quote "A man of most frank…." from: *A History of the Spanish-American War of 1898*, Bibliolife reprint, p. 217.
5. Quote of Garcia from: *The Official War Report of Major General Calixto Ramon Garcia Iniguez*, dated July 15, 1898, translated by Larry Daley, in the website: http://spanamwar.com/Garcia.htm. Note: Most of the older American histories of these events belittle the contributions of the Cuban generals and their armies of volunteers. In his lauded *A History of the Spanish-American War of 1898*, writer Richard H. Titherington—a supporter of American expansionism who, like most of his contemporaries, regarded the Cubans as a lesser, ignoble "mostly black" race, wrote the following about General Garcia's pre-invasion meetings with Sampson and Shafter:

   "*In the afternoon the Seguranca took both commanders to Aserraderos, where they landed – Garcia not caring for another experience afloat – and conferred with the Cuban leader and Generals Rabi and Castillo. It is scarcely probable, if the campaign were to be fought over again, that the American admiral and major general would begin it by a visit to an impromptu camp, while an American army corps waited off shore.*"

   Instead of acknowledging that Shafter accepted Garcia's invasion plan, Titherington wrote: "*It was arranged, at Aserraderos, that at sunrise on the 22d a feint of landing should be made at Cabanas ….*"

   Quotes above, as cited, NY, D. Appleton & Company, 1900, reprint, paperback, BiblioLife, Charleston, S.C., 2012, p. 219.
6. Quote of Lt. Miley, from: T.G. Steward, D.D., *The Colored Regulars in the U.S. Army*, Philadelphia, 1904, paperback reprint, Forgotten Books, Lexington, KY, 2012 pp. 147-48.
7. William G. Mueller, *The Twenty Fourth Infantry, Past and Present*, Regimental

History, 1923, paperback reprint, Old Army Press, Ft. Collins, Colorado, 1972, p.14.
8. Titherington, *A History of the Spanish-American War of 1898,* NY 1900, paperback reprint, BiblioLife, Charleston S.C. 2012, p. 219.
9. It is highly unlikely that the men Kirby shot at were Spaniards. Hundreds of Cuban revolutionaries were camped just ahead of the Americans on the road to Santiago, and it is more likely that Kirby's victims were Cubans out to liberate what they could from the American stores. Quote taken from: Willard B. Gatewood, Jr., *Smoked Yankees and the Struggle for Empire,* University of Arkansas Press, Fayetteville, 1987, pp. 47-48.
10. For the story of Roosevelt's horses being off-loaded, see: Edmund Morris, *The Rise of Theodore Roosevelt,* Random House Trade Paperback, 2010, p 667.
11. Steward, *Colored Regulars in the U.S. Army,* reprint, Forgotten Books, Ky, 2012, p. 127.
12. Quote of W. B. Roberts from Willard B. Gatewood, Jr. *"Smoked Yankees"* paperback, University of Arkansas Press, Fayetteville, 1987, p. 191
13. Titherington, *History of the Spanish-American War,* reprint, BiblioLife, 2012, pp. 222-225.
14. Morris, *The Rise of Theodore Roosevelt,* paperback, 2010, pp. 671-677.
15. Quote "discussing a lunch" Ibid. p. 672.
16. Quote, John R. Conn to his sister, August 24, 1898, from: Gatewood, *Smoked Yankees,* pp. 65-66.
17. Quote of anonymous soldier regarding the night landing at Siboney, taken from Edward Van Zile Scott, *The Unwept—Black American Soldiers and the Spanish-American War,* 1966, Black Belt Press, Montgomery, Alabama, p. 108.

◄Chapter Four►

QUIT YOURSELVES LIKE MEN AND FIGHT!

FAGEN AND THE REST of the 24th Infantry hiked a mile inland and then were ordered to pitch their tents. They had not had a chance yet to fire their newly issued Krag rifles, and it's likely a rudimentary firing range was set-up. If so, a recruit like Fagen would have been coached on how to load, aim, fire and clear his weapon, and would have been shown how to zero his rifle's sights by making corrective elevation and windage adjustments.

On 25 June, the same day that Fagen's outfit landed, General Shafter met again with General Garcia at the latter's headquarters at Aserrederos. Garcia:

> He [General Shafter] gave me my orders to march towards Santiago the next day. He did the same, although some regiments and various cannon went forward that same day.
>
> …At dawn on June 26th the rest of my forces were on the steamships Seneca and Orizaba standing off Siboney. I, with my headquarter staff, and other Jefes by invitation of U.S. General Ludlow who was in charge of our landings, were on the Alamo. At 7 a.m. we started to land and by 10 a.m. we had landed, camping with the rest of the Cuban forces.
>
> There and in the town's immediate vicinity were our forces that had arrived earlier and several thousand of men of the U.S. Army. There were friendly exchanges between the Cuban and American forces. Since we were completely out of food in all our territory the Americans provided the necessary rations for our sustenance.
>
> On the 30th I camped with most of my forces on the Salado, three leagues from Siboney and one and a half leagues from Santiago. General Shafter placed his headquarters in the same place

[on a hill named El Pozo]. At three in the afternoon I received orders to move to Marianaje. This was between El Caney and San Juan, where I was to protect the batteries which were to shell both positions, from any attacks coming from Santiago....[1]

On 29 June, General Shafter finally came ashore. His gout was acting up, so his aides brought him a large mule which he rode to the top of El Pozo. From its crest, he had a view of both of the forthcoming battlefields, so he decided to make the place his new headquarters. On its southern side, El Pozo looked down on the Camino Real highway that connected Siboney to Santiago.

As he sat in the chair his aides had set up for him, Shafter propped his left leg up on a box. Facing westward, he could see the rooftops at the eastern edge of Santiago City, which was situated at the northern end of the bay. Slightly to the right, and considerably closer, stood the fortified mountain ridge called San Juan Hill, and just off its northern end another hilltop could be seen. This one had been named Kettle Hill, after a huge iron cauldron the former plantation owners had used to boil cane. Through his field glasses, Shafter carefully studied the stone blockhouses, trenches and other Spanish fortifications. He must have sensed that Spanish officers were most likely looking back at him through their own field glasses, as they studied all the activity atop El Pozo.

San Juan, Kettle Hill and El Caney were all about 2,400 yards distant from Shafter—well beyond the effective range of his meager artillery. Due to unloading problems, his heaviest guns were still at sea aboard their transports, and the guns that he had were too few to establish differing firing positions. Turning to his right, he lifted his glasses to study the top of El Caney. The hill was named for the town that nestled at the base of the mountain's northern slope. Garcia had told him that the Spanish maintained a garrison there to reinforce and supply the defenders at the crest of the hill.

The city of Santiago was far too large and well-garrisoned to be taken by any assault Shafter could mount with his small force. But El Caney, Kettle Hill and San Juan Hill all looked down on the city and commanded the only reasonable approaches an attacking army could use if it came by land.

With Sampson's fleet positioned just outside the entrance of the bay,

Santiago could no longer be supplied from the sea. However, the city was being serviced by Cobre Road, a major highway which led north and west. It entered the town at about the same place where a rail line led off to the northeast.

Shafter swung around and stared at San Juan Hill once more. The Spaniards had good defensive positions, including stone blockhouses and trenches with rock revetments. All the approaches were laced with barbed wire. Assaulting those slopes under direct fire would be murderous, but if his men finally won the hilltops, he could bring up his big guns. Caught between Sampson's naval cannons and his own artillery, the city of Santiago was doomed.

Spanish barbed wire on the slopes of El Caney. (*US National Archives*)

Shafter planned to begin his attacks on San Juan Hill and El Caney two days later, on 1 July. Garcia would move his forces to block the Cobre Road where, it was believed, a Spanish relief column of from three to four thousand troops was already marching from Manzanillo. Garcia's men were also tasked to seize the rail line that fed Santiago. Once El Caney was in Shafter's hands, he would send another American division to swing north to the village of Cubitas, where they would seize Santiago's water reservoir and cut the aqueduct that watered the city.

With no hope of receiving food, water, ammunition, reinforcements or other supplies, Santiago would wither and die. What Shafter worried about was whether it would do so before Cuba's dreaded fevers (yellow fever, malaria, typhoid, dysentery, and dengue) decimated his little army. Shafter sent the following cable to Washington:

> Advance pickets within a mile and a half of Santiago. No opposition. Spaniards have evidently withdrawn to immediate vicinity of that town. Expect to put division on Caney road, between that place and Santiago, day after tomorrow, and will also advance on Sevilla road to San Juan River, and possibly beyond. General Garcia, with three thousand men, will take railroad north of Santiago at the same time to prevent [reinforcements] reaching city.[2]

Not counting their white officers, there were some 104 black troopers (including Fagen) in H-Company of the 24th Infantry, one of whom was John R. Conn, a sensitive, literate corporal. Soon after the fighting was over, Corporal Conn communicated his experiences in a letter to his sister, Mrs. J.W. Cromwell, of Washington D.C.:

> …We camped here three days, while different parts of the army were marching past us taking their places in columns between us and Santiago. At last our turn came—3rd Brigade, 1st Division—to move forward and go in camp on the same ground made sacred by the blood of the Rough Riders [Las Guasimas] where we stayed in camp three days. June 30, the army was again put in motion, and all day long there was almost a continual column of soldiers passing our camp until about 4 o'clock in the afternoon, when a general call was sounded in headquarters and we struck tents and took our final position in line. We advanced about four miles further west, but the road was so densely choked with soldiers that it was 10 o'clock before we went in camp, and everybody knew what to expect in the morning.[3]

QUIT YOURSELVES LIKE MEN AND FIGHT!

On 23 June, the day before Fagen's outfit landed at Siboney, Spanish Admiral Pascual Cervera met with his captains on board his flagship the *Infanta Maria Teresa* to discuss their worsening situation. Just prior to their meeting, Cervera had sent the following message to the Minister of Marine in Spain:

The Admiral (Cervera) to the Minister (Aunon)
Santiago, De Cuba, June 23, 1898

The enemy took possession of Daiquiri yesterday. Will surely occupy Siboney today, in spite of brilliant defense. The course of events is very painful, though not unexpected. Have disembarked squadron crews to aid army. Yesterday five battalions went out from Manzanille. If they arrive in time agony will be prolonged but I doubt much whether they will save city from catastrophe.

As it is absolutely impossible for squadron to escape under these circumstances, intend to resist as long as possible and destroy ships as last extreme. Although others are responsible for this untenable situation into which we were forced in spite of my opposition, it is very painful to be a shackled actor therein.[4]

Cervera was a realist dealing with madmen. On 25 June, he received the following message from General Arsenio Linares, Commander-in-Chief of the Army of Santiago:

My Dear Admiral and Friend: In a cipher cable received last night the Captain-General says, among other things, as follows: 'I beg that your Excellency will tell Admiral Cervera that I should like to know his opinion and plans. It is my opinion that he should go out from Santiago as early as possible whenever he may deem best, for the situation in that harbor is, in my judgment, the most dangerous of all.

...If we should lose the squadron without fighting, the

79

moral affect would be terrible, both in Spain and abroad.'

Yours, etc.
Arsenio Linares [5]

In Havana, Captain-General Blanco was apparently ready to sacrifice all of Cervera's men and his ships for Spanish honor. Cervera was no magician, and he answered the only way he could:

Santiago De Cuba, June 25, 1898
His Excellency Arsenio Linares,

...The Captain-General is kind enough to want to know my opinion, and I am going to give it as explicitly as I ought to, but will confine myself to the squadron, as I believe that is what he asks for

...The sortie from here must be made by the ships, one by one. There is no possibility of stratagem nor disguise, and the absolutely certain result will be the ruin of each and all of the ships and the death of the greater part of their crews. If I had thought there was even the remotest chance of success I should have made the attempt, although, as I have said before, it would only have amounted to a change of the scene of action unless we had gone to Havana, where things might, perhaps, have been different. For these reasons and in order that my forces might make themselves useful in some manner, I proposed to you to send them ashore, just at the time when the Captain-General made the same suggestion.

Today I consider the squadron lost as much as ever, and the dilemma is whether to lose it by destroying it, if Santiago is not able to resist, after having contributed to its defense, or whether to lose it by sacrificing to vanity the majority of its crews and depriving Santiago of their cooperation, thereby precipitating its fall. What is best to be done? I, who am a man without ambitions, without mad passions, believe that whatever is most expedient should be done, and I state most emphatically that I shall never be the one to decree the horrible and useless hecatomb which will be the only possible result of the sortie from here by main force, for I should consider myself responsible before God and history for the lives sacrificed on the alter of vanity, and not in the true defense of the country.... [6]

While Admiral Cervera and his superiors agonized over the situation, on 1 July Private David Fagen and the rest of the 24th Infantry were awakened early. Corporal Conn describes the morning:

...We were issued rations for three days, and I had just started to eat breakfast when the first gun was fired, at 6:30 o'clock. Very soon the Spaniards began replying and the navy began firing, and in a very short time there was a real and terrible duel with modern arms going on. The navy, as it was situated, could render no assistance, and the Spanish guns by using smokeless powder and being posted in well-masked positions, soon forced our artillery to move from one position to another, to their very great disadvantage, but they still could advance and did advance. I still think the Spaniards had a little the best of it with the artillery the first day.

About 8 o'clock a.m. we started forward, and we were then almost the extreme rear of the army and about four miles from the front, or firing line. Almost immediately our right, I since learned, was hotly engaged, taking a small town called El Caney, on the right of our position. There is where the 25th Infantry distinguished itself....

The fierce sounds of fighting that Conn, Fagen and the others heard coming from the north were from a battle that General Lawton had badly underestimated. Having promised General Shafter to be on top of El Caney within two hours, after which he was to move some of his brigades south to help in the attack on Kettle Hill, Lawton's forces were stalled. The problem was that every time Shafter's guns on El Pozo fired, they emitted clouds of dense white smoke which the excellent Spanish gunners used to target their own cannons. The American artillerymen were being decimated by accurate

Spanish shooting, and were being forced to continually move their guns to new positions under heavy fire. Meanwhile the Spaniards atop El Caney, protected by trenches, rock walls and barbed wire entanglements, swept the Americans with deadly rifle and machine gun fire as they struggled to climb uphill without cover. Lawton's forces were in serious trouble.

Detail of painting by artist Fletcher C. Ransom of 24th Infantry Regiment assaulting San Juan Hill. (*US National Archives*)

Fagen and the 24th Infantry were at the very left of a line of regiments that had just started to advance on San Juan Hill. Corporal Conn's letter tells the story:

> ...As we advanced we could hear the small arms more and more distinctly. After we had advanced about a mile, we began to meet the wounded coming to the rear, and thought seriously of the situation, and then in a short time the road was almost choked

entirely with the wounded and stragglers. Our progress was very slow so when we got into the zone of the small arms firing it was about 11:30 o'clock. It was terrible. There were wounded and dead men lying all along, beside and in the road, and the air seemed alive with bullets and shells of all descriptions and caliber. You could not tell from what direction they were coming; all that we could understand was that we were needed further in front, and we could not shoot, for we could not see anything to shoot at. We advanced until we were assured by our divisional commander [General Jacob Ford Kent] that our mettle was about to be tested; that he was depending on his boys of the 24th to make history, and that the fate of his record and possibly of the nation depended on the quality of the mettle mentioned.

According to historian Richard H. Titherington, "The defense of Caney was the best and bravest bit of fighting the Spaniards did in the whole war. It was worthy of the finest traditions of a nation whose most famous deeds of valor, from the days of Saguntum to those of Saragossa, have been done in defense of beleaguered towns. For more than ten hours General Vara del Rey's five hundred men kept at bay ten times their number of American soldiers...."[7]

The Spanish defenders at Kettle and San Juan Hills were about to be tested. Conn's letter to his sister:

We piled up all our extra baggage and our blanket rolls, nothing but our arms, ammunition, and canteens being needed, and, fully stripped for fighting, we advanced with our regimental chaplain's last words ringing in our ears: "Quit yourselves like men and fight." We were right in it then, in good shape—lots of music and very few drums. From appearance we passed two or three regiments lying in the road, so that we had to stumble over them and pick our way through them to advance. Our colonel took the situation in at a glance and led the regiment down into the bed of the San Juan River until we were in the desired position, and there it was terrible—just one continual roar of small arms, cannon and bursting shells; but our position was comparatively secure on account of the river bank. We were then faced to the right (north), about 900 yards south and right of the now famous San Juan Hill. The order was then: "Third Brigade, (9th, 3rd and 24th Infantry) forward."

The orders from our colonel were: 'Twenty fourth Infantry, move forward 150 yards and lie down.' With a last look at our arms and ammunition—yes and a little prayer—we started and such a volley as they sent into us! It was then that Sgt. [D.T.] Brown was shot almost at the river bank. We had to cut and destroy a barbed wire fence. You may form an idea of how strong it was when I tell you it had five to nine wires strung on it, and the posts were from two and a half to four feet apart. How or by what means it was destroyed no one scarcely knows; but destroyed it surely was, and in that angry mob, nearly all their officers having been disabled, there was no organization recognized. Men were crazy. Some one said: "Let us charge" and someone sounded "Let us charge" on a bugle. When that pack of demons swept forward the Spaniards stood as long as mortals could stand, then quit their trenches and retreated to the trenches around Santiago. When we gained the hill they were in full retreat, and our army just occupied their trenches and commenced to get even.... [8]

Gatling gun at Battle of Santiago. (*US National Archives*)

Spanish prisoners and their captors, Santiago, July 1898.
(*US National Archives*)

By nightfall, Shafter owned the northern railroad, the aqueduct, El Caney, and both Kettle and San Juan Hills. His losses had been heavy and the troops who were now digging in were suffering unrelenting artillery and rifle fire from Spanish positions on the outskirts of Santiago. Rainstorms early in the day had turned the roads to muck, and transporting supplies up to the front lines was all but impossible.

Fagen and his comrades were exhausted. To add to their misery, they were low on ammunition and water, and except for scrounging some rations that the Spaniards had abandoned, they were out of food. Digging sodden trenches in the dark while trying to dodge enemy fire became a literal nightmare.

At his headquarters on El Pozo, Shafter worried that the Spanish would take back San Juan Hill before the night was over.

Defending the hilltop, Fagen and the men around him shared the same perspective. Nobody slept. Under an overcast sky, the night was pitch black and unable to see if Spanish troops were slipping up on them, everyone was listening intently. And the falling rain didn't help.

Suddenly, someone yelled an unanswered challenge. Another soldier fired his rifle, and in an instant the whole line erupted with gunfire.

Sergeants ran about screaming "cease fire, cease fire!" to little avail.

Hearing the heavy gunfire from their front, the Spaniards at their posts on the edge of Santiago assumed that they were being attacked, and replied with their own guns.

Reports from both sides later claimed they had repulsed heavy attacks that night, but no attacks had actually occurred. Only the fear and tension of soldiers on both sides were real.

Corporal Conn:

> We had been on the hill about three hours and my gun was almost red hot. I had fired about 175 rounds of ammunition, and being very thirsty, I gladly accepted the detail [Conn was ordered about 4 a.m. to assist a man to the rear who had been shot in the head], as the hill was ours then and we had been shooting at nothing for about an hour. What a sight was presented as I re-crossed the flat of San Juan. The dead and wounded soldiers. It was indescribable! One would have to see it to know what it was like, and having once seen it, I truly hope I may never see it again ... [9]

General "Fighting Joe" Wheeler later noted that a number of his officers urged him to abandon the San Juan heights and fall back to a more defensible position, which he refused to do. Fearing the same appeal would be made to General Shafter, he sent an urgent message to headquarters claiming that such a withdrawal "would cost us much prestige." He had already requested that trenching tools be hurried forward to him, and Shafter sent him all that could be found. The men on Kettle Hill were also digging in. Another downpour started, and the men were caught in the open without shelters, and many were also without shirts.

General Garcia's war report for the night of 1 July:

> The enemy tried to attack from Cuba [Santiago de Cuba] and was turned back. On that day, in the trenches of Santiago el General Linares, who was in charge of the garrison was wounded and yielded command to Division General Toral....

...General Shafter ordered me to occupy the right flank of his army in the advance on Santiago. I made a night march. At ten that night, after sending some forces directly towards Santiago, I was camped at Quinta de Doucureau.

At dawn of 2nd General Francisco Sanchez advanced along the railroad towards San Luis. The enemy, after light resistance, abandoned the villages of Cubitas and Boniato, and several blockhouses falling back on San Vicente.

All the 2nd there was heavy fire exchanged with the enemy in Santiago. The enemy from his fortifications laid down heavy rifle and cannon fire on our positions....

That day, all the French Colony with the French Consul came out to place themselves under our protection....[10]

Corporal Conn's account continues, telling what happened when he returned to join Fagen and the other men of H-Company on top of San Juan Hill:

When I returned from the hospital five miles [Siboney] to the rear of our position, it was dark [night, 2 July] and as I passed our pile of rolls returning, I took what rations I could find—a few hardtack and a very little raw bacon—and kept on to San Juan in search of my company, which I found busy throwing up entrenchments. We swapped stories of our experiences and I divided my scanty fare. We could not make any fire—so we ate and returned to work, remaining to 2 a.m. July 2, when we lay down in the ditches to get what sleep we could before daylight, as we knew we would have to fight to hold our own.

I was awakened at daybreak by the crack of small arms. It was the Spaniards driving in our pickets. In a short time our whole line was awake, replying to them, and before sunrise the battle was raging furiously. It lasted all day with no intermission, until dark ...[11]

On board his flagship *Infanta Maria Teresa,* as the American and Cuban noose grew tighter around the city of Santiago, Admiral Cervera realized that his plight was steadily worsening. His superiors were urging him to go out and challenge the U.S. Navy, but many of the crew members he had sent to bolster Santiago's defense were still ashore. So were the smaller cannons that had been sent to aid Santiago's protection:

Cervera to Minister of Marine Aunon
July 1, 1898, Santiago De Cuba

The enemy to-day made fierce attack on city with overwhelming forces. Has not accomplished much, as the defense has been brilliant. But we have 600 casualties, among them commander in chief army seriously wounded, and general of brigade killed; captain of navy, Bustamonte, seriously wounded. Crews have not been reembarked because it would entail immediate loss of city. Have asked Captain General [Blanco] for instructions.

Blanco to Cervera:

July 1, 1898, Havana—10:30 p.m.

...You will reembark crews, take advantage of first opportunity, and go out with the ships of your squadron, following route you deem best. You are authorized to leave behind any which on account of slow speed or circumstances have no chance of escaping....

Blanco to Cervera:

Havana, July 1, 1898—10:45 p.m.

In addition to my former telegram of this evening, ask you to hasten sortie from harbor as much as possible before enemy can take possession of entrance....

Cervera to Blanco:

Santiago, July 2, daybreak:

Your urgent telegrams of last night received. Have sent my chief of staff to show them to General Toral, and have given orders to light fires, so as to go out as soon as my forces are reembarked.

Blanco to Cervera:

Havana, July 2 – 5:10 a. m.:

In view of exhausted and serious condition of Santiago, as stated by General Toral, your excellency will reembark landing troops of squadron as fast as possible, and go out immediately.[12]

Admiral Pascual Cervera y Topete, commander of the Spanish Carribean Squadron. (*Library of Congress*)

Early in the evening of 2 July, Shafter conferred with his divisional commanders. Wheeler, Lawton, Kent and Bates disagreed on the issue of withdrawal. Wheeler believed his men could hold Kettle Hill and the San Juan heights, and he finally persuaded Bates and Kent to do the same. Lawton kept his opinion to himself. Shafter argued for withdrawal, but never sent the order. After an hour, Shafter terminated the meeting stating that for the moment he was thinking of holding their present positions.

In fact, Shafter was anything but settled on the issue. The general was in communication with Washington via a coastwise cable from Santiago to Playa del Este, which had been picked up and carried ashore at Siboney and then connected to field telephone lines that ran to his headquarters on El Pozo. Early on 3 July, Shafter wired the Secretary of War Alger at Washington, D.C.:

> ...we have the town well invested on the north and east, but with a very thin line. Upon approaching it we find it of such a character and the defenses so strong it will be impossible to carry it by storm with my present force, and I am seriously considering withdrawing about five miles and taking up a new position on the high ground between the San Juan River and Siboney, with our left at Sardinero, so as to get our supplies to a large extent by means of the railroad, which we can use having engines and cars at Siboney....[13]

Next, under a flag of truce, Shafter sent the following message to Toral, the Commanding General of the Spanish forces at Santiago:

> Sir, I shall be obliged, unless you surrender, to shell Santiago de Cuba. Please inform the citizens of foreign countries, and all women and children, that they should leave the city before ten o'clock tomorrow morning ... [14]

Late in the day, Toral responded: "Sir, It is my duty to say to you that this city will not surrender." Shafter had already ordered his puny artillery pieces to be positioned atop San Juan ridge with orders to open fire at dawn on the nearest part of Santiago City. "We ought to knock that part of the town to pieces in a short time," Shafter optimistically told Colonel McClernand, but this was far more than could have realistically been expected from only a dozen three-inch field guns.[15]

At Washington, Secretary of War Alger and President McKinley waited until 4 a.m. for news from the front. Their last dispatch from Shafter on 2 July had been an urgent request for more surgeons. Concerned that Shafter would withdraw, Secretary Alger cabled him:

> Of course you can judge the situation better than we can at this end of the line. If however, you could hold your present position, especially San Juan Heights, the effect upon the country would be much better than falling back....[16]

Out in Santiago Bay, the sailors and marines whom Cervera had sent ashore to reinforce Santiago's defense were now back on board their ships. Steam was up, and a little before 9:30 a.m. on Sunday, 3 July, Cervera's squadron of six ships, cleared for action, began cruising at full speed for the mouth of the harbor.

Sailors on watch aboard the *Brooklyn* and *Iowa* noticed clouds of black smoke in the air above the entrance of the harbor before the masthead of the first vessel, the *Infanta Maria Teresa*, rounded the last point of land and made directly for the sea. Following her at about eight hundred-yard intervals were the *Vizcaya*, the *Cristobal Colon* and the *Almirante Oquendo*. Twelve hundred yards behind the *Oquendo* came the destroyers, *Pluton* and *Furor*.

As soon as the first Spanish ship came into view, the closest American war ships signaled "enemy ships escaping." To be sure that everyone had been alerted, the *Iowa* fired one of her big guns. Having been patrolling under minimal boiler power, none of the American warships were up to full steam, and were therefore incapable of fast maneuvering. Determined to ram the *Brooklyn*, Cervera swung his cruiser towards the big battleship.

Fagen and the other men of H-Company may have heard the distant booming of big naval cannons off to seaward, but from their position on San Juan Ridge, the sound had little or no meaning.

In his *Official War Report*, Cuban General Garcia described the demise of Cervera's fleet as follows:

> All the morning of the 3rd we engaged in fire fights with the defenders of the city. At ten the Spanish fleet that was in Santiago's bay sailed out and was destroyed in less than an hour by the American fleet. Admiral Cervera, with about 600 of his officers

and men, tried to take positions on land west of Santiago de Cuba. Cuban coastal detachments opposed the action. The Spanish were forced to surrender all their men to Colonel Jose Candelario Cebreco and his men. They were delivered, with receipt, to the American fleet.

On the night of the 3rd of July, using the Cobre Road a column of 5,000 men, led by Colonel Escario entered into Santiago. Colonel Escario, who had left Manzanillo the 22nd of June was harassed from Manzanillo to Baire, by the Manzanillo division. From Baire to Palma this column was forced to fight hard against the [Cuban] column of General Francisco Estrada, this caused the Spanish hundreds of losses, to the extent that all along the route Spanish bodies were found….

…perhaps the entry of this column could have been stopped if I had been able to use most of my forces for this purpose. However, to do this I would have had to abandon my positions to the right flank of the American army. [17]

Wreck of Spanish cruiser *Mercedes* which was sunk during the Battle of Santiago. (*US National Archives*)

The first definitive story of what had happened to the Spanish fleet was the following cable sent to General Blanco by Admiral Cervera, now a prisoner of war:

Playa Del Este, July 4, 1898:

In compliance with your excellency's orders, I went out from Santiago yesterday morning with the whole squadron, and after an unequal battle against forces more than three times as large as mine, my whole squadron was destroyed. Teresa, Oquendo, and Viscaya, all with fire on board, ran ashore. Colon, according to information from Americans, ran ashore and surrendered. The destroyers were sunk. Do not know as yet loss of men, but surely 600 killed and many wounded (proportion of latter not so large). The survivors are United States prisoners. Gallantry of all the crews has earned most enthusiastic congratulations of enemy. Captain of Vizcaya was allowed to retain his sword. I feel very grateful for generosity and courtesy with which they treat us. Among dead is Villamil, and, I believe, Lasaga; Concas and Eulate wounded. We have lost everything, and I shall need funds. [18]

Admiral Cervera's flagship *Infanta Maria Teresa*, sunk by American naval gunfire and beached near Santiago Harbor. (*US National Archives*)

Either late on the third or early on the fourth of July, foreign consuls stationed in Santiago came out to El Pozo to meet with General Shafter. They advised him that there were fifteen or twenty thousand people trapped in the city, and begged him to allow these non-combatants to flee the town and take refuge in the village of El Caney. The Americans would, of course, be responsible for supplying the refugees with food and water. Shafter at once messaged General Toral, advising him that he would not bombard the city until noon of 5 July, if, in return, Spanish forces would make no move against him.

Toral agreed, and an uneasy ceasefire took place for a week as negotiations got underway designed to ensure Santiago's capitulation, sans any damage to Spanish honor. On the night of the Fourth of July, regimental bands on the San Juan Heights tried to enliven the troops by playing a few patriotic tunes. The music had little or no effect on the hundreds of men who had to listen while sitting in trenches whose bottoms were a foot underwater.

The next day, the Americans traded twenty-eight wounded Spanish prisoners, including four officers, for an American lieutenant and a few of his crewmen who had been captured after an unsuccessful attempt to scuttle the collier *Merrimac* and block the entrance to Santiago Harbor.

On 6 July, representing Admiral Sampson, Captain Chadwick met with Shafter. It was agreed that another demand should be made for Santiago's surrender. If it was refused, both the army and the navy would bombard the city on the ninth. Shafter authored the message and sent it to Toral, who replied with a request that the English cable operators who had fled with the refugees to El Caney be sent back to Santiago so that Toral could correspond with Madrid. On the eighth, General Toral offered to evacuate Santiago and the eastern part of the province, on condition that he be allowed to withdraw unmolested to Holguin with his arms, ammunition and baggage.

Aware he had insufficient forces to storm the city without big losses, Shafter forwarded Toral's offer to Washington with his wholehearted endorsement of acceptance. On 9 July Washington replied:

> Your message recommending that Spanish troops be permitted to evacuate and proceed without molestation to Holguin is a great

surprise, and is not approved. The responsibility of destruction and distress to the inhabitants rests entirely with the Spanish commander. The Secretary of War orders that when you are strong enough to destroy the enemy and take Santiago, you do it. [19]

Boiling drinking water, Siboney, Cuba. (*US National Archives*)

Also on 9 July, Fagen and the fellow soldiers of H-company were withdrawn from their trenches on San Juan Ridge and shifted to a new position to the rear.

General Toral refused Shafter's latest demands and the Spanish opened fire at 4 o'clock on 10 July. An hour or so later, the battleships *Brooklyn* and *Indiana* moved closer to the mouth of Santiago Bay and began to lob eight-inch shells into the city. Fagen and his comrades spent this time huddled in muddy trenches listening to the whooshing and roaring of incoming cannon fire, and feeling the ground shake beneath their weary bones. At nightfall, when neither side could see the effects of their shooting any longer, the shooting stopped. In pairs, the men determined who would take the first watch and who would try to sleep. Fagen was no longer a raw recruit.

Notes

1. Quote from Garcia's *Official War Report*, July 15 1898, p. 2 of 8, www.spanamwar.com/Garcia.htm.
2. Quote, telegram Shafter to Secretary of War, 29 June 1898, from Titherington, *A History of the Spanish-American War of 1898*, reprint, paperback, Bibliolife, Charleston, NC., p. 234.
3. Quote from John R. Conn letter taken from Gatewood, *Smoked Yankees*, 1987, p. 67.
4. Cervera to Minister Aunon, June 23, 1898, from: Rear Admiral Pascual Cervera Y Topete, *The Spanish-American War, A Collection of Documents Related to the Squadron Operations in the West Indies*, Office of Naval Intelligence, Washington, Govt Printing office, 1899, p. 108.
5. Ibid. p. 111.
6. Ibid. pp. 111-112.
7. Titherington quote from his: *History of the Spanish-American War of 1898*, Bibliolife, 2012, p. 236.
8. Quote from John R. Conn letter taken from Gatewood, *Smoked Yankees*, 1987, pp. 68-9.
9. Ibid. p. 70.
10. Quote from Garcia's *Official War Report*, July 15, 1898, p. 4 of 8. www.spanamwar.com/Garcia.htm.
11. Quote from John R. Conn letter, taken from Gatewood, *Smoked Yankees*, p. 70.
12. Quotes of messages to and from Cervera from: Rear Admiral Pascual Cervera Y Topete, *The Spanish American War, A Collection of Documents Related to the Squadron Operations in the West Indies*, Office of Naval Intelligence, Washington, Govt Printing office, 1899, pp. 118-120.
13. Shafter to Secretary Alger quote from: Titherington, *History of the Spanish American War*, p. 267.
14. Quote: Shafter to Toral, from: Ibid. P. 267.
15. Quote: Shafter to McClearnand, from: Titherington, *History of Spanish American War*, p. 263.
16. Quote, Alger to Shafter, from: Ibid. p. 268.
17. Quote of Garcia from his *Official War Report*, July 15, 1898, p. 5 of 8, www.spanamwar.com/Garcia.htm.

18. Quote, Cervera to Blanco, July 3, 1898, Ibid. p. 122.
19. Quote, Alger to Shafter from: Titherington, *History of the Spanish American War,* pp. 305-306.

◄Chapter Five►

THE DOUBLE-CROSS

THE AMERICAN SHIPS started shelling Santiago again at dawn and the noise woke Fagen up. He and his comrades huddled in the wet trenches and ate hard tack. This time, the bombarding ships included the *New York*, *Brooklyn* and *Indiana*, which fired barrages continuously until early in the afternoon.

Shafter sent General Toral an exact copy of the instructions he had just received from the War Department," Should the Spaniards surrender unconditionally and wish to return to Spain, they will be sent back direct at the expense of the United States Government.[1]

On 11 July, General Nelson Miles, Commanding General of the U.S. Army, arrived with an American fleet bringing reinforcements, equipment and six additional batteries of artillery. Early the next day Miles rode up to El Pozo. After conferring with Shafter, Toral was sent a message advising him that the Officer commanding the U.S. Army was now present and suggested a personal interview.

General Garcia was informed of General Miles' arrival and he knew when Miles and Shafter went to meet with Toral at a spot half way between the Spanish and American lines. Garcia was increasingly frustrated and alarmed that he had been uninvited to any of these vital meetings:

> During the 12th and 13th the truce continued, we finished placing our cannon, digging our positions in the cemetery and along the front of the city on the north side. On the 14th, firing to begin again at 12 noon; however, the enemy asked for a prorroga (truce extension). As a result of these truce talks the Spanish decided to surrender the city and all the affected areas in the Comandancia General de Cuba…. This was done under the condition that all the

THE DOUBLE-CROSS

Spanish forces were to be taken to Spain by the U.S. Government via the United States....

...the American Government has decided for the time being to occupy the City of Santiago de Cuba with two regiments. Thus General Miles has not given me orders to cooperate in any new operations. (We have been) barred from taking part in peace negotiations or from entering Santiago during or after the truce....

I retire the bulk of forces under my command to their respective home territories....[2]

While American military police barred entry to Santiago by Cuban revolutionaries or civilians, the day before the formal surrender, Shafter sent a personal invitation to Garcia and his staff to witness the surrender ceremony.

Garcia replied by asking if it was intended that the current Spanish civil officials should continue governing Santiago. Shafter's answer was affirmative. Garcia ended the discussion by sternly replying that he would not go where Spain ruled.

The decisions that amounted to the betrayal of Cuba's people and her revolutionary army weren't formulated by General Miles or General Shafter. America's decisions were being made by men in Washington who were driven by leading industrialists and imperialists. What America's businessmen wanted was for the Spanish to be booted from Cuba, and for President McKinley to establish a permanent form of economic hegemony over the country and its people. Such a goal would best be achieved if the United States "guided" the formation of Cuba's new Constitution and the formation of its government. The only thing that stood in the way was Cuba's generals, men like Maximo Gomez and Calixto Garcia [3]

Although Shafter's victory would have been virtually impossible without the aid of Garcia and the Cuban insurgents, the Cubans were no longer on America's welcome list. Garcia recognized that it wasn't just the City of Santiago that the Spanish were giving to the Americans—with the loss of their fleets they no longer had any means of supplying their Cuban garrisons, and their hold on all of Cuba was doomed. Unfortunately for Garcia and the Cubans, it now appeared that they would have to stand by helplessly as one foreign colonial tyranny was supplanted by another. There can be no question of the Cuban fighters' commitment to freedom. If necessary, Garcia and his revolutionaries were prepared to fight the Yankees as they had fought the Spaniards, until they won the freedom that ruled their blood.

However, on the day of the formal surrender of the City of Santiago, Calixto Garcia withdrew all his soldiers in the region. The Americans had no honor.

24th Infantry Regiment, sick call, Siboney, Cuba 1898. (*US National Archives*)

For Shafter, the problems of General Garcia and the Cubans were superseded by a rapid and disastrous onset of debilitating fevers which were now decimating his army. The maladies included typhoid, dysentery, malaria, dengue and the dreaded yellow fever. There were less than seventy doctors and the medical staff was quickly overwhelmed. Although much of their medical equipment was still buried under other military goods in the holds of the transports lying several miles offshore, the medical staff had successfully established tented field and base hospitals, and except for inefficient transport from battlefield to surgery, wounded troops had been quickly and properly treated. The onslaught of hundreds of men in the throes of terrible fevers and diarrhea was a different matter.

The surgeons had only just been informed that mosquitoes were the most likely vector for malaria, but the concept was new and unproven. As for Dengue and Yellow Fever, it would be another three or four years before research would prove that mosquitoes were also their vector. Meanwhile, the doctors supposed that buildings or specific areas were "infected." There was not a single functioning lab available to the medical staff at Siboney which could analyze drawn blood (such capabilities didn't become a reality until 1902). With more than nine hundred seriously ill soldiers bedded in crowded tents, and the load of incoming patients accelerating daily, the problems of the medical staff were exacerbated by doctors and nurses contracting fevers and dropping like flies. The escalating rate of disease so alarmed Lt. Col. Theodore Roosevelt, that on the twelfth of July, one day after the very last American soldier fell victim to Spanish guns, Roosevelt messaged General Shafter alerting him that only three-hundred-fifty of the six hundred officers and men of his Rough Riders were fit for duty.

On the same day, under the direction of the army's commanding surgeon, Colonel Charles R. Greenleaf, the Cuban inhabitants of the city of Siboney were driven from their homes by American troops and, on suspicion that their homes and buildings were "infected," virtually every enclosed building in the city was burned to the ground. The effort, of course, did nothing to curtail the rising numbers of fever victims. On 14 July, Shafter stated that 1,500 soldiers were sick with fever, and it he estimated that ten percent of these men were infected with yellow fever.

Overwhelmed by the volume of ill patients and by the absence of functioning laboratories, the doctors were unable to correctly diagnose and treat the myriad of diseases with which they were faced. Compounding the problem, some patients had combinations of malaria, dysentery, typhoid and dengue. In many cases, men with gut-wrenching cases of diarrhea were treated with large rectal infusions of quinine.

The Cuban weather further weakened the troops and made them even more susceptible to disease. Soldiers in the trenches facing Santiago City lacked adequate shelter and clothing, and heavy rains of short duration fell nearly each day and night. Temperatures fluctuated from 120 degrees in the shade, to the 60s after night fell.[4]

Burning of Siboney by US troops in hopes of eradicating sources of disease.
(*US National Archives*)

Initially there were two tented hospitals established in Siboney: a "base hospital" in which men who had been wounded in battle were treated, and a "pestilence" hospital about a mile away, where men who were ill with unidentified fever or other diseases were isolated and treated. The latter hospital soon became known as a "pest camp."

According to an official U.S. Army Medical History, "After his July arrival in Cuba, Colonel Greenleaf pointed out to the V Corps adjutant general that 500 hospital attendants, 100 nurses immune to yellow fever, and a large number of immune doctors were urgently needed. On the 15th General Shafter initially refused to grant Greenleaf's pleas for the assignment of more men on a permanent basis to the hospital because he did not want to expose those at the front to yellow fever and because their services were vital where they were. Greenleaf immediately appealed to General Miles." Later that same day, presumably after Miles required him to do so, Shafter ordered the 24th Infantry to be withdrawn from the front and sent to Siboney to help Major LaGarde by performing guard duty, police, burial, sanitation and nursing chores. [5]

THE DOUBLE-CROSS

The man who received Shafter's marching orders was the commanding officer of the 24th Infantry Regiment, Major A. C. Markley. His official report to the Adjutant-General, U.S. Army, Washington, D.C., dated 18 September 1898 tells the story:

> ...On July 15th, hostilities having ceased, the regiment was ordered out of the trenches and put its camp in order for sleep and rest. On that day was heard the startling news that yellow fever had broken out in the Army and that Siboney was a great hospital, with a great camp in addition. This had a visibly depressing effect upon officers and men, run down and weakened physically and mentally, all regiments alike, by the unavoidable hardships of a campaign in Cuba in its hottest and most unhealthy season.
>
> About 4 p.m. an order was received directing me to proceed at once with the regiment and report for duty to Colonel Greenleaf, Medical Department, at Siboney, reporting hour of departure. The regiment marched at 5:30 p.m. by which time all had regained their composure and were in better spirits to face the 14-mile night march over that bad road and the serious business at the end of it.
>
> In darkness the tired troops toiled in single file through the mud puddles, un-bridged streams, and thorny thickets, arriving on the hill at Siboney at 3:30 a.m. with eight companies, fifteen officers and 456 enlisted men. At daylight I went down into the camp to get an idea of the situation, finding some 600 patients packed closely, with insufficient protection and attendance, unavoidable and the fault of no one at the time, there being also the large pest camp about a mile out on the railroad. The state of affairs was very poor. [6]

When daylight came, Fagen could not find the Siboney he remembered. Not a building was standing and amidst numerous piles of rubble wisps of smoke were still rising. The last time he and the regiment had camped there, the town had been crowded with Cubans and dozens of smiling men and women wearing little more than rags walked about selling vegetables, melons, fruit and coconuts. Now the place was dead quiet, and any thoughts he may have had of seeing and mixing with the Cubans vanished with the desolate, grim picture of the town's utter destruction. There wasn't a single Cuban in sight, and other than an abandoned dog or two, the streets were empty. A fetid, rank, rotting smell mingled with the odor of smoke permeated the air. Beyond the beach where he had landed, steam launches were towing boats carrying supplies ashore from transports anchored two or three miles out. The only visible habitations were rows of medical tents.

Fagen had been in the U.S. Army now for some forty-two days and while he had not yet been taught close order drill or the manual-of-arms, he was a veteran Buffalo Soldier whose company had lost two officers and ten men during the fighting on San Juan Hill. Nearby, lying somewhere in the clusters of big medical tents were two wounded officers and sixty-seven enlisted men from H-company, all casualties of the battle. As the morning drew on, Fagen and the others ate breakfast and established their camp. No doubt Private David Fagen and his comrades hoped to visit their injured friends. They did not discuss their fear of catching Yellow Fever.

On Sunday morning the troopers were assembled, and Major Markley told them that there was a desperate need for volunteers—sixty-five men were needed at once to work as nurses in the "pest camp." He didn't need to spell out the inherent danger of such work. Another seventy men were needed to work at the Base Hospital, as nurses, cooks, burial parties, sanitation workers, men to set-up and trench tents, and to serve as guards and police.

Major Markley:

> This was the crucial test of the mettle of the men, and an anxious moment indeed. In preparation for it an interview had been had with Captain A. A. Auger, commanding Company H, a man of high and strong character, and a course of action decided on. Captain Augur then explained matters to his men and called for volunteers for the pest camp. Fifteen gallant fellows responded from his company, and this fine example soon produced more than were needed for all purposes.
>
> …The camp was so crowded, so full of rubbish, and in such filthy condition, from previous occupancy by Spanish, Cubans,

volunteers, and by other hospitals, that large fatigue details were necessary. But large details for loading and unloading transports in the harbor and the railroad were also made, and the sick lists of the troops began to be large. The volunteers were unskilled, needing the presence of a regular officer, who could not be spared. The officers of my regiment were rapidly falling sick from disease contracted in the trenches, and the other battalions were wisely ordered away. It was found best—in fact, necessary—to command all fatigue parties, big and little, myself, this labor being an important feature, too long to explain why. Besides, there was not enough officers to command companies and do the regimental work....

...By the end of July yellow fever had overrun all the hospitals, including a new one established in a large railroad shed. All was pest camp; even separation of cases was impossible. All wards had it. Surgeons, nurses, and hospital stewards were now among the patients; and so it continued to about August 20, when determined steps were taken to break up the place.... [7]

A Tampa newspaper of 7 August 1898 reported that in Cuba on 3 August, the total number of sick was 3,778, of which 2,589 were suffering from fever, and there had been reported some 449 new cases that day.[8]

The "breaking-up" of the medical centers at Siboney that Major Markley's report mentions was the result of a conspiracy involving Lt. Colonel Theodore Roosevelt and a collection of General Shafter's divisional and brigade commanders who had been summoned to El Pozo to discuss what to do about the diseases that were destroying their army.

Shafter opened their conference by advising his staff that he had sent an urgent request to Secretary of War Alger, asking permission to evacuate his army on transports and sail them away from Cuba's poisons, and his plea had been refused.

Shafter did not explain the reason for Washington's refusal, which originated from the fact that McKinley's government was not satisfied with the acquisition of the City of Santiago. The Spaniards, after all, were still in control of Havana and had dozens of garrisons situated throughout the country. Spain had not yet surrendered Cuba entire, and would certainly be less inclined to do so if Shafter and his victorious army were to suddenly withdraw. Convoys carrying reinforcements to Shafter were already underway from Florida.

Shafter's commanders concluded that their best response would be to compose a Round-Robin letter to Washington, which all of them would sign. As historian Edmund Morris wrote in *The Rise of Theodore Roosevelt*, "All agreed that it was critical, and that the War Department's apparent unwillingness to evacuate the Army was inexcusable. Somebody must write a formal letter stating that in the unanimous opinion of the Fifth Corps staff, a further stay in Cuba would be to the 'absolute and objectless ruin' of the fighting forces.

"Having reached this agreement, the Regular officers hesitated. None wished to sacrifice his career by offending Secretary Alger or President McKinley. As the conference's junior officer and a Volunteer, Roosevelt was nudged, or more probably leaped, into the breach. The result was a "round robin" letter, drafted by himself and signed by all present, dated 3 August 1898."[9]

> We, the undersigned officers ...are of the unanimous opinion that this Army should be at once taken out of the island of Cuba and sent to some point on the Northern seacoast of the United States ... that the army is disabled by malarial fever to the extent that its efficiency is destroyed, and that it is in a condition to be practically entirely destroyed by an epidemic of yellow fever, which is sure to come in the near future ...
>
> This army must be moved at once, or perish. As the army can be safely moved now, the persons responsible for preventing such a move will be responsible for the unnecessary loss of many thousands of lives.[10]

After having signed the letter, Shafter's officer staff was unable to decide who among them would send it to Washington. Once again Roosevelt volunteered. Having achieved the glory he sought leading the Rough Riders at both Guasimas and San Juan hills, he was no longer concerned with his military career. Later that afternoon, in lieu of mailing the letter to Washington, he made sure it got into the hands of Reporter Richard Harding Davis of the *New York Herald*.

As historian Edmund Morris wrote: "The document, accompanied by a long and even stronger letter of complaint signed by Roosevelt alone, was published [the] next morning. As predicted, Secretary Alger was enraged. So, too, was the President, whose first inkling of the round-robin came when he opened his morning papers.

"As a result of the Round Robin letter, within three days of it's publication in the American press, Shafter's army was ordered to Montauk, Long Island."[11]

Major Markley, of the 24th Infantry Regiment, USCT:

> Of this regiment, Captain Dodge had died; two officers were expected to die; three were dangerously ill, and five more or less so. Out of sixteen present, ten were in hospital; three well, three sick, but doing well; sick and well living mostly within a radius of fifty feet. Officers kept up when they should have gone into hospital, making it worse for them when they did give up....
>
> ...Of the 65 enlisted men sent as nurses to the pest camp July 16, most had succumbed, their places being filled by others. When these went down, the gaps were filled, and the same was the case in all the hospitals and the whole camp the entire time.
>
> ...A trouble was that those who recovered did not get strong. All worked in some way regardless of rank.
>
> The labor required was taking down and putting up tents, changing to new ground, ditching tents, moving the sick, unloading stores, digging graves, cleaning up filth for the multitude of sick, and innumerable other things. Working convalescents was tried until unexpected deaths warned us to stop. Major La Garde and myself worked together as one man.
>
> Of the 456 men who marched to Siboney, only 24 men escaped sickness. All were not down at one time, of course, but on one day 241 were on sick report, although death and "sending north" had reduced the regiment in numbers.

...By August 22, such progress had been made in breaking up the hospitals that the welcome order was received for the regiment to prepare to go north. Six officers were in the hospital, four of whom were sent home on the hospital ship Berkshire, and two were left behind by the regiment, being too ill for removal. Eleven officers and 289 men were able to go with the regiment on the transport, but many were to sick to attempt to march in ranks, so on August 26, its forty-first day at Siboney, the regiment marched to the train, band playing and colors flying, with nine officers and 198 men.

Proceeding by rail to Santiago, the regiment ... embarked on the transport Nueces, and sailed the same day, August 26, arriving at Montauk Point, N.Y. September 2nd with considerable sick, including two officers, but no deaths, and one of the cleanest ships that came to that place.

The regiment went into Camp Wikoff, the finest camp in every respect that I have ever seen, and with the most excellent hospitals possible, in my opinion. Yet, notwithstanding all this and the fine weather, the men began to fall sick in great numbers, several dying.

...The regiment lost in this service one officer (so far) and about thirty men, effectually showing that colored soldiers were not more immune from Cuban fever than white.

Very respectfully, your obedient servant,
A. C. Markley, Major 24th Infantry Commanding Regiment [12]

The records indicate that Private David Fagen was not among the lucky twenty-four enlisted men who escaped coming down with fever of one sort or another.

Rev. Dr. T.G. Stewart, Chaplain, 25th Infantry, witnessed the 24th Infantry disembarking from the *Nueces* at Montauk and he was deeply moved by what he saw:

...As these fever-worn veterans arrived at Montauk, they presented a spectacle well fitted to move strong men to tears.

In solemn silence they marched from on board the transport Nueces, which had brought them from Cuba, and noiselessly they dragged their weary forms over the sandy roads and up the hill to the distant "detention camp." Twenty-eight of their members were reported sick, but the whole regiment was in ill-health.

...Of these shattered heroes General Miles had but recently spoken in words well worthy of his lofty position and noble manhood as a "regiment of colored troops, who, having shared equally in the heroism, as well as the sacrifices, is now voluntarily engaged in nursing yellow fever patients and burying the dead." These men came up to Montauk from great tribulations which should have washed their robes to a resplendent whiteness in the eyes of the whole people. Great Twenty-Fourth, we thank thee for the glory thou hast given to American soldiers, and to the character of the American Negro! [13]

Unfortunately for David Fagen and all the other African-American soldiers who had fought in Cuba, the black chaplain's stirring homage was not echoed by the American press. There was little incentive for white editors to run stories praising a race that most of their readership despised. From what the public gleaned from the newspapers, readers could only have concluded that it was Colonel Roosevelt and his gloriously valiant Rough Riders who had won America's great and noble victory and had paid back the dirty Spaniards for sinking the *Maine*.

Chapter Endnotes

1. Quote from War Department to Shafter from: Ibid. p. 306.
2. Quote of Garcia, from his: *Official War Report*, p. 6 of 8.
3. See *NY Times*, Garcia to Shafter, 7/23/1898.
4. See: U.S. Army Medical Department Office of Medical History, http://history.amedd.army.mil/booksdocs/spanam/gillet3/ch6.html, pp. 6-12 of 27.

5. Ibid., p. 11 of 27.
6. Quote, Major A. C. Markley to the Adjutant-General, U.S. Army, September 18, 1898, in William G. Muller, *The 24th Infantry, Past and Present,* 1923, reprint Old Army Press, Ft. Collins, Colorado, 1972, pp. 20-21.
7. Ibid. pp. 23-24.
8. Tampa newspaper story, from: Edward Van Zile Scott, *The Unwept,* Black Belt Press, Montgomery Alabama 1996, p. 189.
9. Quotes from Edmund Morris, *The Rise of Theodore Roosevelt,* Random House Trade Paperback, 1979, pp. 691-2.
10. Ibid. p. 692.
11. Ibid. p. 692.
12. Quote, Major Markley to the Adjutant General, U.S. Army, Sept. 18, 1898, in: Wm. G. Muller, *The 24th Infantry Past and Present,* 1923, reprint, Old Army Press, Ft. Collins, Colorado, 1972 pp. 24-26.
13. Quote of Chaplain T. G. Steward, from his: *The Colored Regulars in the United States Army,* 1904, Philadelphia, reprint, Forgotten Books, Lexington , KY, 2012 paperback, pp. 248-49.

◄Chapter Six►

WE DON'T NEED NO WHITE OFFICERS

MANY OF THE BLACK AMERICAN SOLDIERS who went to fight in Cuba believed that if they demonstrated extraordinary courage and discipline under fire, their performance would help create a more favorable social climate back home, one that would "bring about a stronger belief in the potential of the black race."[1]

When Roosevelt's 1st Volunteer Cavalry was pinned down at Las Guasimas, it was the black 10th Cavalry who came to their rescue, climbing the steep hillside under continuous fire and taking heavy casualties. Finally, the men of the 10th who survived the assault crested the ridge and dislodged the enemy. The Spanish guns that had been chewing Roosevelt's troops fell silent.

After observing some nine hours of fighting at El Caney, *New York Herald* correspondent Stephen Bonsal wrote: "Afro-American troops of the Twenty-Fifth Infantry emerged from the underbrush and advanced, seemingly oblivious to a hailstorm of bullets, the spang of lead smashing into rocks, the blazing sun, and barbed wire entanglements as they charged the blockhouse. Continuing to move up in spite of heavy fire, they soon saw a white flag sticking out of the window of the fort in a sign of surrender. The Spaniard holding the flag was felled by a bullet, but another took his place. At this point the firing stopped. The Twenty-fifth Infantry entered the fort."[2]

After the fighting was over, Bonsal wrote: "The orders given to the colored regiments brought them well to the front in the different divisions to which they were assigned, and their courage and soldierly efficiency kept them there. The 25th fought at El Caney under Lawton, and shared with the white men of the Twelfth Infantry the honor and losses incident to capturing the old stone fort."[3]

At Kettle Hill, it was the Rough Riders and the black 10th Cavalry who took the summit. In the battle of San Juan Heights, it was the black 9th Cavalry and the Rough Riders who charged the northern slopes while the 24th Infantry Regiment scaled the southern side and drove the Spanish from their positions on the ridge top.

Most big newspapers in the U.S.A. omitted stories attesting to the valiant exploits of the Buffalo Soldiers during the crucial battles for Santiago, because their editors refused to glorify black soldiers to their mostly white readership.

The absence of public acclaim for their courageous accomplishments, coupled with negative stories like the following racist exposé written by Theodore Roosevelt, America's latest and greatest war-star, helped accelerate the Buffalo Soldiers' profound frustration:

> On the hill-slope immediately around me I had a mixed force composed of members of most of the cavalry regiments, and a few infantrymen. There were about fifty of my Rough Riders with Lieutenants Goodrich and Carr. Among the rest were perhaps a score of colored infantrymen, but, as it happened, at this particular point without any of their officers. No troops could have behaved better than the colored soldiers had behaved so far; but they are, of course, peculiarly dependent upon their white officers. Occasionally they produce non-commissioned officers, who can take the initiative and accept responsibility precisely like the best class of whites, but this cannot be expected normally, nor is it fair to expect it. With the colored troops there should always be some of their own [white] officers; whereas, with the white regulars, as with my own Rough Riders, experience showed that the non-commissioned officers could usually carry on the fight by themselves if they were once started, no matter whether their officers were killed or not.
>
> ...None of the white regulars or Rough Riders showed the slightest sign of weakening; but under the strain the colored infantrymen (who had none of their officers) began to get a little uneasy and to drift to the rear, either helping wounded men or

saying that they wished to find their own regiments. This I could not allow, as it was depleting my line, so I jumped up, and walking a few yards to the rear, drew my revolver halted the retreating soldiers, and called out to them that I appreciated the gallantry with which they had fought and would be sorry to hurt them, but that I should shoot the first man who, on any pretense whatever, went to the rear. My own men had all sat up and were watching my movements with the utmost interest, so was Captain Howze. I ended my statement to the colored soldiers by saying: 'Now, I shall be very sorry to hurt you, and you don't know whether or not I will keep my word, but my men can tell you that I always do.' Whereupon my cow-punchers, hunters, and miners solemnly nodded their heads and commented in chorus, exactly as if in a comic opera, 'He always does; he always does!'

This was the end of the trouble for the 'smoked Yankees,'—as the Spaniards called the colored soldiers—flashed their white teeth at one another, as they broke into broad grins, and I had no more trouble with them, they seeming to accept me as one of their own officers.... [4]

Roosevelt's ungracious statements were initially published in *Scribner's Magazine* in their April 1899 issue, and the article deeply wounded the Buffalo Soldiers. Of the eighteen Medals of Honor awarded to soldiers for bravery during the Spanish-American War, none was awarded to an Afro-American. In barracks banter, black soldiers everywhere were now voicing their frustrations over their combat deeds being ignored. For this, and other reasons, the main topic of dissatisfaction shifted, and now focused on the military's apparent insistence that black troops be commanded by white officers. Their irritation manifested itself in what was rapidly becoming a strident movement to serve under men of their own complexion. The NCOs remained mostly in the background. Those veterans understood one thing that all new soldiers have to learn—never let it show when military circumstances throw bad things your way. You can hate something—a rule, a duty assignment, a person, or an officer—but you keep it in because if you let it out, you will always end up losing. Always.

113

John E. Lewis, 10th Cavalry:

...Will this war open up a brighter future for the colored soldier? Have not the non-commissioned officers proved that they are fully capable of commanding? Did 1st Sergt. William Givens of D, 10th Cav. fail when the command fell upon him, when their brave officers were shot down? No! It was forward!... About every troop of the 10th lost its officers... and non-commissioned officers took their places and led the troops on to a victory that has gained the admiration of the world.

...These men showed that they could be depended upon at a critical moment and why not now?

I have it from men who were upon the field that had it not been for the boys in black, the recent victory at Las Guasima would have been a second Custer massacre; yet it is the men of the Rough Riders and gallant 71st New York who get the glory and the promotions. The press fails to state how the 1st, 10th Cavalry and 24th Infantry went through the ranks of the Rough Riders urging them on and how, after they had dislodged the Spaniards, the gallant 71st came up.

John E. Lewis, 10th Cav [5]

Maybe it was Fagen's upbringing: the hateful oppressive acts blacks like him were supposed to tolerate, the fights one faced growing up in the Scrub, the labor union brawls, or perhaps it was just the way he was—but it wasn't part of David Fagen's character to shrug off wrongs. He was noted as one of the most vocal protestors in his company at demanding an end to the policy which prohibited black officers from leading black troops.

Energized by the stories that ran in their own newspapers, black America was proud of what their men had accomplished in Cuba. Not long after their arrival at Montauk, the men of the 24th Infantry were honored by an organization of patriotic black ladies from Brooklyn who came out on a train to present them with a decorated regimental color stand, followed by a sumptuous dinner and a dessert which included some four hundred berry pies.

Fagen and his comrades had been recovering at Montauk for only twenty-one days when, on 23 September, they were ordered to board a steamer to Weehawken, New Jersey. From there, companies A, B, D, G, H and K were directed to go by rail to their old base at Fort Douglas, Utah. Remembering how most of the residents of Salt Lake City had turned out to cheer them off with a parade before leaving for Florida and the war in Cuba, Fagen's H-Company comrades welcomed the transfer. They figured the same folks would be happy to welcome them back. Companies C, E, F, and I were sent to Fort D.A. Russell, in Wyoming.

Not all the black outfits that left confinement at Montauk were blessed with a happy trip. In the Cleveland *Gazette* of October 22, 1898 Chaplain George W. Prioleau, 9th Cavalry (USCT), describes the treatment he and his men had experienced after leaving Long Island:

> While the cheers and the 'God bless you's,' were still ringing in our ears, and before the warm handshakes had become cold, we arrived in Kansas City, Mo., the gateway to America's hell, and were unkindly and sneeringly received. The First Cavalry, U.S.A., arrived a few minutes before we did. The two regiments, regulars of the U.S.A. were there together. Both were in Cuba. The 9th faced the enemy amid shot and shell up San Juan Hill. Its members fought, they bled, some died to vindicate the rights of our country and to revenge the loss of the Maine and 250 brave men. They were victorious, and returned home with victory perched upon their country's banner. The 1st Cavalry, well, let history tell it. However, both were under the same flag, both wore the blue, and yet these black boys, heroes of our country, were not allowed to stand at the counters of restaurants and eat a sandwich and drink a cup of coffee, while the white soldiers were welcomed and invited to sit down at the tables and eat free of cost. You call this American 'prejudice,' I call it American 'hatred' conceived only in hellish minds.[6]

Fort Douglas was Fagen's first real experience at garrison life. Here he was introduced to guard-duty, marching, hiking, inspections, and rifle practice—the full gamut of being a professional soldier. He was finally being taught how to be a proper recruit, and his records make no mention of any disciplinary problems.

The crisp fall air of Utah was a far cry from the tropic weather Fagen was used to, and there should be no doubt that as the winter came on, the ex-Floridian felt its bite. Fortunately, the woolen shirts and the jackets the men of the 24th had been forced to endure during the Battle of Santiago were perfect gear for the Utah climate.

While David was undergoing training at Fort Douglas, events caused by Spain's defeat were taking place on the world stage. On October 31, during ongoing peace talks with Spain, the United States asserted its insistence on annexation of the Philippine Islands, another Spanish territory.

On 10 December 1898, after long negotiations during which America maintained the upper hand, Spain sold the Philippines to the United States for $20,000,000, and signed a treaty that spread U.S. sovereignty over Cuba, Puerto Rico, Guam and the Philippine Islands.

Regarding the American government's plans for Cuba, Washington's policies dictated that U.S. authorities were to guide Cuba to independence—an independence which granted permanent military bases to the U.S. and allowed for American control over virtually all of Cuba's major commercial interests. The arrangement also provided a solid foundation for American control of a long line of puppet governments. The scramble to take over Cuba is illuminated by author Philip Foner:

> Even before the Spanish flag was down in Cuba, U.S. business interests set out to make their influence felt. Merchants, real estate agents, stock speculators, reckless adventurers, and promoters of all kinds of get-rich schemes flocked to Cuba by the thousands. Seven syndicates battled each other for control of the franchises for the Havana Street Railway, which were finally won by Percival Farquhar, representing the Wall Street interests of New York. Thus, simultaneously with the military occupation began…commercial occupation.[7]

Philippine Revolutionary leader Emilio Aguinaldo
(*US National Archives*)

A month-and-a-half before the American invasion of Cuba, McKinley and Roosevelt had already targeted the Philippine Islands. After destroying the Spanish Navy the night of May 1, 1898, Admiral George Dewey lacked enough troops to invade and defeat the Spaniards. Hoping to get the help of Filipino insurgent forces, Dewey's attention was directed to twenty-nine-year-old Emilio Aguinaldo – a Filipino revolutionary leader who had engineered numerous victories against Spanish colonial forces, and who had been exiled to Hong Kong in 1896. Dewey sent agents to contact the exile.

The audacious American naval commander was walking on broken glass—he had been warned by Washington not to attempt anything that could be interpreted as recognizing a Philippine government, and Aguinaldo was the Filipino peoples' most-recognized hero. Dewey decided to take the risk.

At Hong Kong, the sucker-bait Dewey's agents dangled in front of Aguinaldo was an implied promise of U.S. recognition of Philippine independence once the Spanish were defeated. The promises, of course, were all vocal; nothing was on paper. Even so, Aguinaldo was tantalized by the thought of seeing his dream of Philippine independence become a reality. In addition to offering him prestige and free transport back to the Philippines, Dewey's agents turned over about one hundred rifles, and the United States consul in Hong Kong purchased another two thousand—more than enough for Aguinaldo to reassert his claim to leadership of Luzon's independence movement. (The Province of Luzon contained Manila and was the seat of Filipino power and government.) Once Manila fell, the game was over. [8]

On May 17 Aguinaldo was escorted back to the Philippines aboard one of Dewey's gunboats and taken to Dewey's flagship *Olympia*, anchored in Manila Bay. Aguinaldo wrote about the event:

> The Admiral ushered me into his private quarters, and after the exchange of the usual greetings I asked whether it was true that he had sent all the telegrams to the Consul at Singapore, Mr. Pratt, which that gentleman had told me he received in regard to myself. The Admiral replied in the affirmative, adding that the United States had come to the Philippines to protect the natives and free them from the yoke of Spain. He said, moreover, that America is exceedingly well off as regards territory, revenue, and resources and therefore needs no colonies, assuring me finally that there was no occasion for me to entertain any doubts whatever about the recognition of the Independence of the Philippines by the United States. Then Admiral Dewey asked me if I could induce the people to rise against the Spaniards and make a short, sharp, and decisive campaign of it. The Admiral said he ... thought the Filipinos and Americans should act towards one another as friends and allies, and therefore it was right and proper that all doubts should be expressed frankly in order that explanations be made, difficulties avoided, and distrust removed; adding that, as he had already indicated, the United States would unquestionably recognize the Independence of the people of the Philippines, guaranteed as it was by the word of honor of Americans, which, he said, is more positive, more irrevocable than any written agreement, which might not be regarded as binding when there is an intention or desire to repudiate it, as was the case in respect of the compact

I made with the Spaniards at Biak-na-bato. Then the Admiral advised me to at once have made a Filipino National Flag, which he said he would recognize and protect in the presence of the other nations represented by the various squadrons anchored in Manila Bay, adding, however, that he thought it advisable that we should destroy the power of Spain before hoisting our national flag, in order that the act would appear more important and creditable in the eyes of the world and of the United States in particular.

...I again thanked the Admiral for his good advice and generous offers, giving him to understand clearly that I was willing to sacrifice my own life if he would be thereby more exalted in the estimation of the United States, more honoured by his fellow countrymen.

Thus ended my first interview with Admiral Dewey, to whom I signified my intention to reside for a while at the headquarters of the Naval Commandant of Cavite Arsenal.[9]

On 12 June 1898 (at which time raw-recruit David Fagen was aboard the *City of Washington* on his way to fight in Cuba), Emilio Aguinaldo proclaimed Philippine independence. His declaration stated:

Under the protection of the mighty and humane North American Nation, we proclaim and solemnly declare, in the name and by authority of the inhabitants of all these Philippine Islands, that are and have the right to be free men and independent, that they are released from all obedience to the crown of Spain, that every political tie between the two is and must be completely severed and annulled; and that, like all free and independent states, they have complete authority to make war, conclude peace, establish treaties of commerce, enter into alliance, regulate commerce, and execute all other acts and things that independent states have the right to do.[10]

Ten days later, Emilio Aguinaldo announced the formation of a democratic Revolutionary Government, replete with an executive, a congress and courts.

After his meetings with Admiral Dewey, Aguinaldo activated the Filipinos as he had promised, and he and his generals then led them to a string of quick victories over Spanish-controlled towns and provinces. Finally, near the end of July, only the walled city of Manila still held out, surrounded by Aguinaldo's freedom fighters.

By then, thousands of American troops had arrived, led by General Wesley Merritt, who requested that Aguinaldo order his forces to step aside to let the Americans pass through them on their way to Manila. Reluctantly, Aguinaldo agreed. Located on Manila Bay, the three inland sides of the city remained covered by Filipino troops, and in some cases, their lines and American positions faced each other.

Behind closed doors, Spain negotiated with the Americans and pressed for an "honorable" way to surrender Manila without any "real" losses—a solution that would give the Americans Manila, while protecting the Spaniards, their families and loyal Filipino supporters from bloody retribution. Aguinaldo's agents gave him real-time intelligence and he realized that the American promises of Filipino freedom and independence were swiftly fading.

Philippine Army of Liberation troops facing American soldiers in Manila, just prior to breakout of Philippine American War. Filipino officer with sword is General Juan Kauppama Cailles. (*US National Archives*)

WE DON'T NEED NO WHITE OFFICERS

On 12 August 1898, following the American victory at Santiago in Cuba, Spain initiated a peace protocol requesting an immediate end to hostilities between themselves and the United States in Cuba, Puerto Rico and the Philippines, pending the resolution of forthcoming peace negotiations. America agreed, but the Spanish peace protocol was too late to save the city of Manila.

"On the evening [12 August, 1898] before the [faux] attack, [Major General Wesley] Merritt informed Aguinaldo that his forces were forbidden to enter Manila. American commanders were instructed to first overcome the Spanish, and then immediately shift to block Filipino incursions: 'Forcible encounters with the insurgents in carrying out these orders will be carefully guarded against, but pillage, rapine, or violence by the native inhabitants or disorderly insurgents must be prevented at any cost.'

This was the Philippine echo of the scurrilous way the Americans had barred General Calixto Garcia and his staff from attending the Spanish surrender treaty at Santiago Cuba.

As historian Brian Linn wrote "…unexpected Spanish resistance prevented the split-second timing required by such a complicated plan, and thousands of armed insurgents entered the suburbs, where they were confronted by American soldiers demanding that they leave. In several places angry Filipino and American soldiers almost came to blows.…"[11]

In Washington, a vociferous outbreak of anti-war and anti-imperialist protests exploded, led by such notables as former Secretary of State John Sherman, Senator Ben Tillman, presidential candidate William Jennings Bryan, labor leader Samuel Gompers and leading industrialists and celebrities including Andrew Carnegie and Mark Twain. Their strident efforts encouraged a battery of veteran newspaper writers, who roared with their pens that the very essence of America would be lost if the country which became a country in pursuit of liberty was to force its rule over a foreign people.

The anti-imperialist protests were too little and too late. Washington's drive for the acquisition of the Philippines was already underway. Defending his decisions, President William McKinley explained to a group of ministers visiting the White House:

Before you go I would like to say just a word about the Philippine business…. The truth is I didn't want the Philippines, and when they came to us as a gift from the gods, I did not know what to do with them . . . I sought counsel from all sides—Democrats as well as Republicans—but got little help. I thought first we would only take Manila, then Luzon, then other islands, perhaps also.

I walked the floor of the White House night after night until midnight; and I am not ashamed to tell you, gentlemen, that I went down on my knees and prayed Almighty God for light and guidance more than one night. And one night late it came to me this way—I don't know how it was, but came:

1. That we could not give them back to Spain—that would be cowardly and dishonorable.

2. That we could not leave them over to France or Germany, our commercial rivals in the Orient—that would be bad business and discreditable.

3. That we could not leave them to themselves---they were unfit for self-government—and they would soon have anarchy and misrule over there worse than Spain's was; and

4. That there was nothing left for us to do but to take them all and to educate the Filipinos, and uplift and civilize and Christianize them, and by God's grace do the very best we could by them, as our fellow men for who Christ also died. And then I went to bed and went to sleep and slept soundly….[12]

Addressing the United States Senate, Albert Beveridge of Indiana expressed the prevailing point of view:

Mr. President, the times call for candor. The Philippines are ours forever…. And just beyond the Philippines are China's illimitable markets. We will not retreat from either….We will not renounce our part in the mission of our race, trustee, under God, of the civilization of the world.

And we will move forward to our work, not howling at regrets like slaves whipped to their burdens, but with gratitude for a task worthy of our strength and thanksgiving to Almighty God that He has marked us as His chosen people, henceforth to lead in the regeneration of the world.

...It will be hard for Americans who have not studied them to understand the people. They are a barbarous race, modified by three centuries of contact with a decadent race. The Filipino is the South Sea Malay, put through a process of three hundred years of superstition in religion, dishonesty in dealing, disorder in habits of industry, and cruelty, caprice, and corruption in government. It is barely possible that about 1,000 men in all the archipelago are capable of self-government in the Anglo-Saxon sense .

My own belief is that there are not 100 men among them who comprehend what Anglo-Saxon self-government even means, and there are over 5,000,000 people to be governed....[13]

Like Calixto Garcia and the Cubans, Emilio Aguinaldo and the Filipinos were about to share the despicable honor of being betrayed by American politicians.

Filipino outposts on the outskirts of Manila, 1899. (*US National Archives*)

On 28 January 1899, the law under which he had enlisted having expired, Private David Fagen was granted an honorable discharge. According to his records, his character rating was "good." Travelling home by rail from

Fort Douglas, after his train passed into the South, Fagen had to ride in the Jim Crow cars, and was subjected once again to southern prejudice. Somewhere during this long ride, Fagen decided against going home to Tampa. Only twelve days after his departure from Utah, he presented himself at the recruiting office at Fort McPherson, Georgia, where he signed up for three more years. At this time, there were no vacancies in his old outfit, H-Company of the 24th Infantry Regiment, so Fagen was assigned to I-Company and sent by rail to Fort Russell, Wyoming.

At Fort Russell, Fagen continued learning the business of professional soldiering. His Buffalo Soldier mentors were among the most experienced and battle-wise soldiers of the U.S. Army, and their teaching aids were the latest weapons that could be procured. Fagen applied himself to learning his trade and was promoted to corporal. By then, the men of the 24th Infantry Regiment had heard that they were going to be sent to fight in the Philippines, and that it wouldn't be long before they would be ordered to ship out.

On February 4, 1899, just five days before Fagen reenlisted at Fort McPherson, the long-standing stalemate between American troops and frustrated Filipino revolutionaries came to a bloody end. At about 9:00 p.m. Privates William W. Grayson and Orville H. Miller, both of Company D, 1st Nebraska Volunteers, then serving in Manila, fired the first shots of the Philippine-American War. Grayson, an English immigrant and former hotel worker, became an instant celebrity. His story was picked up by numerous newspapers, including the Omaha *Daily Bee*:

> ...I had been doing outpost duty for some time, and was getting rather used to the strained situation. There were four of us on duty at the post in daytime, and the guard was doubled at night. We knew it was coming, and we all wondered who would be the man to fire the first shot. That night my companion on outpost was Orville Miller. During the day I had a talk with a Filipino Lieutenant. He told me that I would have to keep back farther. You see, they were encroaching on our territory every day and because we seemed to stand for it, they got brave and impudent .
>
> I told the lieutenant I did not 'savvy,' Miller and I walked

down to the end of the lane, so that our retreat would be covered in case we had to fall back. We were half-sitting, half-kneeling at the end of the lane when we heard the soft whistle of the Filipino. It was answered by several other whistles, and we knew that mischief was brewing.

Then from the Filipino's block house, No. 7, we saw a red light waving in some kind of signal. We turned our gaze back to where the whistle came from, when up rose a Filipino as if he had come out of the ground. I challenged him and he challenged my challenge. That meant fight. I heard the click, click of rifles, and without a moment's hesitation I let fly, and my impertinent Filipino tumbled over.

Miller and I took to our heels up the lane. Two shots rang out as we ran, and when we had got back about twenty-five yards two Filipinos blocked our path.

They were inside our lines, but they challenged us.

"Shoot!" I cried to Miller, and a second later there was a dead Filipino. In another second I had brought down my second Filipino. At first, I think, was the lieutenant who had given me 'lip' in daytime. I think I killed him. I do not know, but I think he got it right.

We retreated until we reached the pipe line. That was the water main, and it made a fine breastwork, and we needed it. The Filipinos kept firing at us all the time. The entire outpost – there were thirty of us – came into the pipe line and we all peppered away at the enemy.

Then the action spread from right to left, and in fifteen minutes the engagement was general from Caloocan to the bay.[14]

After Grayson and Miller fired their shots, "as they ran back to their post, Grayson shouted, 'line up fellows, the niggers are in here all through these yards.'"[15]

Across the city from where the shooting had started, the rapidly increasing sounds of battle were heard by Colonel Frederick Funston and his new bride, Eva, who had just gone to bed:

Major and Mrs. Whitman, Major Metcalf and Mrs. Funston and myself had started up house keeping in a very passable house in the Binondo district. Our orderlies slept in the same building, and the horses were in a stable in the courtyard. On the night of February 4, we had just retired, and I was not yet asleep when Major Metcalf pounded vigorously on the door and called out "come out here, Colonel. The ball has begun." I scarcely realized at first what he meant but hastily slipped on a few clothes and came out into the hallway. Metcalf conducted me to a window, and asked, "Did you ever hear that racket before?" And sure enough, from a little north of east, floating over the house-tops of the great city, came the distant rattle of the Mausers. There was no mistaking it, and we realized that a war had begun. As the preliminary rattle swelled into a great roar, there were excited voices in the streets, rapid closing of doors and windows, the sound of people running through the streets, and then the city became almost as quiet as death. In the meantime our orderlies had been awakened and were saddling our horses in frantic haste. We dressed hastily, said hurried good-bys, and in a few moments were galloping through the silent streets to the regimental headquarters.[16]

Historian Howard Zinn sums up what happened next: "American firepower was overwhelmingly superior to anything the Filipino rebels could put together. In the very first battle, Admiral Dewey steamed up the Pasig River and fired 500-pound shells into the Filipino trenches. Dead Filipinos were piled so high that the Americans used their bodies as breastworks. A British witness said: 'This is not war; it is simply massacre and murderous butchery.' He was wrong; it was war."[17]

In a letter he sent home dated 23 February, Frank M. Erb of the Pennsylvania Regiment wrote:

> We have been in this nigger-fighting business now for twenty-three days, and have been under fire for the greater part of that time. The niggers shoot over one another's heads or any old way. Even while I am writing this the black boys are banging away at

our outposts, but they very seldom hit anybody. The morning of the 6th a burying detail from our regiment buried forty-nine nigger enlisted men and two nigger officers, and when we stopped chasing them the night before, we could see 'em carrying a great many with them. We are supposed to have killed about three hundred. Take my advice, and don't enlist in the regulars, for you are good for three years. I am not sorry I enlisted, but you see we have had some excitement and we only have about fourteen months' time to serve, if they keep us our full time, which is not likely. We will, no doubt, start home as soon as we get these niggers rounded up. [18]

On the morning of June 22, companies C, E, G & I of the 24th Infantry Regiment (USCT) were among hundreds of other soldiers who were loaded aboard the chartered steamer *Zeelandia*, which departed that afternoon from San Francisco bound for Manila, with scheduled coaling stops at Hawaii and other refueling stations across the Pacific. Once again, Fagen was on his way to war.[19]

Through friendly newspapers, President McKinley and the imperialists at Washington were broadcasting that, among other things, the U.S. was engaged in a noble effort to help the disparate, mostly savage and illiterate people of the Philippines establish a working democratic government. This would lead, they claimed, to better roads, wider water distribution, improved living conditions, modern schools and industry. McKinley's people also spread the propaganda that this endeavor was being ruthlessly opposed by a tyrannical Filipino tribal leader who was dead-set on establishing a Tagalog dictatorship which would, no doubt, be more oppressive to the poor, half-civilized Philippine people than that which they had endured under Spanish control.

Black or white, the American troops being rushed to the Philippines believed they were more than ready to fight the "Gugus."*

*The derivation of this pejorative slang term stemmed from American soldiers bending the Tagalog descriptive for stupid or asshole – "Gago." Eventually, the slang term remained in American usage, having evolved to the word: "Gook."

Notes

1. Quote from: Edward Van Zile Scott, *The Unwept*, Black Belt Press, Montgomery Alabama 1996, paperback, p. 194.
2. Quote, Stephen Bonsal, Ibid. p. 138.
3. Quote, Stephen Bonsal, Ibid. p. 147, see also JSTOR online: http://archive.org/stream/jstor-25105899/25105899_djvu.txt.
4. Quote of Theodore Roosevelt, in his *Rough Riders, Scribner's Magazine,* April 1899, pp. 435-436.
5. Quote of John E. Lewis, from *The Illinois Record,* August 13, 1898, in: Gatewood, *Smoked Yankees,* p. 58.
6. Quote of Chaplain George W. Prioleau, in Gatewood, *Smoked Yankees,* pp. 82-83.
7. Quote of Philip Foner, from his: *A History of the Labor Movement in the United States,* taken from: Howard Zinn, *A People's History of the United States,* paperback, 2003, Harper Collins, NY, p. 310.
8. Quote from, Brian McAllister Linn, *The Philippine War,* University Press of Kansas, paperback, 2000, p. 21.
9. Quote of Aguinaldo's account of his meeting with Dewey, from: Don Emilio Aguinaldo y Famy, *True Version of the Philippine Revolution,* September 1899, reprint, paperback, Valde Books, Lexington, Ky, 2012, pp. 10-11.
10. Quote from Philippine Declaration of Independence from Luis Francia, *A History of the Philippines,* Overlook Press, Peter Mayer Publishers, New York NY, 2010, pp. 139-140.
11. Quotes "First Battle of Manila," and "unexpected Spanish resistance" from: Linn, *The Philippine War,* .p. 25.
12. Quote of McKinley from Howard Zinn, *A People's History of the United States,* 1999, Harper Collins Publishers, paperback, 2003, pp. 312-313.
13. Senator Albert Beveridge quote extractions from: http://websupport1.citytech.cuny.edu/Faculty/pcatapano/US2/US%20Documents/beveridge.html.
14. Grayson quote from: Omaha Daily Bee, August 2, 1899, in Arnaldo Dumindin, http://Philippineamericanwar.webs.com/filamwarbreaksout.htm.
15. Quote "as they ran back", Ibid.
16. Quote from: Frederick Funston, *Memories of Two Wars,* 1911, Board of Regents

of the University of Nebraska, 2009, paperback, p.p. 177-178.
17. Howard Zinn, quote from: *A People's History of the United States,* paperback, HarperCollins Publishers, New York, 2003, p. 316.
18. Quote of Erb letter from: *American Soldiers Write Home About the War in the Philippines,* website: http://historymatters.gmu.edu/d/58/.
19. See Captain William G. Muller, *The Twenty Fourth Infantry, Past and Present,* 1923, reprint, The Old Army Press, Ft. Collins, Colorado, 1972, p. 26.

◄Chapter Seven►

THE NIGGER WAR

June 22 - July 23, 1899

IT WASN'T AS THOUGH FAGEN AND THE OTHERS had no idea who they were facing in the Philippines. In fact, they had a consuming interest to learn about the people they were destined to fight, and imprisoned below decks they had plenty of time to indulge that interest.

Back home, aided by contemporary newspaper cartoons, the popular American perspective of black soldiers was one of a mostly illiterate, happy-go-lucky crowd of hard fighting but ignorant darkies (not unlike the black-faced African Americans being lampooned in minstrel shows during the same period).

With black faces that didn't wash off, the Buffalo Soldiers aboard the *Zeelandia* had in their midst a few veterans who also served as voluntary correspondents to a string of black newspapers. The mail of these men brought them copies of their favored periodicals, all of which were passed around, read, read aloud, and reread. Indeed, with its glaring overhead lights, the hold of the *Zeelandia* was the perfect environment for the readers to enlighten their illiterate brothers. Having spent years chasing and fighting Native Americans in the far west, the majority of these professional soldiers understood that the better you knew your enemy, the better your chances were to kill him when you fought.

Corporal John R. Conn frequently fed letters to the *Washington Evening Star*. Sergeant Major John Galloway contributed letters and columns to the *Richmond Planet*. Sgt. Patrick Mason corresponded with the *Cleveland Gazette*, while Edward Brown and Corporal S.T. Evans of I-company sent stories to the *Indianapolis Recorder*. Sgt. Preston Moore of C-company was a regular contributor to Indianapolis's *The Freeman*.[1]

In addition to the shooting war now underway in the Philippines, across the United States an on-going political war between imperialists and anti-imperialists was taking place. Evidently, a slight majority of white Americans accepted the idea of annexing the Philippine Islands, but black leaders and editorialists were stridently opposed. Some argued that taking the Philippine Islands would only provide a new outpost for Jim Crow.

"If blacks were denied their rights in this country, the same thing would take place in the Philippines once the whites got control." A black editor noted that "when one of the great Christian countries found land it desired, it was quickly seized with a commendable desire to spread the benign influence of civilization over the natives, but what a remarkably small number of natives are left after this process of civilizing has been completed."[2]

In February, 1899, *McClure's Magazine* published a poem written by Rudyard Kipling urging the United States to take up the "burden" of empire, as Britain had previously done. The poem was titled *The White Man's Burden: The United States and the Philippine Islands.* Spread through numerous newspapers, Kipling's poem attracted enormous public attention. McKinley, Roosevelt and the imperialist movement praised Kipling's blatant advocacy of white imperialism. But their opponents used the poem for proof that America's foray into the Philippines was pure evil, and had nothing whatever to do with benevolent assimilation.

The White Man's Burden

Take up the White Man's burden—
Send forth the best ye breed—
Go send your sons to exile
To serve your captives' need
To wait in heavy harness
On fluttered folk and wild—
Your new-caught sullen peoples,
Half devil and half child
Take up the White Man's Burden

> In patience to abide
> To veil the threat of terror
> And check the show of pride:
> By open speech and simple
> An hundred times made plain
> To seek another's profit
> And work another's gain
> Take up the White Man's burden—
> And reap his old reward:
> The blame of those ye better
> The hate of those ye guard—
> The cry of hosts ye humour
> (ah slowly) to the light:
> "Why brought ye us from bondage,
> "our loved Egyptian night?"
> Take up the White Man's burden—
> Have done with childish days—
> The lightly proffered laurel,
> The easy, ungrudged praise.
> Comes now to search your manhood
> Through all the thankless years,
> Cold-edged with dear-bought wisdom,
> The judgment of your peers! [3]
>
> —Rudyard Kipling

Recognizing that the islands' inhabitants were dark races, the A.M.E. *Church Review* called outright for black identity with the Filipinos. The paper suggested that Filipino resistance and black mobilizations in the United States were part of a larger, global pattern. The editor of the *Washington Bee* suggested the same, writing: "There is some analogy between the struggle which is now going on among the colored people for constitutional liberty and that of a similar race in the Orient, and hence a bond of sympathy naturally springs up."[4]

Even before they landed at Manila, Fagen and his comrades understood the war they were about to fight was a racial conflict. But regardless of their personal sentiments, as regulars in the U.S. Army, it was their duty to fight and kill whomever they were ordered to attack. Their war in the Philippines would be no different than when they had fought against warring Navajos, Apaches, Zunis, Comanches and Nez Perce. Veterans like Sgt. Galloway had learned how to manage their emotions. The army was banking on the premise that the training of Fagen and the newer men would assure their compliance. It was a safe bet. The army had no lenience in such matters; soldiers would cope or hang.

Considering the great desire for freedom and independence burning brightly in Aguinaldo and the Philippine people after their victory over Spanish Rule, the Nigger War now taking place was a predictable and logical result of President McKinley's famous *Benevolent Assimilation Decree,* which he authored only ten days after the Treaty of Paris had been signed:

Executive Mansion, Washington

December 21, 1898

The destruction of the Spanish fleet in the harbor of Manila by the United States naval squadron commanded by Rear Admiral Dewey, followed by the reduction of the city and the surrender of the Spanish forces, practically effected the conquest of the Philippine Islands and the suspension of the Spanish sovereignty therein. With the signature of the treaty of peace between the United States and Spain by their respective plenipotentiaries at Paris on the 10th instant, and as a result of the victories of American arms, the future control, disposition, and government of the Philippine Islands are ceded to the United States. In the fulfillment of the rights of sovereignty thus acquired and the responsible obligations of government thus assumed, the actual occupation and administration of the entire group of the Philippine Islands becomes immediately necessary, and the military government theretofore maintained by the United States in the city, harbor, and bay of Manila is to be extended with all possible dispatch to the whole of the ceded territory.

In performing this duty the military commander of the United States is enjoined to make known to the inhabitants of the Philippine Islands that in succeeding to the sovereignty of Spain, in severing the former political relations, and in establishing a new political power, the authority of the United States is to be exerted for the securing of the persons and property of the people of the islands and for the confirmation of all their private rights and relations. It will be the duty of the commander of the forces of occupation to announce and proclaim in the most public manner that we come, not as invaders or conquerors, but as friends, to protect the natives in their homes, in their employments, and in their personal and religious rights. All persons who, either by active aid or by honest submission, co-operate with the Government of the United States to give effect to these beneficent purposes will receive the reward of its support and protection. All others will be brought within the lawful rule we have assumed, with firmness if need be, but without severity, so far as possible.

...Finally, it should be the earnest wish and paramount aim of the military administration to win the confidence, respect, and affection of the inhabitants of the Philippines by assuring them in every possible way that full measure of individual rights and liberties which is the heritage of free peoples, and by proving to them that the mission of the United States is one of

BENEVOLENT ASSIMILATION

Substituting the mild sway of justice and right for arbitrary rule. In the fulfillment of this high mission, supporting the temperate administration of affairs for the greatest good of the governed, there must be sedulously maintained the strong arm of authority, to repress disturbance and to overcome all obstacles to the bestowal of the blessings of good and stable government upon the people of the Philippine Islands under the free flag of the United States.

WILLIAM McKINLEY [5]

Early in January, aware that the Treaty of Paris still had to be ratified by a Senate that was deeply divided, McKinley created the Philippine Commission—a non-partisan group headed by Jacob Gould Schurman, then President of Cornell University. McKinley tasked the committee to study the inhabitants of the islands—their conditions, cultures, resources and economy—and then recommend the best path for American policy.

Safely ensconced within the walled city, Schurman and his fellow commission members (not including General Elwell Stephen Otis who, disdaining the whole affair, absented himself from all its deliberations) conducted all their investigations. The only Filipinos interviewed were a collection of wealthy, elitist "Ilustrados"—educated Filipinos, many of whom had studied in Europe, and whose families had profited immensely under Spanish control. In order to maintain their positions, fortunes and land holdings, these men had deserted Aguinaldo and the Army of Liberation and were now striving to ingratiate themselves with their new American masters. They knew what the Americans wanted to hear, with the acuity and intensity of a hunting shark. They eagerly testified that yes, indeed, it is absolutely true that the peoples of the Philippines were mostly illiterate, separated by dozens of languages, and were inarguably incapable of self-government.

Aware that these sycophants exerted immense economic and political power over thousands of tenant farmers and laborers, and that their loyalty would both weaken the image of the revolutionaries and reduce the amount of money, armaments and supplies they received, Schurman and General Otis were happy to accept and exploit them.

Surprising no one, the Philippine Commissions' preliminary findings corroborated McKinley's opinions. There was no doubt that the Philippine Islands were indeed a collection of disparate, mostly illiterate tribes. The current revolutionary war was indeed the product of a power move by Aguinaldo and his Tagalog tribe, a bid designed to bring them hegemony over everyone else. McKinley was delighted with Schurman's assessment.

While the war of words between the imperialists and anti-imperialists was waged in newspapers and in the halls and bars of Washington and New York, the real carnage of the war—torn flesh, blood and death—continued in Luzon. The American troops had neither the inclination nor the time to spread American benevolence. L. F. Adams, of Ozark, Missouri, a soldier serving in the Washington regiment, describes the scene after the battle of February 4-5, 1899:

> In the path of the Washington Regiment and Battery D of the Sixth Artillery there were 1,008 dead niggers, and a great many wounded. We burned all their houses. I don't know how many men, women, and children the Tennessee boys did kill. They would not take any prisoners.[6]

Howard McFarland, Sergeant, Company B, 43rd Infantry, wrote to the *Fairfield Journal* of Maine in March, 1899:

> I am now stationed in a small town in charge of twenty miles to patrol...at the best, this is a very rich country, and we want it. My way of getting it would be to put a regiment into a skirmish line and blow every nigger into nigger heaven. On Thursday, March 29, eighteen of my company killed seventy-five nigger bolo-men and ten of the nigger gunners...when we find one that is not dead, we have bayonets.[7]

Lt. John F. Hall of the 20th Kansas Volunteers wrote a harsh letter to the Adjutant-General, charging both officers and men of the regiment with violent crimes under the U.S. Code of Military Justice:

> ...Fifth: That on the tenth day of February, 1899, the said Wilder S. Metcalf did maliciously, willfully, and without just cause, shoot and kill an unarmed prisoner of war on his knees before him begging for his life, in violation of the Fifty-Eighth Article of War.
>
> Sixth: That the said Frederick S. Funston, at said date, and thereafter, did issue orders to shoot prisoners, and compounded the crime of the said Metcalf, above mentioned, by protecting and shielding the said Metcalf and using his influence to prevent a fair and impartial investigation of the shooting of these prisoners, in violation of the Fifty-Eighth Article of War.[8]

THE NIGGER WAR

Lt. Hall was quickly transferred to another outfit and no charges were ever filed against Colonel Funston.

Back in the United States, at large assemblies and in the nation's leading newspapers, influential imperialists proclaimed open admiration "for our Anglo-Saxon cousins across the Atlantic. Blood was thicker than water," they chimed, and we Americans "shared Britain's racial genius for empire building—a genius they must exercise for the greater glory of the race, and to advance civilization in general."[9]

While it appeared that imperialists were all racists, both racist and non-racist views drove their opponents. Some of the anti-imperialists opposed annexation of the Philippines because they were convinced that if Filipinos were denied any political rights in the Philippines, the same rights for American citizens would be weakened. On the other hand, if Filipinos were granted full and equal rights as Americans, their numbers and cultural cohesiveness might destroy American institutions. After all, *their* culture and history was alien. No matter how they were dressed or acted, they would never, ever truly become Anglo-Saxon. "If incorporated they would remain a hopelessly heterogeneous element in the population. Our democratic institutions would assuredly degrade."[10]

Mrs. Jefferson Davis claimed she was sure that the Filipinos included "several millions of negroes" who would only exacerbate our own unresolved "negro problem." [11]

Labor leaders feared that the immigration of Filipino workers "might erode the labor rights and racial integrity of white workingmen." [12]

On 6 February, 1899, the day the U.S. Senate was to decide whether to ratify or reject the Treaty of Paris—in which Spain surrendered control of Cuba, Puerto Rico, parts of Spanish West Indies, Guam and the Philippine Islands to the U.S.—Emilio Aguinaldo and other key leaders of the Philippine Republic prayed for a negative result. Despite their prayers, McKinley and the imperialists won by a single vote. The war that had begun by accident two days earlier would continue.

Throughout March, Americans decimated General Antonio Luna's brave—but untrained and undisciplined—Filipino revolutionaries. The Americans were supported by warships patrolling Manila Bay and by heavily armed gunboats plying the many navigable rivers of Luzon. Unable

Town heavily damaged by US Naval gunfire. (*US National Archives*)

to withstand the onslaught of rapid-firing cannons, Gatling guns and Colt machine guns, the Filipinos were forced to retreat. But as the front lines moved inland and northward, the Americans began to outrun their supplies and their advances stalled.

Learning the hard way, the Army of Liberation began to retreat to defensive positions that were unreachable by U.S. naval gunfire. Suffering from heat, foul water, inadequate food, and often a lack of ammunition, the American attacks were blunted and in some cases, U.S. troops were driven back. Casualties increased to alarming levels.

For the Americans, the tropic heat was as much an enemy as the insurgent army. Stripped of all but food and ammunition, a company of seventy-five U.S. infantrymen consumed a ton of supplies every five days. Because a trooper in the field was burdened with a nine-pound rifle, ten pounds of ammunition, a canteen, hardtack biscuits, a few tins of meat and a poncho, supplies had to be hauled in on horses, mules, or on carts pulled by water-buffalos (carabaos). Hundreds of Chinese porters were hired to carry heavily laden packs. All too often, after the first day of an assault, the lead columns had left their supply wagons miles behind and were living on fatty bacon, coffee and dry bread, and were drinking from polluted wells

General Antonio Luna.
(*US National Archives*)

and streams. In three days those fighting at the spearhead of the American attack would run out of food.

As with any war, it was the residents of the country being fought over who bore the brunt of the savagery. Neither of the opposing armies showed them much compassion. General Luna hanged civilians for failing to supply his army with foodstuffs, and did the same to anyone who refused to burn their homes before the advancing Americans. Intending to leave nothing of any use to the enemy, he ordered dead animals and even human bodies tossed into wells. Operating in what appeared to be a permanent state of rage, Luna was equally severe with his troops: officers or men who fled their positions under heavy fire were condemned, and forced to stand and be shot before firing squads.

The American march to Malolos (the then current seat of the Philippine Republic's government) followed the Manila-Dagupan Railway, and the first troops to enter the town, which had been shelled frequently, received deadly fire from Filipino snipers hidden in the rubble. American ingenuity provided an answer to this problem, which, for reasons of delicacy, General Otis did not reveal to reporters at his daily press briefings in Manila. The solution was to convert a fire-fighting steam engine into a machine that could spray villages with burning petroleum, in effect a type of giant flame thrower.

During daily press conferences attended by attentive newsmen who, under military law were required to have all their copy reviewed and approved before any of it could be cabled back to America, General Otis repeatedly proclaimed that, for practical purposes, the war was all but over.

In a carefully planned attack on the coastal town of Bacoor, the U.S. Navy was to bombard the place with their big guns just prior to General Lawton's assault. For one reason or another, the warships opened fire long before the army was able to reach the town. According to the *San Francisco Call* of June 16, 1899:

> General Lawton rode five miles along the coast without discovering the enemy, to Bacoor, and found the town full of white flags. But there were no soldiers. The women and children who had fled the bombardment, were camping in the ruins of their homes. The shells had almost knocked the town to pieces. The big church was wrecked and many buildings were ruined. Even the trees and shrubbery were torn as by a hailstorm.[13]

Despite General Otis's claims of success, what had become apparent in Washington and in the American press was that all the predictions of a war that wouldn't last more than a few weeks were pipe dreams. American casualties were now in the hundreds, and thousands of men had been wounded or incapacitated by tropical diseases. In constant movement outward and away from Manila, the Americans had insufficient troops available to hold and control captured areas. Worst of all, no one foresaw an end date to the conflict.

Powerful editorials on June 16 and 20 in the *San Francisco Call* summed up the disillusionment of the anti-imperialists. They had patriotically held back their criticisms of the war for the first four months or so, but they could no longer contain their silence:

> The undeclared war in the Philippines has now been nearly twice

THE NIGGER WAR

as long as the war with Spain. The Filipinos, without effective artillery and [with a] lack of military form, have proved their touch and common feeling with all people who are fighting for the soil they were born on and for independence and self-government against an invading host.

Our superior arms, aim, and formations, our great guns and support of warships that with one broadside can destroy a town and leave its men, women and children heaped in a mass of torn flesh to spume in the sun ... our inadequate forces have destroyed the country by raiding ... and their hosts have closed in behind advancing columns, as water closes after a hand that is drawn through it.

Meanwhile General Otis has been dealing "crushing blows." He has ended the "rebellion" repeatedly, but the "crushing blows" do not crush. We have probably killed thousands. There is much mourning in American homes where the first born of many a house has died under the blistering tropical sun . . . Our troops have pushed the unavailing butchery of war with uncomplaining endurance and dash. Yet the barefooted enemy, remembering his hut burned and his paddy field destroyed, lurks in the jungle and fights.[14]

One veteran recalled that as the Americans pulled back "a long black column of smoke sprang up . . . canoes were dragged up to the fires, and burned and the entire district destroyed so that it would seem necessary not only for a bird but even a Filipino to carry his rations while crossing it."[15]

Frederick Funston's outfit was one of the leading regiments of the attack on the insurgent capital at Malolos. He wrote down his experiences on March 31:

We were now less than a mile from the Nipa houses [Philippine native houses with walls of woven straw] in the suburbs of Malolos. I was on the railroad tracks with the division commander (MacArthur), when he asked me if I would like to take a few men and feel my way into the town? I said I would be glad to, and took

Lt. Ball and about a dozen men from Company E, leaving the regiment in command of Lt. Col. Little for the time being. Moving rapidly over to the left of the regiment, our little detachment found a narrow road leading into the capital, and we went it up on the jump, now and then halting for a few seconds to peer around the corners. The road soon became a street and here we were joined by the ubiquitous Mr. Creelman, quite out of breath from his exertions in overtaking us, he having "smelled a rat" when he saw us leave. We were fired upon by about a dozen men from behind a street barricade of stones, gave them a couple of volleys, and then rushed them. A minute later we were in the plaza or Public Square, and exchanged shots with a few men who were running through the streets starting fires. The buildings occupied by Aguinaldo as a residence and as offices and the Hall of Congress were burning. We gave such cheers as few men could and I sent back to General MacArthur that the town was ours. In a few moments, troops from all the regiments of the brigade, as well as the brigade commander himself joined us.[16]

By the time Malolos fell, General Luna's army was no longer standing and fighting from fixed defensive positions. His latest tactics sacrificed territory in order to kill, wound and demoralize American soldiers. For every foot the Americans advanced, their logistical problems increased proportionally. Applying tactics he had learned in Europe, Luna's army was now fighting from well-prepared interlacing trenches and bunkers. These positions were camouflaged with straw and brush, and in many cases, the trenches had been roofed over with sandbags. Luna's men would hold their fire until the advancing Americans were close, and then open up on them with their Mausers. Suffering severe losses, the Americans would halt; bring up their reserves or artillery, fire a barrage, and then advance. When they reached the enemy positions, they would see that their enemies had withdrawn via escape trenches to new, unknown locations up ahead where they were lying in wait for them. Luna's new hit-and-fallback tactics were paying off and the Filipino leaders were banking that the Americans could not afford to allow such losses to continue.

THE NIGGER WAR

Firing squad executing Filipinos. (*US National Archives*)

Spanish using garrote to kill Filipino man. (*Courtesy Anthony Powell, Jr.*)

By this time most Filipinos saw little difference between living under Spanish or American rule.

US troops waterboarding Filipino. (*US National Archives*)

Filipinos held in stocks. (*US National Archives*)

By this time most Filipinos saw little difference between living under Spanish or American rule.

On 28 March, hoping to bolster their spirits, Luna sent out telegrams to several provincial chiefs:

> ...in barrio Malibay, the troops of the Republic discovered and surprised 111 Americans, 90 of whom were killed, and from whom they got 111 rifles, 28 revolvers, thousands of rounds of ammunitions, and four thousand pesos in gold; in a second encounter, another group of Americans, 60 in number, were all killed in a barrio of Marikina, and from whom the Filipinos took 50 rifles and a large amount of ammunition.[17]

Although his tactics were working, Luna's logistic problems were becoming a nightmare. The Republic was rapidly exhausting its resources; and ever more frequently, his troops were running out of ammunition and then being forced to withdraw. Meeting with Aguinaldo, Luna sharply advocated for a rapid transition to guerilla warfare—a style he was convinced he could afford to fight however long it might take to win. The general was convinced that American support for such a never-ending war would gradually erode.

Although Aguinaldo agreed with many of Luna's arguments, he felt that the timing was wrong. The main American reason for subjugation of the Philippines was based on the assumption that the people of the Philippines were half-civilized savages, wholly incapable of self-government. President Aguinaldo believed that the longer the Army of Liberation was able to fight formal, "civilized" war, adhering to all its rules, the more effectively they would counter that perception. In addition, at that very moment there were a number of capable and talented Filipino diplomats touring Europe, working to gain international recognition for a Philippine State. It was simply too early to reduce the revolution to uncivilized guerilla warfare.

Luna sensed that Aguinaldo wasn't about to budge. Abandoning the argument, he returned to his headquarters still convinced that his position was correct. If Aguinaldo was incapable of dealing with reality, so be it. On his own, Luna began preparations for transitioning to guerilla warfare.

While Aguinaldo and Luna were arguing at Cabanatuan, Commissioner Schurman was in Manila, working in consultation with his leading Filipino

Ilustrados. As a group, they began to develop a peace offering which coupled autonomy with an acceptance of American sovereignty. Presenting his draft to the wealthy Filipino elitists who had sworn their loyalty to the United States, the response was overwhelmingly positive. They electrified him by predicting that even Aguinaldo would accept such an offer. They were so sure of it that some of them volunteered to personally carry it to the president. With his accord, the costly, bloody and tragic war would be brought to an immediate end. Tantalized by the thought that he might soon be honored for creating a diplomatic masterpiece that would save thousands of American and Filipino lives, Schurman quickly cabled a draft of his plan to Secretary of State John Hay in Washington.

Hay was a realist who had absolutely no faith that General Otis could conclude the current conflict in the foreseeable future, and although his approval of Schurman's peace plan was a direct slap to the general's face, he quickly endorsed the proposal.

While there were many in Washington hoping for a peaceful settlement of the conflict, neither the American or Filipino generals who commanded the opposing armies were among that group. Craving victory as the crowning achievement to his long military career, General Otis was determined to resist any sort of settlement short of a full Philippine surrender. In his view, the Filipinos would have to lay down their arms before he would even discuss peace.

General Luna was equally committed to reject any sort of settlement with the Americans that would result in anything but complete Philippine independence.

After Malolos fell, the insurgents fled to the province of Nueva Ecija, where their government was seated at San Isidro. The head of Aguinaldo's cabinet was Apolinario Mabini, a young fragile man, with a subtle and logical intellect. He was dedicated to the cause of Philippine independence and had a fierce, irreconcilable hatred of the government of the United States.

When Commissioner Schurman's peace proclamation reached the Filipinos at San Isidro, many of the leaders perceived that under American sovereignty they would enjoy greater liberties than they had ever dreamt of under Spanish rule. If not full independence, they would have surer self-government than their own Philippine Republic could ever guarantee.

According to Commissioner Schurman:

> ...if not a nominal independence, at least a firmer and surer self-government than their own Philippine Republic could ever guarantee. The demoralization of the Philippine army was meanwhile going on apace, thanks to the continuous victories of General Lawton and General MacArthur. And the commission, who had timed the issue of the proclamation after conference with General Otis so that the hand of conciliation might be felt at the same time as the hand of force, watched anxiously for the result on the insurgent authorities. Nor had we long to wait for the realization of our most sanguine expectations.
>
> On May 1st the Congress of the Philippine Republic voted for the cessation of war and the adoption of peace on the basis of our proclamation! Mabini's cabinet was overturned, and a new cabinet was formed, pledged to peace and reconciliation, with Paterno at its head and Buencamino as his most important colleague...[18]

Believing the commission's peace offer had ended the war, Schurman's hopes were dashed by General Luna, who had all the delegates arrested before they could proceed to Manila and sign away Filipino independence.

The outcome was now centered on the conflict between Aguinaldo who wanted to make peace, and Luna who was determined to continue the fight for independence.

Informed by friendly Ilustrados of the conflict between Aguinaldo and Luna, General Otis ordered an attack on the city of Iloilo. Inwardly, there could be little doubt that Otis was grateful for Luna's revolt.

What happened is revealed best by Philippine historian Vivencio Jose, in his *The Rise and Fall of Antonio Luna*:

> ...Luna earlier, upon learning that a new Commission, this time composed of Gonzaga, Barreto, Zialcita, and del Pilar was formed and was already dealing with the Schurman Commission, went later to Cabanatuan to inquire. He proceeded to the convent of the town where Aguinaldo held office. A dinner was then being tended

to the members of the council and other ranking officers of the Republic, with Aguinaldo's family present. Luna strode into the room and upon being invited, took his seat. Not for long, he was discussing heatedly with his colleagues, berating their willingness to negotiate peace with the Schurman Commission. In the course of their arguments, Luna cast a murderous look at Buencamino, the most passionate and incorrigible defender of the autonomy policy of the government. Luna could not conceal his hatred of this autonomist, who he believed, was selling the country to the Americans. Turning to his side, Luna spoke loud enough to be heard in the room: "There is another traitor whom we should be permitted to eliminate!"

Stung to the quick, Buencamino fumed: "I deny your accusation, as, for me, if there is any traitor at all among those who form the government and Army of the Republic, it is you because if you would not have taken the one thousand soldiers armed with Mauser guns from Calumpit in order to subdue General Mascardo without permission of the Capitan General [Aguinaldo], until now the American Army would be surrounded at Malolos. This accusation of yours is as false as that denounced by you to Captain General Aguinaldo! . . .

[Luna] lunged swiftly at Buencamino. Severino de las Alas, then Secretary of the Interior, caught Luna by the arm and led him away.

...Back at his own headquarters, convinced more than ever that the Paterno-Buencamino clique would not desist from its dealings with the Schurman Commission, Luna ordered a unit of his troops to arrest the members of the cabinet on charge of treason -- an order to this effect he issued officially. Later, he hurriedly saw Aguinaldo and firmly proposed to the latter "the exile of all of them to Bayambang [prison] as traitors to the country." [19]

Aguinaldo, who found the entire proceedings disturbing and distasteful, answered Luna that the "accusation was very serious and that it was necessary for him to prove it before taking such a severe measure. " Nevertheless, he assured Luna that they would be "detained in the meantime pending the result of the investigation which he would conduct immediately for that purpose.

When Luna's back was turned, having left for the front, Aguinaldo for reasons of his own released the prisoners. Fearfully agitated at the disastrous turn of events Aguinaldo and these autonomists held on May 27 a meeting in the Presidential Quarters at Cabanatuan. Buencamino … affirmed that Luna's actions tended to overthrow Aguinaldo from his position with the object of substituting him in power, he being of the opinion that Luna had to be condemned to death. Aguinaldo admitted, however, that he was convinced that Luna's ambition does not amount to what he was presently accused of. Buencamino and Paterno then, in concert, chorused to sway Aguinaldo to their belief. "In the presence of Your Honor, they said, "he laid hands on the face of one of your ministers, and then without the knowledge of Your Honor, he arrested your Cabinet wholesale. After such aggressive acts to the person of Your Honor and to your authority, what more is wanting?[20]

President Aguinaldo was being torn apart. On one side, two of the wealthiest and most powerful men in his country were urging him to make a deal with the Americans that would allow him to retain political leadership of the country. At his other ear, true patriots, including a majority of generals and provincial leaders, demanded that he remain loyal to Philippine independence because "it was better to die for freedom than live on his knees before the Americans." Aguinaldo spent two weeks pondering his options.

Luna received two telegrams on 4 June; one from Angeles and the other from Cabanatuan. The first, from a commander who was to participate in a planned counterattack against the Americans at San Fernando, requested reinforcements. The second message was from Aguinaldo, inviting Luna to come to Cabanatuan to form a new cabinet that he would preside over, a cabinet which was to resist any compromises with the Americans and would be strongly militant in its policy of struggle. Excited by the prospect, Luna sent a positive answer back to Aguinaldo and hurriedly assembled his travel party. Accompanied by his aide-de-camp, Colonel Francisco Roman, staff officers Colonel Simon Villa, and Captains Licuanon, Rusca and Jose Bernal, Luna also had a seventeen-man cavalry escort. After loading their mounts aboard a special train, Luna and his party departed for Tarlac. At Victoria, they mounted their horses and rode for Liclab, Nueva where they took a light breakfast. Continuing on, their next stop was Aliaga, where they ate lunch. Apparently, in a light, happy mood, Luna ordered Second Lieutenant Juan Paz to remain there with the cavalrymen and await their return from Cabanatuan. Securing three carromatas (single horse-drawn two-wheeled carts commonly rented for town travel) Luna set out for his destination, with Colonel Roman and Captain Rusca riding beside him. At the ferry landing leading to downtown Cabanatuan, two of Luna's three carromatas either suffered mechanical problems or, because the ferry was quite small, were forced to wait for the next crossing. Telling his men to come to the town as soon as they could, Luna and his two companions continued on and arrived at the town plaza at two o'clock in the afternoon, stopping on the street adjacent to the main entry of a former convent. Alighting from his mount, Luna turned and instructed Roman and Rusca to wait for him there, since he planned to return quickly once he had seen Aguinaldo, after which they would travel in haste for Tarlac and the coming attack.

There are more than a half-dozen accounts by Filipino and American historians about what happened next. What they all agree on is that Cabanatuan and the convent now serving as Aguinaldo's headquarters were manned entirely by members of the Kawit Company—a special guards' unit sworn to protect Aguinaldo and his family, and to take orders from no one else.

Luna was assassinated by assailants wielding bolos, bayonets and revolvers. Colonel Roman was gunned down on the street. Captain Rusca was felled by a rifle bullet that struck his leg, but managed to survive by crawling to safety in a nearby church.

Drawing close to Luna's fallen body, the general's assailants approached him warily, pointing their weapons. Luna's eyes were open and staring, but he was completely motionless. Two of his assassins knelt down to strip off his bloody jacket and search the pockets. The only document they discovered was Luna's copy of Aguinaldo's telegram inviting him to Cabanatuan.

THE NIGGER WAR

At Aguinaldo's direction, Luna and Colonel Roman were buried the next day with full military honors. There was a perfunctory investigation but no one was ever tried or held accountable for their murders.

The man who had ordered the death of Andres Bonifacio, the founder of the Katipunan, and one of the Republic's greatest revolutionary leaders, had now brought about the death of its greatest field general.

There were numerous repercussions. Troops and officers formerly loyal to Luna were investigated and some were imprisoned. In the weeks following Luna's assassination, what Aguinaldo came to recognize was that most of his generals, as well as the people of the countryside, were adamantly opposed to any form of autonomy under U.S. rule. They were determined to continue the struggle for freedom.

Appraising the presiding mood, Paterno and Buencamino swiftly adjusted their positions and swore new, invigorated loyalty to the revolution. Ironically, just as Luna had suggested, the Philippine Army of Liberation quickly transitioned to full scale guerilla warfare. The American response was to wage a war of racial extermination. Their rationale was that now the Filipinos were fighting like savages, the same way the Sioux had done at Wounded Knee and the Cheyennes at Sand Creek, the extermination of their uncivilized opponents was once again the proper strategy. The definitions between Filipino combatants and non-combatants blurred. Butchery was the new theme and the Americans were encouraged to use all their weaponry and conclude the fighting as swiftly as possible.

As Paul A. Kramer writes in his *The Blood of Government*: "The heart of the United States' emerging imperial racial formation was rich in contradictions; the people of the Philippines did not possess enough of what General Arthur MacArthur (father of Douglas MacArthur of WWII fame) would call 'ethnological homogeneity' to constitute a nation-state, but they did have enough to be made war upon as a whole."[1]

This then was the state of the Philippine-American war when Fagen and about half of the 24th Infantry Regiment arrived at Manila aboard the *Zeelandia* on the evening of July 23, 1899. They disembarked the next morning. Within hours, Fagen and the other Buffalo Soldiers came to understand that their real purpose in the Philippines was to help fight America's Nigger War.

Notes

1. Letters from these soldiers that were published in black newspapers appear in Gatewood, *Smoked Yankees,* pp. 65-71, 251-255, 257, 273-4, 276-77, 288-290.
2. Quotes of *Indianapolis Recorder,* taken from Paul A. Kramer, *The Blood of Government, Race, Empire, the United States, & the Philippines,* University of North Carolina Press, Chapel Hill, 2006, pp. 119-120.
3. Quote, Kipling's Poem, online http://historymatters.gmu.edu/d/5478/.
4. Quotes of A.M.E. *Church Review* and *Washington Bee* taken from Kramer, *Blood of Government,* p. 120.
5. McKinley decree of Benevolent Assimilation taken 11/17/2012 from: http://filipino.biz.ph/history/benevolent.html.
6. Quote of L.F. Adams, from *Marked Severities, Secretary Root's Record in Philippine Warfare,* originally published by Geo. H. Ellis Co. Boston, 1902, p. 10 from Google Books, online, 11/17/2012.
7. Quote, Ibid. p. 10.
8. Quote, Ibid. pp. 11-15.
9. Quote Ibid. p. 121.
10. Quote Ibid. pp. 117-18.
11. Quote from Paul A. Kramer, *The Blood of Government,* University of North Carolina Press, paperback, 2000, pp. 117, 119.
12. Quote Ibid. p. 119.
13. San Francisco Call quote taken from: Stuart Creighton Miller, *Benevolent Assimilation,* Yale University Press, 1982, p. 72.
14. San Francisco Call quote of June 16 and 20, 1899, taken from Miller, *Benevolent Assimilation,* p. 72.
15. Quote from, Brian McAllister Linn, *The Philippine War,* University Press of Kansas, paperback, 2000, p. 95.
16. Quote, Frederick Funston from his *Memories of Two Wars,* in Vivencio Jose, *The Rise and Fall of Antonio Luna,* 1972, pp. 271-2.
17. Quote from: Vivencio Jose, *Rise and Fall of Antonio Luna,* University of the Philippines, Quezon City, 1972, p. 278.
18. Quote from Jacob Gould Schurman, *Philippine Affairs, A Retrospect and Outlook,* (an address Schurman gave to the student body at Cornell

University), published 1902 by Charles Scribner's Sons, NY, pp. 10-11.
19. Quote, Vivencio Jose, *Rise and Fall of Antonio Luna,* 1972 p. 352-353.
20. Ibid. p. 353.
21. Quote from Paul A. Kramer, *Blood of Government,* Univ. of N.C. Press, 2006, p. 90.

◀Chapter Eight▶

VICTIMS

EARLY THE NEXT MORNING, Fagen and his comrades marched from the docks to a barracks inside Intramuros, the walled, ancient inner-city of Manila. Aware they were watched, they marched with an extra sharpness and snap, their heels striking the roadway all together as one. They marched down cobbled streets lined on both sides by classic Spanish buildings. The architecture was much the same as Fagen had seen in Santiago, Cuba, but fancier. Staring down at them from second floor balconies were small, dark Asians and on the roadway, horse-drawn carriages and carts piled high with goods pulled over to the curb to let them pass.

24th Infantry, USCT, arrives in Manila.
(*Anthony Powell, Jr. Collection*)

The Filipino men wore shirts, trousers and shoes, and the women had billowing dresses and carried brightly colored umbrellas to shade them from the blistering sun. All stared with wonder as the "Negrito" soldiers marched by in four arrow-straight columns. Not yet 9:00 a.m., it was already as hot and humid as Tampa in July. In groups of two and three, white American soldiers also stood and watched, their faces as unfriendly as their thoughts. Some hurled insults.

In his book *Smoked Yankees and the Struggle for Empire,* Willard B. Gatewood, Jr. wrote:

> ...The men of the Twenty Fifth Infantry had scarcely landed in 1899 when as they marched into Manila, a white spectator yelled: "What are you coons doing here?" White troops not only refused to salute black officers but also delighted in taunting Negro soldiers by singing, 'All coons look alike to me' and 'I don't like a nigger nohow.'[1]
>
> When the question 'What are you coons doing here?' rang out, the following retort came back from one of the marching soldiers: 'We've come to take up the White Man's burden.'[2]

The following morning, C, E, G and I companies of the 24th IR boarded an armored train and steamed their way along the Manila-Dagupan rail line to Caloocan. After leaving the suburbs of Manila, the scenery abruptly changed. The small towns were mostly rubble and the few people they saw there were emaciated, shoeless, and clothed in rags. Their faces wore apprehensive expressions. To Fagen and all the men watching from the train, these Filipinos were much the same as the locals they remembered from the war-ravaged towns and villages in and around Siboney, Cuba, only smaller in stature.

Three days later, Companies C, E and G were sent by rail to Marikina, or El Deposito, the main Manila water pumping station located four miles north of the city. Just above El Deposito, Fagen and the men of I-Company went into camp to perform guard and outpost duty on the Balic-Balic road.[3]

At first, the locals were afraid of the black troopers. Some Filipinos exclaimed, "These are not Americanos; they are Negritos." It did not take

155

long for their fear to dissipate. Within a few days the people came to accept black American troops as "very much like ourselves, only larger."[4]

Historian Willard B. Gatewood, Jr. describes the situation:

> Most of the Negro soldiers reciprocated their good will and in many instances quickly established a bond of racial identity with their Filipino "cousins." It was generally agreed that in towns and districts "garrisoned by colored troops the natives seem to harbor little or no enmity toward the soldiers and the soldiers themselves seem contented with their lot and are not perpetually pining for home."
>
> ...Most white Americans in the Philippines did not echo such praises. Particularly disturbing to the whites were the close ties of friendship which developed between the "Negritos Americanos" and the Filipinos. "While the white soldiers, unfortunately, got on badly with the natives," the correspondent Stephen Bonsal reported, "the black soldiers got on much too well." White military personnel came to suspect that black soldiers had more sympathy for the Filipinos' aspirations of independence than for American policy regarding the islands.[5]

A thoughtful letter written by a black soldier of the 25th Infantry, which later appeared in the *Cleveland Gazette*, illuminates the subject:

> ...As far as I can note from casual observance, I should class the Filipinos with the Cubans. They are intelligent and industrious, and although some of their habits are unclean, their clothes are always spotless and neat. They are eager to learn American ways and customs, and even if they don't understand would rather have one speak English to them as they think they can learn quicker that way. They are friendly and hospitable.... There are here some of the best mulatto people I have ever seen in my life. They are handsome. It is common for the women to wear their hair hanging down, and when they pass anyone on the street, they have to take hold of it and get it out of the way of the

passerby as the American ladies do their dresses....[6]

- C. W. Cordin, Co. B, 25th Infantry

Nevertheless, while relations between the Filipinos and the men of the 24th tightened, the truth is that most of the Filipinos Fagen and his comrades encountered fully supported the armed resistance toward the American invaders. Regardless of their color, American soldiers were regarded as unwelcome replacements for their former Spanish overlords. By day, the Filipino men who remained in the garrisoned towns and villages (mostly older men and farm workers) behaved in a manner profoundly polite and friendly to the American troops. But at night, these "Amigos" often joined the Insurrectos in swift and deadly attacks against isolated outposts, guard stations and supply wagons. In fact, the guerilla war was swiftly becoming known as "Amigo Warfare." It was the innocent civilians who suffered most. The guerillas continually demanded food, money, weapons and ammunition, and were quick to severely punish or execute anyone deemed *too* cooperative with the Americans.

Men like Fagen, charged with garrisoning population centers, had the near impossible task of protecting civilians while at the same time steadfastly pursuing and attacking insurgents. Black American soldiers faced the reality that in order to prove their loyalty and patriotism they had to suppress freedom for the Filipinos, "with whom they had ideological and racial ties."[7]

The need to locate and destroy guerilla bands required the ongoing collection of information from the very same people that the U. S. troops were supposed to be protecting and befriending. Village leaders, elected mayors and other minor officials were frequently subjects for brutal interrogation. In their mission to deny the guerillas weapons or food, the Americans were forced to repeatedly pressure Filipinos by searching them and their homes. When stored grains or other foodstuffs were discovered in quantities larger than required to meet the immediate consumption of one or two families, the food was collected and hauled to a guarded building.

Whether garrisoning towns or villages, or actively pursuing and attacking rebel bands, the Americans had a vital need for knowledgeable guides and interpreters. How one selected such confidants was crucial:

make the wrong choice and men on patrol would be led into an ambush, or spend their day on an exhausting, dangerous trek to nowhere.

One solution to this problem came in early July of 1899, when a young lieutenant named Matthew A. Batson requested permission to recruit a single company of Macabebe Scouts to be used as guides and interpreters. Batson's request was based on sound historical fact. As natives of the city of Macabebe, an area about ten miles square located in Pampanga Province just to the east of Calumpit, these men had formerly comprised an elite unit within the Spanish Army. Legend suggests that the original Macabebes had served as an effective, aggressive fighting unit of the Spanish Army in Mexico, and were later brought to the Philippines to enforce Spanish authority. Some Filipino historians claim the original Macabebes were Yaqui Indians, who, after one or two hundred years of marrying Filipinos, were as Asian in their appearance as their hated, traditional Tagalog enemies. If they proved to be loyal, it was more than likely that recruiting these superb fighters (all of whom had been trained in the latest European methods of warfare and were good shots with the Spaniards' rifles), was a good idea.

Macabebe scouts. (*US National Archives*)

VICTIMS

Disenfranchised by Spain's surrender, and hating the idea of an independent Philippines led by Tagalogs, the Macabebes offered their loyalty and fighting skills to the Americans. Their initial efforts were met with scorn by military authorities like General Otis who was, by now, suspicious of all Filipinos. Even so, as the dire need of his field commanders for reliable guides or scouts grew, Otis finally relented. A company of one-hundred Macabebe Scouts was formerly organized, provided with a short course in drill and tactics, equipped with Krag carbines, and sent into the field.

The Macabebes swiftly proved their loyalty and effectiveness by demonstrating a degree of barbarity against Tagalog guerillas and civilians that their American officers were forced to curtail. Both the Macabebe Scouts and American troops in the field commonly utilized a brutal form of torture to force captives to give up information. Called "the water cure," this painful abuse was the grandfather of today's "waterboarding" technique. The victim was forced to lie on his back on the ground with several men pinioning his outstretched arms and legs. A stick or bayonet or any such object was then forced between his teeth to fix his jaw open, and then a pipe or funnel tube was inserted. The helpless victim was then made to imbibe large amounts of salty or dirty water. Sometimes the water was also spilled into his nostrils as well as his mouth, adding to his distress by giving him the sensation of drowning. When his stomach was fully and painfully distended, it would be kicked or pummeled or sat upon, causing the water to be forcibly ejected. The victim's screams were disregarded, and the process would be repeated until the man broke or, in some cases, died.

Sergeant Leroy Hallock, who had witnessed the "cure" being administered to "at least a dozen insurgents," was more graphic:

> They would swell up—their stomachs would swell up pretty large—and I have seen blood come from their mouth (sic) after they had been given a good deal of it."[8]

The question of just how common and popular this particular torture became is demonstrated by the fact that the "water cure" was portrayed in poems, comedy sketches and even in a song composed by American soldiers:

The Water Cure in the P.I.

Get the good old syringe boys and fill it to the brim
We've caught another nigger and we'll operate on him
Let someone take the handle who can work it with a vim
Shouting the battle cry of freedom.
(Chorus)
Hurrah Hurrah We bring the Jubilee
Hurrah Hurrah The flag that makes him free
Shove in the nozzle deep and let him taste of liberty
Shouting the battle cry of freedom [9]

Some prisoners were shot to death or hanged. Assailed by everything he was witnessing, Fagen's attitude steadily darkened. The white officers of I-Company became the targets of his frustration and he was made to pay for his transgressions. According to historians Michael C. Robinson and Frank N. Schubert: "During his first months in the Philippines, Fagen

American Buffalo Soldiers hanging Filipinos.
(*Courtesy Anthony Powell, Jr.*)

experienced difficulties with his superiors." Details of the specific incidents remain unknown, but by mid-November Fagen had received some seven Court-Martials, and had applied no less than three times to be transferred to some other unit. Sergeant Major John W. Galloway later recalled that "Fagen might have been picked on and was made to do all sorts of dirty jobs."[10]

Robinson and Schubert speculated that the punishments Fagen may have received "probably included such tasks as night soil removal and kitchen police."[11] But "Night soil removal" and "kitchen police" are terms later used to describe World War I or II penalties for minor military infractions. Fagen's punishments may have been significantly more severe. Sentences resulting from courts-martials in all-black military units of the U.S. Army for this time period included one called the "Hanging Act," and another called the "Spread Eagle." With the Hanging Act, a rope was suspended from the ceiling of the guard house and tied tightly around two thumbs. The prisoner was then drawn up so that his toes would just touch the floor. Eventually, the entire weight of his body was borne by his thumbs and the pain became excruciating. The exercise continued until the subject indicated he was willing to comply with the court order, after which he was forced to perform hard labor for as long as his immediate superiors decreed.

In the "Spread Eagle," the prisoner was placed face downward on the ground with his arms and legs outstretched and tied to stakes that prohibited any movement. Every twelve hours, a sentry posted to watch over the subject asked him if he was willing to obey all his orders now. If so, the man was released and compelled to perform some difficult physical duty like digging latrines or clearing a road or trail in the hot sun.[1]

On September 28, C, E, G, and I-Companies of the 24th Infantry Regiment were relieved at El Deposito and carried by rail to San Fernando, where they continued to perform guard and outpost duty. The rest of the regiment, along with several other outfits, was now actively engaged in a major northeastward campaign. Put into motion by Brigadier General Samuel B.M. Young, the objective was to trap Emilio Aguinaldo and what was left of his fleeing army.

Amidst heavy, almost incessant rain, the soldiers were often forced to take part in long marches through mud so deep it prohibited the passage of any of their supply wagons. Living much of the time on what they could forage from the field or in captured villages and towns, the bulk of General Young's attacking army began to suffer debilitating diseases. He begged for supplies from General Lawton, who repeated his appeal to General Otis in Manila.

With roads so mired that even carabao carts got stranded, the army now relied on the transport of supplies by boats and barges up the deeper rivers. Unfortunately, due to frequent rainstorms, the rivers rose and fell unpredictably. Many of the craft that General Otis had provided drew too much water and stranded in the shallows. The American campaign to trap Aguinaldo during the rainy season was becoming a disaster.

Garrisoning the captured town of San Fernando, Fagen's outfit had it relatively easy, and the men had ample time to mingle with the locals. For use in an article he would eventually send to the *Richmond Planet*, Sergeant Major John W. Galloway interviewed a Filipino doctor about how his people viewed black soldiers:

> Question: 'Do the Filipinos hold a different feeling toward the colored American from that of the white?'
> Answer: 'Before American occupation of the islands and before the colored troops came to the Philippines, Filipinos knew little if anything of the colored people of America. We had read American history in the general, but knew nothing of the different races there. All were simply Americans to us. This view was held up to the time of the arrival of the colored regiments in Manila, when the white troops, seeing your acceptance on a social plane by the Filipino and Spaniard was equal to, if not better than theirs…they began to tell us of the inferiority of the American blacks—of your brutal natures, your cannibal tendencies—how you would rape our seniotitas, etc., Of course, at first we were a little shy of you, after being told of the difference between you and them; but we studied you, as results have shown. Between you and him, we look upon you as the angel and him as the devil.'
>
> 'Of course, you both are Americans, and conditions between us are constrained, and neither can be our friends in the sense of

friendship, but the affinity of complexion between you and me tells, and you exercise your duty so much more kindly and manly in dealing with us. We can not help but appreciate the differences between you and the whites.'

-Interview of Senor Teodorico Santos, a Filipino physician.

By the difference in "dealing with us" expressed is meant that the colored soldiers do not push them off the streets, spit at them, call them damned "niggers," abuse them in all manner of ways, and connect race hatred with duty, for the colored soldier has none such for them....[13]

Having learned by now what the derisive term "nigger" meant, Filipino leaders began to aim psychological warfare at the Afro-American soldiers. Aguinaldo wrote propaganda sheets directed at them which were printed and distributed at night by guerilla agents. Written in Spanish, the one mentioned in the following newspaper article was discovered nailed to a tree and was quickly translated:

To the colored American soldier:

It is without honour that you are spilling your costly blood. Your masters have thrown you in the most iniquitous fight with double purposes. In order to be you the instrument of their ambition. And also your hard work will make soon the extinction of your race. Your friends the Filipinos give you this good warning. You must consider your situation and your history. And take charge that the blood of your brothers Sam Hose and Gray proclaim vengeance.[14]

Among the eighty-five black lynchings that took place in America in 1899, the torture and murder-by-mob of both Sam Hose and Edward Gray were particularly gruesome. As such, the two killings became food for headlines in America and Europe. Hose had been arrested for murder and was forcibly taken from jail by a mob, which then mutilated and burned him alive. Charged with burglary, Edward Gray was hauled to court in front of a white mob that had gathered to lynch him, after what they assumed would surely be his conviction. Instead, Gray was found innocent. The mob lynched him anyway.[15]

The Filipino leaders frequently received newspapers from Europe and the United States, sent to them clandestinely via Hong Kong and Tokyo and smuggled in on merchant ships bound for Manila and other Philippine ports. That the names of Sam Hose and Edward Gray, and the brutal circumstances of their deaths were known to Aguinaldo, illustrates just how astutely Filipino leadership was in tune with the American political scene.

Presidential candidate William Jennings Bryan was basing his campaign on ending what he argued was an evil, unwinnable war which besmirched America's image, and both Aguinaldo and the leading American anti-imperialists were counting heavily that he would win the election.

Aguinaldo's attempts to influence African-American soldiers went beyond demoralization. Indeed, there were hopes that some of them could be recruited.

On 10 October, I-Company marched from San Fernando to a town called Mexico, where it rejoined the main battalion. Early the next morning, the 24th Infantry, one squadron of the 4th Cavalry and a battery of 3" mountain guns, all under the command of Brigadier General Young, proceeded to Santa Ana, where they pitched camp just before nightfall.[16]

Sometime after the end of September, Fagen realized he no longer wanted to kill Filipinos. Shortly thereafter, he began to contemplate desertion and defection. He understood the consequences; once he deserted there would be no going back. But what was there for Fagen to go back to? Tampa? He had joined and rejoined the army to escape Tampa. Then, in Cuba, he had seen how America's army abused the black and brown people who lived there, and now he was in the Philippines fighting their "Nigger-war."

On 12 October, General Young's army left Santa Ana at daybreak with the 24th Infantry spear-heading the attack. Companies A, H, F and K formed the firing line, with C, E, G and I-company in reserve. At 8:00 a.m. they engaged several hundred insurgents near Arayat. An hour and a half later, the insurgents withdrew and units under Young entered the town. The only American casualty of the morning was one of Fagen's fellow members of I-Company, Private James B. Turner, who had been wounded in the throat.[17]

The regiment remained at Arayat performing outpost, guard, escort, and scouting duty until 18 October, when the Rio Grande was crossed and the town of Cabiao was occupied. They remained there for nine days and it appears that somewhere within this timeframe Fagen made secret contact with the insurgents. He learned that if he joined them, he would be welcomed as a brother to his new homeland and awarded the rank of Lieutenant. And he would not be ordered to fight against his former black comrades. These were among the things he was promised if he joined the guerrillas.

On 27 October, companies C, E, G and I marched to San Isidro, the capital of Nueva Ecija Province. On 17 November, Headquarters Company, the regimental band and companies E, G, and I were scheduled to march to Cabanatuan. They did so without David Fagen who, before fleeing, had broken in to a weapons room and stolen several revolvers and a quantity of ammunition. Fagen then took a horse and rode off.

The deed was done. From this moment enemies of the Filipinos were his enemies also. So be it.

Notes

1. Quote from Gatewood, *Smoked Yankees*, paperback, 1987, p. 244.
2. Ibid. see footnote 15, p. 244.
3. Mueller, *The Twenty Fourth Infantry, Past and Present*, p. 26.
4. Gatewood, *Smoked Yankees*, p. 242.
5. Quotes: Ibid., pp. 242-43.
6. Quote of C.W. Cordin, Co. B, 25th Infantry, in Gatewood, *Smoked Yankees*, pp. 250-51.
7. Quote of Gatewood, from *Smoked Yankees*, p. 245.
8. Quote from Luis H. Francia, *A History of the Philippines*, Overlook Press, NY, NY, 2010, p. 155.
9. Song quote from Paul A. Kramer, *The Blood of Government*, paperback, University of North Carolina Press, 1968, p. 141.
10. See: Michael C. Robinson and Frank N. Schubert, *David Fagen: An Afro-American Rebel in the Philippines, 1899-1901*, in *Pacific Historical Review*, Vol. 44:1 (Feb. 1975) p. 74.

11. Quote "night soil and kitchen police," etc., Ibid. p. 74.
12. Punishments-see Gatewood, *Smoked Yankees,* pp. 217-18.
13. Quote from a letter by Sgt. Major John W. Galloway, 24th U.S. Infantry to Editor, *Richmond Planet,* in Gatewood, *Smoked Yankees,* p. 251-253.
14. Quote from *Richmond Planet,* November 11, 1899, War in the Philippines, p. 8.
15. Lynchings: http://faculty.berea.edu/browners/chesnutt/classroom/lynching_table_year.html; Sam Holt: http://historyengine.richmond.edu/episodes/view/502; Edward Gray: http://www.louisianadigitallibrary.com/cdm/compoundobject/collection/LWP/id/6588.
16. Mueller, *Twenty-fourth Infantry, Past and Present,* pp. 29-30.
17. Ibid. p. 30.

◀Chapter Nine▶

PAYBACK AND AUDACITY

THERE ARE NO RECORDS that detail Fagen's daily activities over the next six months, but, as had been promised; upon his arrival at one of the guerrilla strongholds the Philippine National Army of Liberation inducted him as a lieutenant. Fagen was assigned to the *Brigada Lacuna,* a guerrilla army under the command of General Urbano Lacuna. The general's theater of operations encompassed hundreds of square miles of jungle and forested mountains in Nueva Ecija Province, and his secret headquarters was situated near Mt. Arayat.

A day or two after Fagen's arrival at the guerrilla camp, the soldiers were assembled in his honor and he was formally introduced (they pronounced his name as "Pagain"). Briefed by their officers, the soldiers were urged to make the Americano feel at home. Compliance was immediate. The freedom fighters offered Fagen the same warmth, courtesy and respect they traditionally extended to a welcome and important guest. Their incentive was genuine. They knew this Negrito Americano was a well-trained, combat-experienced, professional soldier who had risked his own life to join their war for independence. This brother could teach them how to win battles and survive. They also understood that if they were caught by the Americans they could expect to be imprisoned, but if Pagain was captured, he would be executed.

For the first time in his life, Fagen's skin color seemed to have no significance. He was among people who respected him for who he was and what he knew, and his daily interactions with the Filipinos convinced him he had made the right decision. Fagen understood that part of the reasons the United States was making war on these people was because they were brown. Now his future, and theirs, was inextricably linked.

The new lieutenant had a lot to learn. An ability to make himself understood in Spanish as well as Tagalog was vital. And, as it was with most American army units, officers of the Philippine Army of Liberation rode horses, something Fagen had never done in his life. Among the many things he needed to know were the guerrilla chain of command, their officer corps' rules and regulations, and the operational make-up of General Lacuna's forces. He also had to learn the spy networks, the terrain, the security organization, the regional politics and the complex multi-leveled task of logistical support.

The social separation between the educated, upper class officers and their mostly illiterate peasant troops was severe. But because of Fagen's special status (his primary responsibility was the training of the guerrilla fighters), and his friendly, outgoing personality, he cheerfully mixed with both classes without interference or remonstration.

As time passed, Fagen began to absorb the Filipino language and customs. By the spring of 1900, when accounts of his military activities first begin to appear in American newspapers and military and civil records, Fagen had developed a working fluency in both Spanish and Tagalog.

General Gregorio del Pilar (second from left), and other officers of the Philippine Liberation Army. (*US National Archives*)

Guerrilla soldiers, Philippine Liberation Army. (*US National Archives*)

By early 1900, American military leaders recognized they were no longer facing an entrenched enemy who would stand, fight and allow themselves to be destroyed by overwhelming U.S. firepower. Now the insurgents were fighting a guerrilla war. To counter the new situation, the Americans began to garrison all the larger towns and cities in Luzon. Every day each base was required to send out scouting patrols to search for, locate and destroy the guerrilla camps. Tasked with denying the enemy sustenance, arms, ammunition and money, the garrison commanders were ordered to foster, support and protect local Filipino officials and business leaders who pledged American loyalty.

Simultaneously, the Americans cajoled, bribed and coerced these people to provide useful intelligence on enemy activities. In some cases, when an American officer came to believe that a mayor or other civil authority was providing the enemy with food, money or weapons, instead of having the duplicitous man hanged or shot, the officer met with him in private and advised him that his crimes were known. This provided a powerful lever.

The Filipino leaders the Americans sought to exploit were at the same time being threatened by the guerrillas, who administered public beatings and executions of Filipinos they believed were collaborating with the enemy.

The Americans expanded considerable effort creating secret spy networks, and funds were regularly distributed to their favored agents. As could be expected, sometimes the same people the Americans were exploiting were being used as sources by the guerrillas.

More and more American forces began to arrive, and when combined with ever-improving avenues of supply, the war that began to evolve put terrible pressure on both the guerrillas and the civilian populations. Curfews and the searching of homes and public buildings became commonplace, and whenever bulk foods and grains were discovered, they were seized and hauled to guarded warehouses inside the garrison compound. These foods were then distributed by American officers at their discretion.

Filipinos were frequently assembled so that a masked informant could be marched in front of them, pointing out people accused of helping the insurgents. These unfortunate individuals were immediately arrested, frequently tortured, and in many cases, hanged or shot. Their homes were destroyed and their families made to suffer. The Philippine-American War had become a stage for egregious cruelty by all combatants.

The following quote from author William Pomeroy in his book *The Forest,* illustrates the agonizing situations which resulted from such actions:

> A young girl in a white dress, frightened, sits before a ring of men, answering questions. This is Virgie, the courier, who, when captured by the enemy, pointed out our posts in Longa and other towns. Several people were arrested and tortured because of her revelations, and much dislocation of activity occurred. She was in the Santa Cruz jail at the time of the raid there and was released from her cell. Her brother was killed in the attack on the PC [Philippine Constabulary] barracks. Now she is here. She is undergoing revolutionary trial.
>
> Yes, she admits, she talked. She went with the enemy… and pointed out the posts in the towns. But the [men] should understand that she was tortured. They raped her and they did things to her…. Her wide eyes that are moist go around the circle of faces before her that nod and say little, but ask the next question.

The quiet questions and the answers go on and the shadows of late afternoon gather in the hut. Then the talk trails away all that is written on the papers is placed in front of her and she signs it.

Outside it is late afternoon and blue shadows pool at the bottom of the forest. A small group of armed men is standing there in the dusk, leaning on rifles, silent. They are the firing squad, for betrayal has a penalty in this struggle. [1]

Lieutenant Fagen and his guerrillas practiced hit and run warfare. Their favored targets were American outposts, supply wagons, trains, boats and barges. All the major guerrilla bases were surrounded by networks of sentry outposts, whose various signaling methods were generally successful at providing adequate warning of approaching American patrols.

Utilizing his knowledge and skills, Fagen eagerly invested himself in training Lacuna's fighters. Not all the men carried firearms. Those who did bore an assortment of guns, including the superb Spanish Mauser rifle, ancient Remington single-shot weapons, captured American Springfield 45-70s and even a few of the new Krags. Men who had no firearms carried machetes or bolos.

The guerrillas were deplorable marksmen. As members of an army whose ammunition supply was and would remain woefully inadequate, this problem was more than ominous. Some of the untrained fighters had filed off the end sights of their rifles because they snagged brush and other debris when the men were hurrying through jungle or tall grass. For these men, the concept of lining up a target by using both the rear and front sights of his weapon was incomprehensible. With limited ammunition available for training (they frequently went into battle with less than five rounds per man), teaching such soldiers to shoot was beyond difficult and Fagen worked tirelessly to correct the problem.

Even when the men had learned how to adjust and zero the sights of their rifles, the ammunition itself proved unreliable. Makeshift ammo and gunpowder manufacturing operations were established in a few of the most remote guerrilla camps, and here, without access to new cartridge cases, old fired shell casings that had been collected by women and children from former battlefields were reprocessed. Shell casings originally manufactured to the exacting specifications of a particular caliber were frequently shortened or reformed to fit another. There was no standard formulation for the manufacture of gunpowder and this factor resulted in unpredictable accuracy, and all too often during the heat of battle a soldier's rifle would jam or even blow-up in his face.

Because of the donations of wealthy patrons, Aguinaldo's army was able to purchase arms and ammunition from foreign suppliers who delivered their goods via small cargo ships which were unloaded at friendly harbors during the night. Fagen's tactics—a swift and deadly attack from cover, followed by rapid withdrawal—included the rapid retrieval of any American arms or ammunition that could be salvaged and was an important source of new armaments.

The results of Fagen's efforts were soon noted by military leaders on both sides of the war. In his memoirs, General Jose Alejandrino, General Lacuna's immediate commander, mentioned Fagen whom he liked and respected:

> Fagen was a Negro giant of more than six feet in height who deserted the American Army, taking with him all the revolvers that he could bring, and who served in our forces with the rank of Captain. He did not know how **to** read or write, but he was a faithful companion. He was very affectionate and helpful to me, going to the extent of carrying me in his arms or on his shoulders when I, weakened by fevers and poor nutrition, had to cross rivers or ascend steep grades. The services which he rendered to me were such that they could only be expected from a brother or a son....
>
> ...Fagen was very fond of carousals and drinking. In some of his escapades he arrived in a small village on the banks of the Rio Chico of Pampanga. He looked for a guitar, and with some members of his guerrilla, he began to drink and to serenade the women of the place. When the night was already very late, he went to bed in a small hut, sleeping with a companion. After a short while his companion woke him up, telling him that he was hearing footsteps and voices of Americans. Fagen, who was half-asleep, answered him that he was dreaming and that his fear induced him

to hear and see visions. Inasmuch, however, as his companion insisted, Fagen reluctantly stood up to peep out the window, and there he really saw that the hut was surrounded by Americans. He lost no time in jumping out of the window and, taking advantage of the circumstances that the Americans could not fire for fear of wounding their own men in the dark, he selected the site nearest to the forest and with a revolver he shot his way out and escaped.

...I had heard narrations of the feats of valor and the intrepidity of Fagen, but his most outstanding characteristic was his mortal hatred of the American whites.

Fagen spoke Tagalog very vividly and lived in the camp with a woman. [2]

Although it appears that Fagen was the first African-American deserter to join and fight with Philippine forces, some twenty-plus desertions from black units occurred during the war, with nine of these men (including Fagen) choosing to fight American imperialism. In Albay Province, John Dalrymple, Edmond DuBose, Lewis Russell, Fred Hunter, Garth Shores and William Victor joined the Filipino forces. However, due to newspaper coverage of Fagen's deeds both in the Philippines and the United States, it was he who rapidly became America's most famous traitor.

By the summer of 1900, General Frederick Funston had been given command of all the American forces in Northern Luzon. His immediate enemies included General Lacuna's Brigade. A daring, aggressive little man who was addicted to action, Funston frequently rode out on patrols with a retinue of some eighteen to twenty-five hand-picked scouts. Most of these men were former cowboys, including one with a literary bent named Jack Ganzhorn, a native of Arizona. Others had been former lawmen from the southwest, and admittedly, some had been outlaws. To say that Funston and his cowboy scouts were an audacious, wild-bunch would be an understatement.

Because much of their shooting would take place from horseback, proficiency with a sidearm was an absolute requirement. At the time, the standard army-issue pistol was a double-action .38 caliber revolver. Due to its better man-stopping performance, Funston's cowboy scouts preferred the older, heavier, single-action .45 caliber pistol—the famous Colt's Six-Shooter with which they were all familiar. Funston equipped his scouts with the pistols they preferred.

In 1910, Jack Ganzhorn's book *I've Killed Men* was published, in which he memorialized a number of his encounters with Fagen (whose name he spelled as "Fagan"). Although greatly dramatized, these encounters serve well to illustrate Fagen's notoriety:

July 1900

>...Still getting around on crutches, I missed the fighting of July 4. Taking advantage of the rainy season, and wanting revenge for his defeat at Peneranda, General Lacuna attacked the garrisons of Peneranda, Gapon and Manacling simultaneously.
>
>Peneranda had no trouble repulsing the enemy, but the fight at Manacling was different. That very day, July 4, forty negro soldiers of the Twenty-Fourth, under Lieutenant Mitchell ... arrived to garrison the town. While General Lacuna with four hundred men attacked the Manacling, Fagan, a deserter from the Twenty-Fourth, now an officer under Lacuna, ambushed two four-mule wagons under the escort of a few negro soldiers. After killing all but one of the escort, the ambushers burned the wagons in the road.
>
>The only mounted troops in San Isidro at the time were the Scouts, and under the command of Lieutenant Richard C. Day, they crossed the Rio Chico and raced for Manacling. Fagan, the American renegade, cunningly awaited in ambush near the burned wagons.
>
>As the nine Scouts with Lieutenant Day galloped up to the scene of ambush, the gugus met them with a volley. Quickly hitting the ground and deploying, their backs to the swollen river, the Scouts made their fight. Death by gunfire or drowning was their only choice.
>
>Driving his gugus to the attack, creeping closer behind shelter of brush and trees, the renegade Fagan kept up a string of taunting boasts.

"Captain Fagan's done got yuh white boys now," he jeered. [Actually, at this time Fagen was a lieutenant]. "Less'n you all surrender, my little gugus is gonna chop on yuh with their meat cutters!"

Lieutenant Day leaped to his feet. Hartzell and Bates pulled him back down as he shouted "Go to hell, you black scum!"

When other troops arrived to support the Scouts, they found the boys had fired their last Krags and had their six shooter shells in their hats beside them, waiting for the end. In the vicious fight of the next few minutes Private Johnson was killed. Fagan got away with a few of his men, but many lay on the scene of their murdering ambush. [3]

Stories of Fagen's treachery began to flood the newspapers of Manila, and the United States. As Fagen's reputation grew, stories and even cartoons of General Funston's inability to capture and hang the renegade were pushed by the press, humiliating the egoistic Kansan.

In their essay *An Afro-American Rebel in the Philippines,* Michael C. Robinson and Frank N. Schubert wrote:

> ...The ambitious and aggressive Kansan general must have revealed his frustrations to his family, for his sister-in-law, Magdalene Blankart, confided to a relative that 'for sometime he and his men have been trying to capture "Fagen."' At Christmas time in 1900, while Funston was probably still fuming at his lack of ammunition at a key moment, she chided him with a bit of dinner table doggerel:

> > By Jiminy Christmas Fred
> > What's this I see?
> > Poor old Fagen
> > Hanged to a tree? [4]

The following is another recollection of Jack Ganzhorn of one of the eight skirmishes with Fagen that he experienced that summer:

On July 22 we caught up with Pablo Tecson [Tecson was one of the guerrilla leaders operating under Lacuna]. Fully three hundred strong, his force made stand on a sharp ridge and opened up on us while we were in the canyon below. We did not total eighty-five men. From that ridge less than one hundred yards above us, the gugus would have soon slaughtered us had we not charged.

Twenty yards from the top the withering fire increased. Directly above me, deliberately firing his piece, grinning and mocking us, still wearing parts of the uniform he had disgraced, I saw the leering features of Fagan, the deserter. In trying to crawl around a projecting hummock, Fryburger had slid over against my left side, his head and shoulders just ahead of mine. He lifted his rifle to shoot at the grimacing black face of the American renegade. I heard Fagan's bullet hit Fryburger's right shoulder. Clinging to the grass with one hand, the wounded man turned his eyes to my face: "For God's sake Ganzie," he screamed, "Kill that black devil!"

Hanging on with one hand and clawing for my six-shooter, I saw Fagan's carbine level, puff smoke, and heard a sickening thud. Blood and brains from a terrible hole in poor Fryburger's head spattered into my eyes. His body slithered back, struck a clump and tumbled to the bottom of the hill. Sobbing for breath, crazy mad, I wiped the warm sticky mess from my face.

Years have not dimmed that awful picture. I've seen it in the long, dark nights, over and over again. Down through the years, I've heard Fryburger's agonizing cry for me to kill Fagan. God, how I wanted to! But when I could see to shoot, Fagan was not in sight....

...During the long, sad trip back to San Isidro, the bitterness of our loss seemed greater because we knew it was largely due to the experience and training received by Fagan while a soldier of the United States.

Upon many occasions in the past we of the Scouts had found placards offering a large reward in pesos to the gugu bringing in the head of one of Funston's Scouts. The General, too, had received insulting letters. These letters and reward posters had all been signed by "Major Fagan." At those times, while the name of

Fagan was despised, we made light of his bragging. Now it was different. Every man in that fight prayed for a chance to kill the traitor.⁵

On October 29, 1900, the *New York Times* published the following article:

AMERICAN DESERTER
A FILIPINO GENERAL

David Fagin of Twenty-Fourth Infantry an Insurgent.
Has Particular enmity Toward his former Company
Recently Captured Twenty Americans

MANILA, Oct. 28 – A private launch towing a barge loaded with merchandise near Arayat was attacked by a force of 150 insurgents under David Fagin, a deserter from the Twenty-fourth Infantry. The American troops, on hearing the firing, turned out in force before the boat could be looted and recaptured it.

Fagin, who holds the rank of General among the insurgents, has sworn special enmity toward his former company. Of the twenty men he captured a month ago seven have returned. One was killed in a fight, his body being mutilated. Fagin sends messages to his former comrades threatening them with violence if they become his prisoners. It was Fagin's men who captured Lieut. Fredrick W. Alstaetter, who is still a prisoner....⁶

In his autobiography, *Memories of Two Wars*, Frederick Funston wrote:

August 1, 1900

During one of these actions Lt. Colonel Manuel Ventus, one of Lacuna's subordinates, was wounded and captured, being placed in our hospital for treatment. As soon as he was near recovery I wrote Lacuna stating that while I could not arrange an exchange of prisoners with him, I promised to release Ventus if he would do the same with Alstaetter. [Lt. F. W. Alstaetter had been captured by Lacuna's men.] A few days later the latter was escorted to our outposts and Ventus was released at the same time, but was allowed to remain in the hospital until his recovery.

For months we had known of the presence with the insurgents of this region of an American negro named Fagan, a deserter from the Twenty-fourth Infantry. This wretched man was serving as an officer, and had on two occasions written me impudent and badly spelled letters. It was mighty well understood that if taken alive by any of us he was to stretch a picket rope as soon as one could be obtained. Fagan was prominent in the fight in which Alstaetter was captured and appropriated Alstaetter's West Point class ring, declining to give it up on the eve of the latter's release.[7]

As more and more troops were made available to him, Funston was able to garrison most of the small towns in his immediate command area. In an effort to keep tightening the noose around Lacuna and his guerillas, he began to establish small detachments of mounted scouts at all of his outposts.

Late in October 1900, Funston and his scouts were out searching for insurgents some fifteen miles east of San Isidro. Just before sunrise, near the crest of a remote mountain, they halted to search a suspicious solitary Nipa hut. Jack Ganzhorn rode up to peer in through the front window and was startled to find an insurgent inside, leveling a rifle at him. Ducking low over his horse's neck, he frantically drew his revolver as the guerrilla fired. Ganzhorn's cheek felt the heat from his opponent's rifle blast. The Filipino was working the bolt on his rifle to chamber another round when Ganzhorn's six-shooter bullet killed him.

Another insurgent took advantage of the firing and escaping from the hut through a back window ran to nearby cover. It turned out that the man who escaped was General Lacuna himself. Entering the hut, Funston and a few of his men discovered a large number of documents the general had been forced to abandon. Among these were several blank sheets of stationery bearing the general's stamped letterhead. Funston was delighted with his haul.

PAYBACK AND AUDACITY

On 6 September 1900, in recognition of his bravery, loyalty and his many successful operations against the Americans, General Jose Alejandrino promoted David Fagen to the rank of captain.

In the United States, the anti-imperialists were still protesting. On 15 October, Samuel Clemens (Mark Twain) fired a salvo in the *New York Herald*:

> I left these shores, at Vancouver, a red-hot imperialist. I wanted the American eagle to go screaming into the Pacific. It seemed tiresome and tame for it to content itself with the Rockies. Why not spread its wings over the Philippines, I asked myself? And I thought it would be a real good thing to do.
>
> I said to myself, here are a people who have suffered for three centuries. We can make them as free as ourselves, give them a government and country of their own, put a miniature of the American constitution afloat in the Pacific, start a brand new republic to take its place among the free nations of the world. It seemed to me a great task to which we had addressed ourselves.
>
> But I have thought some more, since then, and I have read carefully the Treaty of Paris, and I have seen that we do not intend to free, but to subjugate the people of the Philippines. We have gone there to conquer, not to redeem.
>
> It should, it seems to me, be our pleasure and duty to make those people free, and let them deal with their own domestic questions in their own way. And so I am an anti-imperialist. I am opposed to having the eagle put its talons on any other land.[8]

General Funston had another encounter with Fagen on 5 December:

> We swung in a curve, first north-east, then gradually to the southeast and south, just at day break striking a tributary of the Penaranda near where it emerges from the foot hills. We crossed the stream to its south bank and then hurried down it, straight west in the direction of San Isidro, thus having made a wide circle of the enemy, and were coming in on his rear. Just an hour after striking the stream, we approached the unsuspecting

enemy, and dismounted for the attack, as the country was so close that a mounted charge was impossible. We had to dash straight across the stream under a hot fire, as they discovered us as we were dismounting. We killed four men and captured two wounded, besides getting five rifles and some ammunition. In this fight I got a fairly good look at the notorious Fagan at a distance of a hundred yards, but unfortunately had already emptied my carbine. [9]

Lieutenant J. D. Taylor, 24th Infantry (Fagen's old outfit) commanded the company garrison at Pantabangan, situated some sixty miles northeast of the western slope of the mountain range between Luzon and the Pacific coast of the island. On 8 February, 1901, escorted by the town's mayor, a small band of insurgents had surrendered themselves to him voluntarily. Their leader claimed he was a messenger and that letters he was carrying were from Aguinaldo to his cousin Baldomero, along with others meant for Jose Alejandrino, Urbano Lacuna, Pablo Tecson, and Teodoro Sandico. All were important insurgent leaders. It turned out the letters were in cipher and could not be immediately read. Taylor telegraphed the story to General Funston, and added that the letters appeared to be signed fictitiously, although he believed the handwriting resembled that of President Aguinaldo.

The incident would prove to have a profound effect on both David Fagen and the Philippine-American War. There was no question but that Emilio Aguinaldo was the commander of all the insurgent forces, and up to this moment, virtually every effort the Americans and their Filipino sycophants had made to ascertain Aguinaldo's whereabouts had failed. If this messenger who had surrendered to Lt. Taylor was telling the truth, Aguinaldo was at Palanan – a small town not far from Luzon's northeastern coast, isolated from the rest of Isabela Province by the Sierra Madre Mountains.

If Aguinaldo was truly where the Filipino messenger claimed, he was in Funston's region of command. The wolf from Kansas began to salivate.

It should be remembered that Funston was the same man who many years ago while working a summer job as a train conductor had been driven off by a cowboy who aimed a six-shooter at him when he asked for the man's ticket. A few hours later, approaching from behind where the man was seated, the 5'3" conductor pressed a rifle into the man's neck. "I came back to punch your ticket," Funston said softly. The cowboy's face blanched and he meekly produced his ticket.

The American General who was now contemplating killing or capturing the President of the Philippines, was the same man who in 1896 had schemed his way into joining the Cuban revolutionary army and who had fought with them for two years against Spanish forces.

It wasn't much of a stretch for Funston to reason that if he captured or killed Aguinaldo, the deed might very well bring an end to the current conflict. If that became reality, it would make him the greatest American hero of the Philippine-American War.

Funston wired Lt. Taylor and ordered that the Filipino messenger and all the documents he had been carrying were to be strongly guarded and quickly brought to him at San Isidro.

The man arrived in less than two days, and gave his name as Cecilio Segismundo. Speaking in Spanish, Funston interrogated him himself. Funston:

> ...During this recital he looked me squarely in the eyes, answered all questions frankly and apparently without reserve, and seemed to be telling the truth and keeping back nothing....
>
> ...On the 14th of January, accompanied by a detachment of twelve armed men of Aguinaldo's escort, he had left with a package of letters to be delivered to Urbano Lacuna, the insurgent chief in Nueva Ecija Province, who was to forward to their final destinations those [letters] that were not meant for him. After a terrible journey down the coast and through mountains he had in the vicinity of Baler encountered a small detachment of our troops out on a scouting expedition and had lost two of his men....
>
> ...finally, twenty-six days after leaving Palanan, had reached the outskirts of the town of Pantabangan. Here, foot weary and hungry, he communicated with the local presidente, or mayor, who had formerly acted in the same capacity for the insurgent government that he was now filling under American rule.

181

> ...He told Segismundo that he was in the service of the Americans, and strongly counseled him to present himself to the commander of the local garrison, give up the correspondence in his charge, and in fact attach himself to the chariot of progress and be an Americanista....
>
> ...It took much diplomacy on the part of Lieutenant Taylor, the presidente at first acting as go-between, to get him to surrender, but he finally did so. Lieutenant Taylor deserved the greatest credit for the excellent judgment he used in the whole matter. Of course, any attempt to capture the band would have spoiled everything, as the most of them would probably have escaped.[10]

Segismundo told Funston that Aguinaldo had several officers on his staff and a personal guard or escort of fifty uniformed and well-armed men, all of whom had been at Palanan for several months. The leader was in constant communication with all the guerrilla leaders by means of a network of trusted messengers. According to Segismundo, the citizens of the town and indeed, most of the soldiers of his escort were unaware of his identity. He was known as Captain Emilio, and those who did not know him to be Aguinaldo thought he was a subordinate officer of the insurrection.

Suspecting that Aguinaldo was indeed at Palanan, Funston and Captain E.V. Smith and Lazaro Segovia (a Spaniard who served as Funston's secretary) plunged into the task of deciphering all of the letters and documents Segismundo had surrendered. They worked all night and finished the next day at noon.
Funston:

> ...from their context these communications could come only from one who was recognized as the leader of the insurrection, as they gave positive orders to officers of the highest military rank.
>
> ...Not one of the communications, either official or personal, intimated the name of the obscure town in which Aguinaldo had taken his refuge.
>
> ...The most important letter, and the one that was the final undoing of its writer, was to his cousin Baldomero Aguinaldo, then

in command of the insurgent bands operating in Cavite Province just south of Manila.

This directed the person to whom it was addressed to proceed at once to the "Centre of Luzon," and, using this communication as authority, to supersede in command Jose Alejandrino, who evidently was not giving satisfaction to his chieftain. As soon as he had established himself in command, Baldomero was to direct his subordinates, that is, Lacuna, Mascardo, Simon, and Pablo Tecson, and possibly one or two others, to send him detachments of men until the aggregate should reach about four hundred.

These were to be made up of picked troops, and might be sent by whatever routes their respective commanders thought best....

...After translating the letters we went to bed, but I had great difficulty in sleeping, as plans began to evolve themselves. About four o'clock I got up and sent for Segismundo.[11]

Before dawn, Segismundo explained that Aguinaldo had dozens of lookouts at numerous locations who would immediately alert him of any overland approach by American troops. There was no way an American force could approach Palanan without being seen. And once alerted, Aguinaldo could be quickly moved to another remote hiding spot in the Sierra Madre Mountains.

Funston started on a new tack. He asked whether an expedition from the sea, one which landed on the beach at night some seven miles from Palanan might succeed.

Segismundo thought that the presence of any big vessel off the coast would surely be reported, and that even if the landing was successful, it would be discovered and reported before reaching Palanan.

Funston dismissed Segismundo and went back to bed, his mind racing.

Funston:

...By morning I had thought out the general features of the plan which was eventually to succeed, and on asking Segismundo whether it was in his opinion practicable, he replied in the affirmative.

>...The only recourse was to work a stratagem, that is, to get to him [Aguinaldo] under false colors. It would be so impossible to disguise our own troops that they [methods] were not even considered, and dependence would have to be placed on the Macabebes, those fine little fighters, taking their name from their home town, who had always been loyal to Spain and who had now transferred that loyalty to the United States. As it would be absolutely essential to have along some American officers to direct matters and deal with such emergencies as might arise, they were to accompany the expedition as supposed prisoners who had been captured on the march, and were not to throw off that disguise until there was no longer necessity for concealment.
>
>...In order to pave the way for the bogus reinforcements, which were supposed to be those from Lacuna's command, it was considered essential to have them preceded by letters from that individual.
>
>...Stationery captured in Lacuna's camp had at the top of each sheet the words Brigada Lacuna—in English, Lacuna's Brigade – they having been put on with a rubber stamp. [12]

A year earlier, Funston had employed a former insurgent officer named Roman Roque to serve at his headquarters as interpreter and clerk. The man was an excellent penman, and Funston set him to work practicing at signing Lacuna's signature. After a few days, Roque's forged signatures were excellent, and one of them was placed at the foot of each of two sheets of the stamped *Brigada Lacuna* writing paper. For security purposes, Funston determined that the bodies of the two forged letters were not to be filled in until he and all his raiders were at sea.

To join him in playing the role of captured American prisoners, Funston chose Captain Harry W. Newton, 1st Lt. Burton I. Mitchell, Captain Russell T. Hazzard, and the latter's younger brother, 1st Lt. Oliver P.M. Hazzard. Funston also determined to take his secretary, Segovia, as well as Cecilio Segismundo on the mission.

Squad of Macabebe Scouts chosen for the secret mission to capture Aguinaldo. (*US National Archives*)

General Funston and the four officers he chose to go with him on mission to capture Aguinaldo, all of them to be disguised as captured American privates. L to R: 1st Lt. Burton I. Mitchell, Capt. Russell T. Hazzard, Brig. Gen. Frederick Funston, Capt. Harry W. Newton, 1st Lt. Oliver P.M. Hazzard. (*US National Archives*)

Funston recalls the moment:

> ...General Wheaton had selected as the main part of the expedition Company D of the First Battalion of Macabebe scouts. This organization contained about one hundred men and had seen much service in the field....
>
> ...A weeding out of the Macabebe company so that we would have in it only men who could speak Tagalo, and so pass themselves off as belonging to that race, and the leaving behind of a few who it was thought might not be able to make the long march anticipated, brought the number actually embarked down to eighty-one.
>
> Of course, it was absolutely essential for them to discard everything in the way of their equipment as American soldiers.... So before sailing we obtained a sufficient supply of the clothing of the country, the most of it being second-hand material, as it would not do for the men to look neat.... It was considered unnecessary to clothe the Macabebes in insurgent uniforms, as the time when the great body of insurgent troops wore uniforms had long gone by.
>
> ...There was also obtained from the Manila arsenal a sufficient number of Mauser and Remington rifles with the necessary quantity of cartridges, all of this being material that had been captured in the field.
>
> ...Admiral Remey had designated the gunboat Vicksburg, Commander E.B. Barry commanding, to carry the expedition, the object of which even he did not know.
>
> ...The greatest secrecy had been maintained, as, outside of Generals MacArthur and Wheaton, two or three officers of the district staff left behind at San Isidro, the officers who were to go on the expedition, Segovia and Segismundo, not a single man had been informed.
>
> ...At last everything was ready. [13]

Funston's plan echoed the classic Trojan horse scheme used by the

Greeks against the Trojans at Troy. It was a charade that required cunning, audacity, stealth and considerable luck. Like the Greek legend, the march to Palanan was also a do or die affair for all involved, since no quarter could be expected from the Filipinos for any of the Macabebes.

The gunboat USS *Vicksburg*. (*US National Archives*)

On the night of March 6, the *Vicksburg* sailed out from Manila Bay. Soon after her departure, Funston sent for the three leading Macabebe officers and informed them the nature of their mission. Startled by the audacity of the operation, the Macabebes quickly warmed to the idea and swore to do their part. They were then told the false story they and all their men were to use with any civilians or enemy soldiers they encountered before Aguinaldo was captured. The account told how they had marched north from Nueva Ecija and had surprised ten American soldiers who were making maps of the country. A brief fight had ensued, during which two Americans were killed, three were wounded, and the remaining five were captured. Funston made sure that the Macabebe leaders understood that virtually all their men were to memorize the details accurately.

Segismundo had told Funston that any armed vessel approaching the coast would be noticed and its presence quickly reported. Accordingly, in order to draw the least notice, it was decided to acquire some large native sailing bancas (outrigger canoes) at a port not too far from where the landing was to take place. The innocent looking bancas would be towed behind the *Vicksburg,* and while still offshore, Funston and his force would transfer to the canoes which they would then sail in to land ashore in the darkness.

Three Bancas (sailing canoes) that sank during storm being towed by USS *Vicksburg.* (*US National Archives*)

On the night of 12 March, a fierce, unexpected gale blew-in and riled the seas through which the Vicksburg was towing the three bancas they had obtained. One by one, the boats swamped and as they began to sink their towlines had to be cut. A new plan was devised in which the *Vicksburg's* boats would be used to land at a protected area of the coast before daylight. The mission would depend upon the men being put ashore well before sunrise, and that the *Vicksburg* would be well offshore and out of sight by first light.

Funston's plan was dependent on his force being able to convince any Filipinos they encountered that they had marched north by land. If Funston's beach landing was observed even by one local Filipino, the mission was doomed.

Funston:

The time had now come when it was necessary to write the two bogus letters from Lacuna to Aguinaldo…. These letters were held until the opportunity should come to send them in advance of us. Fortunately for us, the weather was thick and squally, and at one o'clock on the morning of the 14th, the Vicksburg having very carefully approached the coast, with all her lights screened, we were landed in the ship's boats. We were inside the entrance to Casiguran Bay, and so fairly well protected, with the consequence that we had no surf work. The darkness was intense, however, and it was raining so that we did not feel particularly comfortable or cheerful. It would have been impossible to carry out the plan of deception if we had landed with a supply of the food ordinarily used by American soldiers, so that we brought ashore one day's ration of rice. All of us Americans were dressed as private soldiers of our army, that is, in campaign hats, blue shirts, khaki breeches, and leggings. As I looked our crowd over the next morning I thought that we were a pretty scrubby-looking lot of privates.

…So it happened that eighty-nine of us, counting Filipinos and white men, landed on that dreary coast. I do not recall that we had any particular emotions or sensations, as we were too busy trying to make ourselves comfortable.[14]

Funston and his men spent several miserable hours sitting around and trying to keep out of the incessant rain. At first light, scouts were sent out to locate fresh water, and when a stream was found the raiders went there, drank and filled their canteens. Some small fires were built so that rice could be boiled.

There were no trails through the mangroves and forest, and they had landed at about the same point where a force coming cross-country from Nueva Ecija would have come.

Funston believed their landing had not been observed, and that everything was now in their favor. They made their way through the mangrove swamps, heading for the town of Casiguran and their first confrontation with locals. The place was about ten miles distant.

Around noon they came to the mouth of a small creek and discovered a small banca capable of carrying six men.

Funston:

> ...As soon as we discovered the banca we concocted another letter. This was addressed to the presidente of Casiguran, and was written by Segovia. This communication stated that the writer was under command of Lacuna and on their way north to report to the 'Dictator.' It was requested that the recipient would immediately send a guide to meet the column, and have all arrangements for the housing and provisioning of the force. After the letter had been written I invited my corpulent friend Hilario to sign it. This he did without batting an eyelash. I doubt he ever read it. We sent this missive by Segismundo, he being accompanied by Gregorio Cadhit and two armed Macabebes. The last named men had their instructions as to what they were to do in case of treachery.
>
> ...The four men sailed straight across the head of the bay, delivered the letter to the Vice-presidente, the presidente being absent, and then became the guests of the village. Really, there were some ridiculous features about the whole business....[15]

Funston and his raiders resumed their march. Around 4 o'clock the guide sent to them by the vice-president of Casiguran met up with them and Funston knew his plan was working. As he and his men entered the little town, crowds of happy locals came to meet them. These peasants fully believed they were greeting freedom fighters who had some American prisoners that they had captured. Absurdly, the village band assembled and began to play.

The Macabebes had previously been instructed that upon making contact with the people of Casiguran, they had to be seen to treat Funston and the other white officers roughly, as real prisoners.

Funston:

> ...Among those who met us as we entered the town was the badly

fooled Vice Presidente. He was a man of good appearance and address, and seemed somewhat solicitous regarding the welfare and comfort of the supposed American prisoners. I am glad to be able to state that the general attitude of the people of the town toward us was not hostile.

...They crowded around us, and there were some black looks, and some remarks not of a complimentary nature, but in general there was nothing in their conduct to criticize. Finally, we entered the plaza, the local band exuding some lively, if not very inspiring music. The whole situation was so ludicrous that it was with difficulty we could keep from laughing, despite the peril of our position.[16]

The American prisoners were confined in a room within the municipal building. Meanwhile, continuing their charade, Segovia and Tal Placido—one of the three commanding officers of the Macabebes—met with the Vice President and learned that the trek to Palanan would be arduous, and there would be very little food available for their use unless they could wait four or five days for such supplies to be acquired.

Funston didn't have time to wait—the *Vicksburg* was scheduled to pick-up the raiders at Palanan Bay on the 25th of the month. Funston and his companions spent the 15th in their prison, grateful for the chance to rest.

Funston:

> ... The Macabebes, supposed to be rigidly guarding us, laid it on pretty thick in telling how they had captured us. Once I saw a sergeant, whose eye I had caught, start to laugh but he got a look and a shake of the head that brought him to his senses. It would be essential, in order that Aguinaldo and those with him might not be alarmed at the approach to Palanan of an armed body, to send word to him in advance. So Segovia and I concocted another letter advising Aguinaldo they were coming. ... Meantime, the Vice Presidente obtained two of his townsmen and an Ilongote to carry this letter and the two supposed ones from Lacuna.
>
> They started on the morning of the 16th and beat us to Palanan by two days.[17]

Ilongot warriors. (*US National Archives*)

Early on the gloomy and rainy morning of the 17th, Funston's force began the last leg of their exhausting journey. The only food available to them was a few bags of cracked corn, a small quantity of dried carabao meat, and a dozen live chickens. In order to carry their food supplies and cooking-pots, twelve men from the town were obtained, along with an Ilongote native to serve as guide.

Following the Ilongote over a muddy trail through the forest they reached a sea-beach by early afternoon at which time their guide suddenly ran off into the forest deserting them. One of the Casiguran men who were accompanying the group said he knew the way and he volunteered to serve as guide. Starting out again, their course generally followed the beach which was covered in soft and deep sand. The rain continued to pour and the march drained what remained of their energy. Five days later, Funston and his men were exhausted. They had waded more than sixty streams, most were small but others were so deep and swift they had to put their hands on each other's shoulders and the water was up to their armpits. Their food became a sodden mess. By the 22nd their food had run out and they stumbled along half-dazed. The column was now scattered a mile long across the beach. At five o'clock, some of Funston's men saw a man ahead on the beach, watching them approach. Segovia went ahead to meet him. Funston:

> ...We breathlessly watched Segovia and the man while they were talking and saw the latter hand the former a letter. Segovia came limping back down the column, and as he passed us Americans he said in Spanish, "It is all right. We have them." What a load it lifted of our minds! We were now ten miles of our quarry. The letter, which Segovia opened and read at once and then passed to me, was from Simon Villa, Aguinaldo's chief of staff, and was addressed to "Lieutenant-Colonel Hilario Tal Placido." Although it showed that our ruse was working and that our real identity was not even suspected, there was in it one thing that disturbed us greatly, this being an order that the five prisoners would not be brought into Palanan, as they might find out that the "Dictator" was there....[18]

Somehow the column marched on to a place called Dinundungan, about eight miles from Palanan. Here Funston and his four disguised officers were left under the watchful eye of an old man and a few Negritos who were just finishing building a couple of grass-roofed open sheds. Watched by armed guards, Funston and the other Americans were placed in the first shed. In whispers, Funston and his men discussed their situation. They and the Macabebes were in desperate need of food without which the remaining march of eight miles would have been impossible. Funston told Hilario to write a note to Villa reporting his arrival at Dinundungan, and stating that in the morning he would resume the march to Palanan, but that food was necessary or the men could not go on. Hilario's note also mentioned that the American prisoners would be left where they now were. The letter was carried to Palanan by one of the local Negritos and the next morning enough cracked corn arrived to provide everyone a satisfactory meal.

Using another forged letter, the Macabebes were able to scam the old man at Dinundungan. Not long after the main force had started the march to Palanan, Funston and the other American "prisoners" were allowed to follow after them. The trails were muddy and despite having eaten a meager breakfast, Funston and the others were so weak it took nearly six hours for them to cover the eight miles. Funston and Mitchell were in the worst shape. Every few hundred yards, Funston had to lie down and rest a moment or two. Their course forced them to cross and re-cross a branch of the Palanan River. Half-way to Palanan, Funston and his little group were met by a Macabebe sergeant and another scout, coming back along the trail as fast as they could. They motioned for Funston and the others to follow them immediately, get off the trail and hide in the woods. When they were hidden, the sergeant explained that some real insurgent soldiers were on their way to Dinundungan to take charge of the American prisoners, so that all the men of the Lacuna party from Nueva Ecija might be able to come to Palanan. Funston and the other Americans hid on the ground. After a few moments, they heard some men who were laughing and talking pass by on the trail. When their voices could no longer be heard the Americans rose silently and continued on their way to Aguinaldo's headquarters. Up ahead of them, less than a mile from Palanan, the Macabebe raiders, including Segovia, Hilario and Segismundo, were met by a couple of insurgent officers who greeted them and explained that they were to escort them the remainder of the journey. At three in the afternoon they reached the Palanan River which at that place was a hundred yards wide and quite deep. The only way to cross was aboard a good-sized *banca*. Hilario and Segovia crossed with the first load, leaving instructions for the men to follow as rapidly as they could. As soon as they reached the far bank, they were to march right up to Aguinaldo's house, where they would find him.

The details of the actual capture are told by Funston:

> ...The boat was to be sent back to await our arrival. Segovia and Hilario now had a most trying half-hour. They called on Aguinaldo at his head-quarters, and found him surrounded by seven insurgent officers, all of them armed with revolvers. Outside, the fifty men of the escort, neatly uniformed and armed with Mausers, were drawn up to do the honors for the reinforcements that had made such a wonderful march to join them. Segovia and Hilario entered those present with stories of the march from

Lacuna's head-quarters, and were warmly congratulated on having made it successfully. Segovia took his position where he could look out of one of the open windows and see when the time had arrived. Finally, the Macabebes under Dionisio Bato and Gregorio Cadhit marched up, Segovia stepped to the head of the stairway outside the house, for they were in the second story, and signaled to Gregario, who called out, "now is the time Macabebes. Give it to them." The poor little "Macs" were in such a nervous state from their excitement over the strange drama that they were playing a part in that they were pretty badly rattled. They had loaded their pieces and were standing at "order arms," as were the men of the escort facing them on the other side of the little square. They fired a ragged volley, killing two men of the escort and severely wounding the leader of Aguinaldo's band, who happened to be passing between the lines when fire was opened. Aguinaldo, hearing the firing, and thinking that the men of his escort had broken loose to celebrate the arrival of the reinforcements, stepped up to the window and called out, "Stop that foolishness. Don't waste your ammunition." Before he could turn around Hilario had grasped him about the waist and thrown him under a table, where he literally sat on him, and Hilario was a fat man. I had given the most positive orders to the effect that under no circumstances should Aguinaldo be killed, and that no lives should be taken unless it was absolutely necessary. But as Segovia dashed back into the room several of the officers started to draw their revolvers, and he opened fire on them, hitting Villa three times, who was tugging to get a Mauser automatic pistol out of its holster, and also wounding Major Alhambra. Villa surrendered, as did Santiago Barcelona, treasurer of the so-called republic. Alhambra and the other officers leaped from one of the windows into the river, the house standing on the bank, and escaped by swimming. As Hilario grasped Aguinaldo, he had said, "you are a prisoner of the Americans," so that the fallen "Dictator," as he now called himself, had some sort of a vague idea of what had happened to him.[19]

Having finally crossed the river, Funston and his companions heard the firing and ran up the bank toward the house. They were met by Segovia who was wearing a broad smile and called out in Spanish "It is all right. We have him!"

The general and his four officers hurried to the house. Costumed as a private, Funston walked directly to Aguinaldo, introduced himself, and advised the Filipino leader that the Americans who were with him were officers of the American army, and that all the other men were his troops and not Aguinaldo's. Funston advised Aguinaldo that he was now a prisoner of war and need have no fear of miss-treatment.

Funston:

> He [Aguinaldo] said in a dazed sort of way, "Is this not a joke?" I assured him that it was not, though, as a matter of fact, it was a pretty bad one on him. While naturally agitated, his bearing was dignified, and in this moment of his fall there was nothing of the craven. He is a man of many excellent qualities, far and away the best Filipino I ever was brought in contact with. It was well known that he was a man of humane instincts, and had done all he could to prevent the horrible atrocities committed by some of the guerrilla bands that now made up his forces; but under the circumstances his control over them was limited. The wounded Villa was more inclined to stand aloof, but we dressed his wounds, thereby mollifying him somewhat. Barcelona was as mild as could be. There was some difficulty in getting under control the wildly excited Macabebes. A lot of them insisted on throwing their arms around us. [20]

At this point in time, no one other than Funston and his raiding party knew that the mission to capture Aguinaldo had succeeded. In Nueva Ecija, Fagen and his commanders Alejandrino and Lacuna intended to continue their hit-and-run war until the Americans decided that the costs in blood and money were simply too expensive.

The impact of Aguinaldo's capture came in early April. The man who had once proclaimed the existence of the Republic of the Philippines, and

Photo taken within an hour of Aguinaldo's capture.
Left to right: Villa, Aguinaldo, Funston (disguised as American private), and a Filipino named Barcelona. (*Arnaldo Dumindin Collection*)

Left to right: Emilio Aguinaldo and unknown Filipino officer as captives aboard USS *Vicksburg*. (*US National Archives*)

Company of Macabebe Scouts who captured Aguinaldo, aboard USS *Vicksburg*. (*US National Archives*)

who had started the war against the United States of America, was now being held at General MacArthur's headquarters. There would be no more orders from Aguinaldo, no more intelligence or supplies from outside, and no more money coming from the top. The decision to continue the fight or to surrender was now up to the individual guerrilla commanders.

On 19 April, the revolutionary crisis dramatically accelerated when Emilio Aguinaldo issued the following proclamation:

To the Filipino People:

I believe that I am not in error in presuming that the unhappy fate to which my adverse fortune has led me is not a surprise to those who have been familiar day to day with the progress of the war. The lessons thus taught, the full meaning of which has recently come to my knowledge, suggested to me with irresistible force that the complete termination of hostilities and a lasting peace are not only desirable but absolutely essential to the welfare of the Philippines.

The Filipinos have never been dismayed by their weakness,

nor have they faltered in following the path pointed out by their fortitude and courage. The time has come, however, in which they find their advance along the path impeded by an irresistible force—a force which, while it restrains them, yet enlightens the mind and opens another course by presenting to them the cause of peace. This cause has been joyfully embraced around the glorious and sovereign banner of the United States. In this manner they repose their trust in the belief that under its protection our people will attain all the promised liberties which they are even now beginning to enjoy.

The country has declared unmistakably in favor of peace; so be it. Enough of blood; enough of tears and desolation. This wish cannot be ignored by the men still in arms if they are animated by no other desire than to serve this noble people which has clearly manifested its will.

So also do I respect this will now that it is known to me, and after mature deliberation resolutely proclaim to the world that I cannot refuse to heed the voice of a people longing for peace, nor the lamentations of thousands of families yearning to see their dear ones in the enjoyment of the liberty promised by the generosity of the great American nation.

By acknowledging and accepting the sovereignty of the United States throughout the entire Archipelago, as I now do without any reservations whatsoever, I believe that I am serving thee, my beloved country. May happiness be thine! [21]

Aguinaldo's painful plea for an immediate end to the war for independence, and for all Filipinos to surrender to the Americans, was broadcasted by newspapers that were carried by couriers to guerrilla leaders throughout the country. Word of Aguinaldo's capture and submission quickly spread through every village and barrio.

Initial responses indicated that the remaining guerrilla leaders were looking favorably at obeying Aguinaldo's call for an end to the war. Without their leader and the supplies he made possible, there was little sense in continuing the fight.

Funston's audacious mission to Palanan had succeeded beyond his wildest dreams. A little more than a year earlier (February 14, 1890) the little general had received the Medal of Honor for his actions during a river crossing under fire. Now he had captured Aguinaldo and, in essence, won the war. Surely, he would be promoted again, and back home he could look forward to parades, speeches and glory.

As for Aguinaldo, Funston truly admired the Filipino leader. He had always viewed the man as a decent, humane individual who had dedicated himself to his peoples' freedom and independence. Having now spent many hours in Aguinaldo's company, Funston had come to genuinely like the man.

Funston had but one thing left to do before he was sent home a hero: he was determined to find, capture and hang that black traitor bastard named Fagen. Focusing on the issue, he began to plan just how he would do it.

Notes

1. Quote: William Pomeroy, *The Forest*, Seven Seas Books, Seven Seas Publishers, Berlin, 1965, paperback, pp. 81-82. Pomeroy's journal is taken from his experiences as an American volunteer during the Hukbalahap Rebellion, which took place from 1946 thru 1954. Pomeroy and his Filipino wife fought with the Huks from 1950 through 1953, fighting over much of the same terrain in Luzon and Nueva Ecija that had been the scene of the earlier conflict in which Fagen took part. Since most of the fighters in Lacuna's Brigade were illiterate, very few records exist to reveal the daily lives of peasant guerrillas, who, with Fagen, fought against American imperialism. Unlike Fagen who was illiterate, Pomeroy was an educated American who, before his experience with the Huks, had first fought against the Japanese in WWII as a member of General MacArthur's forces. His book *The Forest* provides a livid insight into the conduct of guerrilla warfare by a mostly peasant Filipino army of people fighting against overwhelming odds for what they believed was a noble and worthy cause. As Professor and fellow historian E. San Juan, Jr., pointed out when I queried him: "Filipino peasant culture and the nature of Philippine

guerrilla war was and is no different today than it was at the time of the wars against Spain and the United States, or during the Huk Rebellion. Philippine idealism, passion, and the burning desire for independence are very much a part of our heritage. Use Pomeroy's book as you see fit to help tell Fagen's story."

2. Quote: Jose Alejandrino, *The Price of Freedom, Episodes and Anecdotes of our Struggles for Freedom*, M. Colcol & Co., Quiapo, Manila, 1949, PDF format, from Library of Congress, Washington, D.C. pp. 174-176. Note: Regarding General Alejandrino's comment that Fagen's height was above six feet, anyone above 5'5" in height in the Philippines is considered to be tall. Also, during the period of the Philippine-American War, Filipinos measured height in metric format, not inches and feet. By comparison to General Alejandrino and most Filipino men, at 5'10" height, David Fagen was indeed a giant.
3. Quote: Jack Ganzhorn, *I've Killed Men*, 1910, Robert Hale, Ltd., London, pp. 190-192.
4. Quote: Robinson and Schubert, *An Afro-American Rebel in the Philippines*, Pacific Historical Review 44:1 February 1975, pp. 68-83. Quote: p. 76.
5. Quote: Ibid. pp. 193-197.
6. Quote: *NY Times*, October 29, 1900.
7. Quote: Frederick Funston, *Memories of Two Wars*, N.Y. 1911, C. Scribner's Sons, paperback, reprint University of Nebraska Press, Lincoln and London, 2009, p. 376.
8. Quote: Mark Twain, *New York Herald*, October 15, 1900.
9. Funston, *Memories of Two Wars*, pp. 379-380.
10. Quote: Ibid. pp. 385-389.
11. Quote: Ibid. p. 395.
12. Quote: Ibid. pp. 396-398.
13. Quote extracts: Ibid. pp. 402-408.
14. Quote: Ibid. pp. 412-413.
15. Quote: Ibid. p. 412.
16. Quote: Ibid.
17. Quote: Ibid. pp. 414-416.
18. Quote: Ibid.
19. Quote: Ibid. pp. 418-421.
20. Quote: Ibid. pp. 421-422.

21. Quote, Aguinaldo proclamation, online: http://filipino.biz.ph/history/ag010419.html.

◀Chapter Ten▶

FAGEN'S FATE

GENERAL JOSE ALEJANDRINO, David Fagen's commander, was now forced to decide whether to keep fighting or surrender. In his book, *Price of Freedom,* Alejandrino recalls:

> Following the capture in Palanan of Aguinaldo and the surrender of almost all generals who operated in the northern and central Luzon, I stayed with the Lacuna Brigade which operated in the mountains of Penaranda sometime in April, 1901.
> ...Officers and soldiers abandoned us, and in our moments of desperation, I began to discuss with Lacuna the convenience of our surrendering.
> We finally agreed to present ourselves and I offered to discuss the conditions of our surrender with the Americans. If they would guarantee our lives and personal liberty, I would return to notify Lacuna and his men.
> I presented myself to the American detachment in Arayat, reporting to its commander, Mr. Baldwin, my purpose. A few hours later, General Funston arrived and without much ado and in a brusque and authoritarian manner told me: 'You cannot surrender yourself without first delivering Fagan.'
> 'The surrender of Fagan is an infamy which I cannot commit because I know that if you get to catch him in your hands, you would be capable of bathing him in petroleum and burning him alive. You have soldiers. Why don't you catch Fagan yourselves?' I answered.
> 'Then, you will remain a prisoner,' General Funston said.
> I replied; 'I came here because of my confidence in the honor

of the American Army and because I believed that you will permit me to return to our camp as what General MacArthur did in case we did not arrive at an agreement. If I was mistaken and you insist in my remaining a prisoner, I will, of course, have to resign myself to force, but you should know, General, that neither Lacuna nor his men will surrender once they come to know the unjust treatment that I have merited from you.'

'You are under arrest,' General Funston ended.

Accordingly, that evening they compelled me to sleep in the house of Don Clemente Santos in the town, then occupied by an officer, with sentinels with fixed bayonets inside my room. But on the following day, it seems that they received orders from General MacArthur for they notified me that I was free and could discuss the conditions of our surrender....

The conditions of my surrender having been accepted, I returned to the camp of Lacuna to fix the day for his surrender at San Isidro, Nueva Ecija. [1]

Early in the morning of April 29, 1901, General Alejandrino and all his troops surrendered to General Funston. At that very moment, on horseback, Fagen with his woman and a few followers were miles away escaping into the mountains.

A week after he had returned from his heroic Palanan expedition, Funston returned to San Isidro and sent a lengthy letter to Lacuna. The letter set forth a statement of surrender conditions that would have to be met, and mentioned the recent capitulations of several prominent Filipino officers. Lacuna quickly responded, informing his opponent that he was ready to consider any reasonable proposition. A mutual decision was made by the principals, and all hostilities in the 4th District ceased.

In Mid-May, Funston and his aides and a dozen of his Scouts rode to Papaya and entered the guerrilla camp without incident.

General Funston:

...We dismounted, the men of the Scouts holding our horses and their own, and were met by an officer whose face was strangely familiar to me, though it was impossible to place him. We were conducted to a rather large, grass roofed shed, the guard of some twenty men coming to "present arms" in very good style, and at last were face to face with Lacuna. He shook hands with all of us, introduced us to a number of officers who were with him, and then had some coffee and cake brought in. Naturally, for a time nothing was said about the object of our visit. We found him to be an apparently full-blood Malay, very dark, of medium stature, and possessed of the quiet dignity of his race. He was a man of about middle age, and had enough knowledge of Spanish to be able to speak the language fairly correctly, so that we understood each other without difficulty. On this occasion he was in the uniform of his rank, but it was evident to all of us that these articles of clothing had but recently been prepared for the occasion....

...But it was not very long before we got down to business. I explained very carefully to Lacuna that all of his officers and men would be allowed to surrender provided they turned in all arms and ammunition in their possession and took the oath of allegiance to the United States, and that all crimes against their own countrymen would be overlooked. It might be best to explain that in doing this I was carrying out the orders of higher authority, which was also the case when it came to the question as to what steps would be taken against any persons whom subsequent developments might show to have been implicated in the murder of American prisoners of war, it being made plain that they could expect no immunity...

...Lacuna himself yielded the point, having nothing to fear; and then came up the question of Fagan, the negro deserter from our army, who was serving as an officer with the force concentrated at this point. It was made clear that this man could not be received as a prisoner of war, and that if he surrendered it would have to be with the understanding that he would be tried by court-martial, in which event his execution would be a practical certainty. Lacuna recognized the fact that any other solution was out of the question, and it was finally agreed that with the exception of Fagan all of his men were to march to San Isidro, deliver up their arms, and take the oath of allegiance to the United States, after which all would be released, but that any who should later prove to have been guilty of killing American prisoners would have to stand trial. The terms were then reduced to writing and signed by both of us. [2]

After Lacuna decided to surrender, Alejandrino remembers:

...When our surrender was effected, I really felt very sorry in having to leave Fagen. I left him some twelve rifles for his defense....[3]

Surrounded by friendly peasants, General Cailles' troops march in to surrender to Americans at Santa Cruz, Laguna Province, June 24, 1901.
(*US National Archives*)

Fagen had already decided against joining with any of the remaining diehard guerrillas. He no longer saw any value in fighting for Philippine independence against insurmountable odds. Fagen understood that General Funston's Scouts and Constabulary would relentlessly pursue him, and he was right.

General Funston:

After the surrender of Lacuna, Fagen had for a time disappeared, but now he began to be heard from, he having in some way obtained two or three rifles and, with a couple of unreconstructed natives, taken to the bosque [jungle], whence he had made a few forays for the purpose of committing robberies. I made a trip to Manila to discuss the matter with General Wheaton, and came back with the authority to offer a reward of six hundred dollars for Fagan, dead or alive. Whatever he had been before, he was now a bandit, pure and simple, and entitled to just the same treatment as a mad dog; which is what he got. A proclamation, written in Spanish and Tagalog, offering a reward of six hundred dollars for the head of David Fagan, American negro, deserter from the United States army, was posted in every town in Nueva Ecija....[4]

From May until December 1901, Fagen eluded capture. During that period, the American authorities announced that the former rules of warfare concerning insurrectos no longer applied. Any insurrectos now captured were to be considered robbers or criminals (*ladrones*), and would be treated as such.

On December 6, the following report announcing Fagen's beheading was posted by 1st Lieutenant R. C. Corliss, of the Philippine Scouts:

Bongabong, Nueva Ecija, P. I.   Adjutant General
December 6, 1901   2nd Separate Brigade
    San Fernando, P. I.

Sir:

I have the honor to submit the following statement of Anastacio Bartolome, corroborated by Sinsorco Habiendo, Feliciano Fortuna and Elisio Fernandez as told to me:

Anastacio Bartolome left Barrio Santos, Bongabong, Nueva Ecija, P.I. about November 15th 1901 for Umiray river where he intended to hunt, fish, and buy "bejacos" from the Negritos. On his arrival at Umiray he met his companions Juan Domingo,

Sinsorco Habiendo, Dionicio Domingo, Feliciano Fortuna and Elisio Fernandez who were fishing in river. Work continued until December 1st, 1901 when David Fagan, his native wife and two Negritos arrived at river. Both Negritos and Fagan were armed. Through fear and to keep on good terms with Fagan, Anastacio and his party prepared them a meal. Knowing that Fagan was an insurgent and ladrone they secretly arranged to kill him.

When the meal was prepared, about 10 a.m. and all were eating, Anastacio and his party suddenly turned on Fagan and his men with bolos. Fagan was mortally wounded and ran about 100 yards and dropped dead. Both Negritos escaped badly wounded. Fagan's wife ran for the ocean, jumped in and drowned herself.

Party then cut Fagan's head off to present here as evidence of their story and buried his body on south bank of Umiray river near its mouth.

The next day they left for Yrurulong bringing Fagan's head and effects. Arriving at Yrurulong Anastacio left remainder of party and brought head and effects to me.

Three of party, namely Sinsorco Habiendo, Elisio Fernandez, and Feliciano Fortuna arrived here on 8th instant and corroborate this statement.

Very respectfully
R. C. Corliss
1st Lieut. Philippine Scouts
Commanding Station [5]

Lt. Corliss sent a second letter on the same date to the Adjutant General:

Sir:

I have the honor to submit the following report regarding [the] killing of David Fagan:

On December 5th, 1901, about 2 p.m., one native, Anastacio Bartolome presented himself at this station bearing the head of an American negro which he claimed was David Fagan's. The head was partly decomposed, but the following features could be recognized – Complexion; dark; -- Hair; curly; Teeth; good and regular; nose; large and flat, forehead; receding; ears, set close to head. Features seemed to correspond with photographs brought in, presumably Fagan's.

Bartolome also presented the following items: two Remington rifles, one Winchester rifle cal. 44, one Colts revolver, U.S. Army model 1894 cal. .38, no. 64788, one Revolver holster, U.S. Army model, one trumpet Spanish model, nineteen cartridges,--12 Remington, 3 Winchester and 4 revolver, one pr. field glasses, one Military Academy class ring marked: "Frederick W. Alstaetter, Class of '97," one pr. gauntlets, three coats, one vest, one pr. shoulder straps (insurgent), two photographs, and two written communications in Spanish.

The place where the killing took place is Umiray, a river flowing into the Pacific Ocean south of Dingalan bay.
Presidente of Bongabong states that it is customary for people from Santos to go there hunting, fishing and trading with Negritos.

The time of killing was December 1st 1901 about 10 a.m. Circumstances are given in report of Anastacio Bartolome, who is well known here as a resident of Santos, by both natives and Americans, He has good recommendations from Capt. C. N. Cabiness, 24th Infantry, U.S.A.

On December 8th, 1901, three of his companions, Sinsorco Abiendo, Elisio Fernandez & Feliciano Fortuna arrived here and corroborated his statement. The other two cannot be found as yet as they are still at Yururulong. All of the party are Ilocanos.

Very Respectfully,
R. C. Corliss
1st Lieut. Phil Scouts [6]

After obtaining permission from General Wheaton, Funston notified the press of Fagen's death. Here's how Funston remembered the situation in his book *Memories of Two Wars*:

> A proclamation…offering a reward of $600 for the head of David Fagan, American Negro, deserter from the United States Army, was posted in every town in Nueva Ecija, and at Bongabong was read by one Anastacio Bartolome, a Tagalog who for years had made his living as a deer hunter. Having heard rumors of the recent movements of Fagan and his companions, and not being averse to earning an honest penny, Anastacio took to the woods with one companion and two days later found Fagan, two Filipino men and three women in camp on the beach of the Pacific Coast of the province at the place known on the maps as Dingalan Cove. The party was just sitting down to a dinner of comotes and fish, and invited the visitors from Bongabong to join them. The opportunity for Anastacio to carry out his plan not being favorable at the time, he accepted. He knew Fagan by sight, having himself been an insurgent soldier, and so was sure he had the right man. The meal being half finished, he gave his companion a look; the two sprang to their feet and in a few strokes beheaded the three men, sparing the three screaming women. Fagan's head, the only one of importance, was brought to Bongabong and delivered to Lieutenant R. C. Corliss….
>
> …Only a short time later Lacuna told me that we got the right man, though there was never any doubt on the subject, as all of the colored soldiers who had been captured had been in one way or another accounted for. Anastacio received his money in less than two weeks, and it was more than he could have saved in many years of following his useful but not very lucrative occupation; and Fagan was at least one American traitor who got what was coming to him. Let us hope that after his return to his home Anastacio did not bet all of his winnings on the wrong bird. [7]

Newspapers across the United States ran the story of Fagen's beheading, vindicating General Funston's persistence in pursuing the Negro traitor. As far as Funston and the U.S. Army were concerned, the Fagen records were now closed.

The *Scranton Tribune*, December 8, 1901:

Scouts at Bengabon
Kill Negro Deserter

David Fagan, Formerly an American Soldier.
Is Decapitated by Filipinos

By Exclusive Wire from the Associated Press. Manila. Dec. 8 – Native scouts from Bengabon, province of Neuva Ecija, have killed the American negro David Fagan, a deserter from the 24th Infantry who for more than two years has been leading Filipinos against the American troops. The native scouts decapitated their prisoner. The man's head, however, was recognized as that of Fagan's. They also secured his commission in the insurgent army. Fagan had on one of his fingers the class ring of Lieutenant Frederick W. Altstaetter, of the engineers, who was captured by Filipinos supposedly under the command of Fagan himself, Oct. 28, 1900.

Fagin has been reported killed upon several occasions. The authorities are satisfied that former statements of his death were erroneous and that he has not been killed. [8]

African-American newspapers were for the most part strongly anti-imperialist, and the Fagen obituary in the *Indianapolis Freeman* of December 14, 1901 illustrates their point-of-view:

David Fagin a Negro, who deserted the U.S. army to serve the Filipino cause, has been caught and beheaded by the natives for his desertion. Fagin was a traitor, and died a traitor's death. But he was a man, no doubt, prompted by honest motives to help a weaker side, and one to which he felt allied by ties that bind. Fagin,

211

perhaps, did not appreciate the magnitude of the crime of aiding the enemy to shoot down his flag. He saw, it may be, the weak, the strong, he chose, and the world knows the rest.⁹

Official U.S. records suggest that the decomposed Negro head Bartolome turned into the Constabulary outpost at Bongabong was *most likely* that of Fagen. But, in their well-researched essay, Army historian Frank N. Schubert and his co-author, Michael C. Robinson, wrote: "...The army released reports of positive identification of the 'slightly decomposed head,' and the press echoed the military's eagerness to announce Fagen's demise. However, officers on the scene expressed doubts about whose head Bartolome had delivered, and sought a precise description of the rebel from members of his former company. The information received from the Twenty-fourth Infantry did not enable the army to dispel uncertainty. The official file in the Adjutant General's Office on the incident is titled 'the supposed killing of David Fagen,' and there is no record of payment of a reward to Bartolome."¹⁰

My research indicates that the only reward actually paid to Bartolome was for his turning in two rifles and a revolver. At the time, military authorities in the Philippine Islands were accounting for every nickel being spent. If Bartolome received a $600 reward for Fagen's alleged head, it wasn't army money. It had to have come from Funston's private funds.

The situation mandates closer scrutiny of Anastacio Bartolome. Lt. Corliss asked the mayor and several of the townspeople about Bartolome, and all of them claimed he was an honest and reliable person. Their appraisal doesn't ring true with the character of a supposed murderous bounty hunter.

Bartolome also admitted that he had served as an insurgent under either Lacuna or Alejandrino in the Nueva Ecija zone of operations. In that case it would have been virtually impossible for him to have done so without knowing the American black Filipino guerrilla hero referred to fondly by his men as "General Fagen." In addition, there are references that record that Bartolome himself served as an officer under Lacuna.

In Lieutenant Corliss's reports to the Adjutant General about Bartolome allegedly killing Fagen, there is a list of Fagen's effects that were turned in by the killer to prove his story. Meticulously recorded, these articles include insurgent coats, jackets and other military clothing supposedly taken by Bartolome after he had killed Fagen. We know from General Jose Alejandrino's recollections that Fagen suffered nightmares about being captured by American soldiers. If you were the most notorious American traitor being hunted by Philippine Constabulary Forces, would you wear or carry clothing that would identify you as a Filipino insurgent officer? Would you travel with your wife and Negrito followers while carrying documentation and a West Point class ring that would decisively identify you as David Fagen? Would you choose to camp and fish in a leisurely manner in an area frequented by travelers? Only if you were suicidal would the answers to these questions be "yes."

In all his conversations with Lt. Corliss, Bartolome never asked him to keep his identity as Fagen's murderer a secret. I think I know why; it didn't matter. Apparently, everyone *except* the Americans knew that Fagan was still alive. Fagen was, after all, the Filipinos' famous Negrito hero. He had risked everything for their independence and freedom and he was well-loved and respected by a people whose friendship and loyalty ran deep.

If Fagen had been murdered for the American reward-money, and his Filipino killer's identity was known, how long do you think such a man would have retained his own head?

For years, when asked about Fagen, the people from Nueva Ecija Province claimed he was still alive and living with his wife and a growing family at a distant, remote hideaway in the mountains. Many individuals admitted that they had seen him from time to time.

The natives were not the only ones to report sighting Fagen long after his alleged beheading:

Philippine Constabulary Dispatch sent by Inspector Bates to Lieutenant Rubio, during pursuit of insurgents under Fagen:

November 30, 1902
Lieut. De Rubio

I had a big scrap this afternoon. I want you to come at once here with all your men, and plenty of arms I am out and have four wounded and 2 of my men captured. Come at once I am about surrounded.

Bates - Insp. [11]

The above sighting is only one of several that occurred long after Fagen was supposedly beheaded in December of 1901.

Some forty-three years later, in 1944, during the Japanese occupation of the Philippines, Major Edwin Price Ramsey—American guerrilla commander of the forces fighting the Japanese invaders in Luzon—secretly travelled to a small village on the island of Mindoro to retrieve a long-range radio brought in by submarine from Australia. Ramsey tells the following story in his biography:

…For the rest of the day we tacked back and forth, running before a capricious wind. As darkness fell I told the captain to put in to land, for I had no intention of spending another night on board. There was a little cove at the village of Pinamalayan, and we eased into it. While I waited on the beach my men went inland to scout a handful of shacks among the coconut palms.
In half an hour they emerged from the jungle some fifty yards farther up the beach. With them was a tall, skinny black man dressed in native clothing, well into his sixties, his skin deeply wrinkled and his hair ashen white. When he saw me his face burst into a smile of anticipation and disbelief. He hurried to me, leaving my bodyguards behind, and threw his arms out to greet me.

He was a startling apparition, another bizarre encounter on this endless trip, and I stood stunned a long minute in his embrace before I managed to free myself.

'Sir,' the old black man panted out before I could speak, 'If I didn't know you was an officer, I'd kiss you.'

His name was White, he told me, Sergeant White, from New Orleans. He drew himself up and saluted.

'Tenth U.S. Horse Cavalry,' he announced. 'Buffalo Soldiers.'

He explained that he had arrived in the Philippines in 1907 with an expedition sent to put down the Moro insurrection. 'I served under Arthur MacArthur,' White declared proudly, 'General Douglas MacArthur's father.' After his term was up, White had chosen to remain behind on Mindoro. For over thirty years he had lived in a remote village in the jungle, where he had married several Filipino women and sired dozens of children.

'You're the first American I've seen in all this time,' he told me. 'I can't hardly believe it. What branch you from, sir?'

I told him that I, too, was cavalry.

He paused a long moment, his yellowing eyes clouding. 'Well, now, I'll just be damned,' he said at last, and the tears brimmed over.

White took us to his village, which indeed was populated by his sprawling family. There were children everywhere whose bright faces reflected that of the old trooper. Three or four of his wives made a feast for us, and for the rest of the evening we sat swapping stories of the cavalry, the guerillas, and our shared loneliness for fellow Americans.

White knew little about the war. He lived in almost total isolation among his family and had not been bothered by the Japanese. His clan was completely self-sufficient, with ample rice, chickens, pigs, and fruit. Since nearly everyone in the vicinity was related to him, he had no worry over spies who might denounce him or bandits who would steal his produce.

He was eager for details of the Twenty-sixth Cavalry and on Bataan, he wagged his head in sympathy.

'What became of your horses?' he asked me.

'When the food ran out they were butchered.'

He nodded and lowered his head. 'My, my,' he sighed. 'Now that is a terrible thing. Surely terrible. I do feel most keenly for you, sir. I mean, a cavalryman without his horse, now, what is he? Just another footslog, sir, ain't that so?'

'No, White, I don't think that's true,' I said. 'I think the cavalry can survive the loss of its mounts. I think it has to. Because one way or another they're going to take away the horses—that's inevitable.'

White nodded ruefully, and then his face brightened. 'But they can't take away the spirit, can they, sir?'

'No,' I answered. 'Old troopers like us are proof of that.'

I spent the night at White's village, and when it came time for me to go in the morning he was again in tears, and it was a long while before he would leave off hugging me and shaking my hand. He pressed food and herbal remedies on us, and he and a dozen of his children accompanied us to the beach.

'God bless y'all,' he cried as we climbed again onto the batil. 'I'd volunteer to join you, but I fear that I'm too old to fight. But I'm at peace, Major; I have my home here, and I'll die among my family.' He looked at me a long moment in thought. 'That's what we all fight for, ain't it, Major—to live in peace in our home, among our own people. I pray that God may bring you safely to it, sir.' [12]

Sergeant White's blissful life-in-hiding suggests that the same possibilities existed for Fagen. Maybe he too was surrounded by his extended family, living happily in some self-sufficient, remote, isolated jungle paradise, seldom visited by strangers.

I surely hope so.

Notes

1. Quote from: General Jose Alejandrino, *Price of Freedom*, (La Senda Del Sacrificio), *Episodes and Anecdotes of our struggles for freedom ---- Original in Spanish, Translated into English by Atty. Jose M. Alejandrino*, Manila, 1949, pp. 172-174.
2. Quote from, Funston, *Memories of Two Wars*, pp. 428-431.
3. Quote from: Alejandrino, *Price of Freedom*, p. 176.
4. Quote from: Funston, *Memories of Two Wars*, p. 434.
5. Corliss to Adjutant General, Second Brigade, Bongabong, N. E. P.I. December 6, 1901, AGO file 431081, NARA, RG 94.

6. Ibid.
7. Funston, MOTW, p. 435.
8. Newspaper quote of *Scranton Tribune,* December 8, 1901.
9. Newspaper quote, obituary of David Fagen, *Indianapolis Freeman,* Dec. 14, 1901.
10. Quote from Robinson and Schubert, "David Fagen: an Afro-American Rebel in the Philippines, 1899-1901," Pacific Historical Review, vol. 44:1 (Feb. 1975) p. 81.
11. Dispatch, Bates to Lt. De Rubio, from Vic Hurley, *Jungle Patrol, the story of the Philippine Constabulary, 1901-1936,* p. 77 sub-title and photo of dispatch.
12. Quote: Edwin Price Ramsey and Stephen J. Rivele, *Lieutenant Ramsey's War, from Horse Soldier to Guerrilla Commander,* NY, First Brassey Five-Star paperback edition, 1996, pp. 228-230.

EPILOGUE

EVENTUALLY, REPORTED SIGHTINGS of David Fagen disappeared from military and civil records.

General Funston returned home to the States and, capitalizing on his fame as the heroic capturer of Emilio Aguinaldo, toured the country and performed a number of speaking engagements. During his talks, he enthusiastically justified American military policy in the Philippines because the Filipinos were "too uncivilized" to manage a true democracy. Reminding his audiences of savage atrocities committed by Filipino insurgents, he protested the accusations and trials of American officers accused of genocide. He readily admitted to ordering the execution of insurgent prisoners, and he vociferously claimed that American anti-imperialists who spoke against the war were aiding the enemy and should be arrested and hanged for treason. His speeches also included mention of business opportunities that our conquest of the Philippine Islands had made possible.

Funston's assumption of smooth sailing after his return from the Philippines was smashed by the anti-imperialists and others who castigated his capture of Aguinaldo as a supreme act of treachery, not bravery. Among the facts they cited in newspapers, was how Funston and his men were starving and had been saved by the grace of their quarry. Their versions of the event glorified Aguinaldo, not Funston.

Editorial, *Boston Post*, May 1902:

> When the capture of Aguinaldo by Funston was announced by cable, it was held as a great exploit. President McKinley lost no time in making him a brigadier-general. But, as the details have come to light, contempt and disgust have taken the place of admiration. The American people accepted, though not without some qualms of conscience, the forgery, treachery and disguise with which Funston

EPILOGUE

prepared his expedition. But until recently the full infamy of his conduct has not been understood. The historian of his expedition, Edwin Wildman, thus describes the last stage of Funston's march: 'Over the stony declivities and through the thick jungle, across bridgeless streams and up narrow passes, the footsore and bone-racked adventurers tramped, until their food was exhausted and they were too weak to move, though but eight miles from Aguinaldo's rendezvous. A messenger was sent forward to inform Aguinaldo of their position and to beg for food. The rebel chieftain promptly replied by dispatching rice and a letter to the officer in command, instructing him to 'treat the American prisoners well.'

This incident was passed over lightly in the earlier reports. Its full significance has just begun to dawn upon the American people.[1]

Funston's speeches which expressed his open hatred for anti-imperialists, including his remarks that people who spoke against the war should be hanged as traitors, were brought to the attention of the president:

THE WHITE HOUSE
WASHINGTON
April 21, 1902
To the Secretary of War:

I call attention to the enclosed report of a speech by General Funston. The reference to the senior senator from Massachusetts is entirely improper in a general of the army. I think that General Funston will have to be requested not to make any more public speeches. I appreciate to the full his great services. I am in cordial sympathy with his general view on the Philippines, but he expresses himself at times in a way that is very unfortunate.
(signed) T. Roosevelt [2]

Following his tour in the Philippines, Funston was assigned to command the Presidio in San Francisco, where he played an instrumental role after the 1906 earthquake. In 1917, just before America entered

EPILOGUE

World War I, Funston was favored by President Woodrow Wilson to command the American Expeditionary Force, but at age fifty-one the general died from a heart attack in San Antonio, Texas. Kansas still honors him as a hero.

John W. Calloway, the Battalion Sergeant Major who signed David Fagen's initial enlistment papers in Tampa in 1898, felt just as strongly as Fagen that the war America was waging against the Filipino people was cruel and immoral. Indeed, just after Fagen's defection, interviewed by a reporter, Calloway listed the severe punishments the defector had endured for expressing his anger at how the Filipinos were being mishandled. However, unlike Fagen, despite his misgivings about America's invasion and occupation of the Philippines, Calloway remained loyal to his country and his uniform. A former printer, educated and articulate, Calloway was a tireless letter writer who fed stories of the war to the *Richmond Planet* (an African-American newspaper from his home town). In many of these stories, the highest ranking non-commissioned officer of the 24th Infantry Regiment disparaged America's imperialism and racism succinctly and well:

Calloway to Editor, *Richmond Planet*, 16 November 1899 (the day before Fagen defected):

> …Since dropping you a few lines from El Deposito, we have been constantly on the jump. First at San Fernando, then Mexico, Santa Anna, Prayal Cabiel, [and] San Isidro. Advantage was taken of these "hikes" to study the Filipino and the Filipino question from the point that follows. The whites have begun to establish their diabolical race hatred in all its home rancor in Manila, even endeavoring to propagate the phobia among the Spaniards and Filipinos so as to be sure of the foundation of their supremacy when the civil rule that must necessarily follow the present military regime, is established.
> …I felt it worth while to probe the Filipino as to his knowledge and view of the American colored man that we might know our position intelligently. What follows is a

EPILOGUE

condensed account of the results....

Q: Do the Filipinos hold a different feeling towards the colored American from that of the white?

Calloway then provided his subject's answers, which the reader may recall ended with the following dramatic statement: "Between you and him, we look upon you as the angel and him as the devil."[3]

Apparently, Calloway was convinced that as long as he performed his duties as well as he could, he had a right to express his opinions about the war. Indeed, his feelings and opinions on this subject were well known to his fellow soldiers. At the time, most of the Buffalo Soldiers serving in the Philippines felt the same way he did.

As friendly relations between African-American soldiers and the Filipinos blossomed, military authorities headquartered in Manila became increasingly alarmed. The driving force behind the Army's apprehensions stemmed from the fear that if this trend were allowed to continue, there would be more "David Fagens".

By the summer of 1900, Sergeant Major Calloway had made up his mind to retire in the Philippines and go into business there. In early October, he married Mamerta de la Rosa, of Santa Rosa, Nueva Ecija.

Among the several elitist and wealthy Filipinos whose friendships Calloway cultivated, was Don Antonio Consunji and his son Tomas, wealthy planters from the San Fernando, Pampanga Province.

Long suspected by US security agents of aiding the insurgents while professing loyalty to the United States, Consunji's home was raided by military police on October 29. Among the papers they confiscated was a letter from Calloway to Tomas Consunji, dated 5 February 1900:

My dear Mr. Consunji:

After my last conference with you and your father, I was constantly haunted by the feeling of how wrong morally we Americans are in the present affair with you. What a wrong to crush every hope and opportunity of a youth of a race of which you, your brothers and our esteemed friend Thomas Paras form such brilliant examples.

221

EPILOGUE

Would to God it lay in my power to rectify the committed error and compensate the Filipino for the wrong done! But what power have I? If I could muster every youth of the race under my hand I would say to them be not discouraged. The day will come when you will be accorded your rights. The moral sensibilities of all America are not yet dead; there still smolders in the bosom of the country a spark of righteousness that will yet kindle into a flame that will awaken the country to its senses....

...Bring up the masses. Teach them. The capacity of a people is measured by its masses – not its exceptions. Teach them to know that a man who can do a common thing in an uncommon way is the man the world respects most. I know you will feel this is very long drawn in the face of your being denied liberty of action, but that will come. Mark my words, Yours Truly, John W. Calloway. [4]

Major Arthur Williams, 3rd Infantry and Provost Marshal General, Pampanga wrote the first reports of the case:

I enclose herewith a letter found in the house of Antonio Consunji, a man who after having taken the oath of amnesty, has acted as a political agent for the insurgents. The letter is addressed to a son of Antonio, who is well known to be opposed to the United States occupying these islands. The writer is, to say the least, very indiscreet. He is John W. Calloway, Sergeant Major 24th Infantry, and I think it would be well that the colonel of that regiment should see the letter. [5]

Calloway's commander, Colonel H.B. Freeman, was enraged by the news of the sergeant-major's actions. Assembling all of his troops on the Parade Ground, Freeman stood Calloway in full uniform before the men, and broke him in rank to private, recommending that he be confined, discharged from the Army without honor, and transported back to the United States.

At first, Calloway was confined at Tayug, Pangasinan where he was

EPILOGUE

stationed, and then he was transported to Bilibid Military Prison in Manila. Thus began a long-drawn saga of trumped-up charges and attempts to court martial the accused, without producing a single conviction. Calloway, it turned out, had not committed treason or any real crimes. His career was being destroyed not for what he had done, but for what *he might do* if (like Fagen) he defected.

In January 1901, Callaway was taken to Manila harbor, locked in the brig of a transport ship and sent to San Francisco. Upon arrival, he was imprisoned at The Presidio. Three months later, he was released. He had no career and no employment, but a few months later he somehow secured passage on a freighter back to Manila, where he slipped ashore quietly and reunited with his wife and his daughter Juanita, who had been born the previous year. Unfortunately, in late August, Calloway was recognized in Manila by the Band Leader of the 24th Infantry Regiment, who turned him in to the Provost Marshal General.

Calloway was arrested again, confined, and soon after transferred to the transport *Grant* which carried him back to San Francisco. After several months, and numerous unsuccessful attempts by Calloway to plead his innocence by letter to the Adjutant General in Washington, DC, Calloway was again set free and made his way back to Manila to reunite with his family. This was in 1902, after President Roosevelt had declared an end to hostilities, and the US military in Manila no longer cared about Calloway's presence.

Left on his own, Calloway raised fourteen children with his wife Mamerta, succeeded in the printing business, and remained in his adopted country until his death on April 21, 1934. Unlike Fagen, Calloway had been able to live his life in the open.

In 1902, military authorities in Manila were able to convince the then Governor-General (and future President) William H. Taft, that relations between African American soldiers and the Filipinos were altogether too friendly. Taft ordered all the Buffalo Soldier regiments shipped back to the US, and barred any future service of colored regiments in the Philippine Islands. Taft's orders were later dropped and units of Buffalo Soldiers were brought back to serve again in the Philippines.

Recognizing the hardships and abuse they would face in their home country under Jim Crow, like John W. Calloway, many of the Buffalo Soldiers elected to muster out and remain in the Philippine Islands.

Today, large numbers of racially mixed Filipinos are living in Nueva Ecija Province.

What happened to Cuba and the Philippines under US Control?

As set forth earlier in this history, US business interests were the driving force behind America's decision to invade Cuba and overthrow Spanish rule.

In 1900, General Leonard Wood, the new US military governor in Cuba, helped draft a constitution which included an amendment by US Senator Orville Platt, which guaranteed America's right to intervene in Cuban domestic affairs. It also forced Cuba to lease in perpetuity to the USA a naval base at Guantanamo Bay and required the Cuban government to 'maintain a low public debt; refrain from signing any treaty impairing its obligations to the United States; to grant to the United States the right of intervention to protect life, liberty, and property; validate the acts of the new military government; and if requested, provide long-term naval leases. Platt would later write 'Cubans are incapable of stable self-government. In many respects, they are like children.' [6]

1903. The United Fruit Company is allowed to buy 200,000 acres on Cuba's cost [sic] for $400,000. ...In March, Cuba and the USA signed a commercial reciprocity treaty that ensured American control of Cuban markets.

...1905. One quarter of all Cuban land is owned by Americans. [7]

On 21 August 1960, the *New York Times* published a piece about Castro's opinion of the American presence in Cuba:

...[Castro] complained that when...the country was being

EPILOGUE

'sacked' during the Batista era, it never occurred to the "Yankee oligarchy…to have its press write of the horrors in which Cuba lived" or to demand a cut in Batista's sugar quota. The Yankee oligarchy failed to do these things, Castro asserted, because it 'was owner of our lands, our mines, our factories, our commerce, most of our banks, our public services and withdrew millions of dollars from our economy yearly.'[8]

The cause of the breakup of Cuban-American relations in 1960 was entirely due to the rapacious actions of American "interests" since imposing US rule from 1900. The wealthy Cuban elite who fled Cuba and settled mostly in Miami when Fulgencio Batista was overthrown, have benefitted greatly from US governmental sympathy. According to a RAND corporation paper by Leland L. Johnson, published in June 1964:

…Seventy-five percent of an agricultural country the size of England, with a population half again that of Ireland, was owned by eight percent of the property holders, a few dozen rich Cuban families and the giant US and Cuban sugar and cattle companies. Tens of thousands of rural Cubans lived in misery on marginal lands, in swamps and in the trackless mountains where their fathers and grandfathers had been driven by relentless expansion of the sugar monoculture, which produced sugar to rigid quotas and let millions of acres of land lie fallow to become overrun by brush and weeds.[9]

On April 11, 2015, Presidents Barack Obama and Raul Castro (brother of Fidel) shook hands at the Summit of the Americas in Panama. Their hand shake opened the door to renewed relations after the severing of all ties between the two nations 54 years ago. It appears that the United States is at last willing to forgive Fidel Castro's nationalization of so many American businesses back in 1960. However, as of this writing, the American trade embargoes which have punished Cuba's economy for so long remain in place—although steps to re-establish trade have already been taken—including American tourism to Cuba. On November 25,

2016, Fidel Castro died of natural causes. His ashes are buried at Santiago.

In the Philippines, retaining control over the Filipinos' defense and trade from 1902 until 1942, the United States slowly increased the rights of the Filipinos to participate in their own government, with a promise of eventual independence. In 1942, Japanese invaders took control of the Philippines until their defeat by US military forces in 1945. On July 4, 1946, the US government afforded the people of the Philippines genuine independence. However, by the terms of the agreement, the US was to retain military bases there in perpetuity, and would benefit from rules of trade that gave American businesses distinct advantages.

On the positive side, among the things Filipinos received from American colonialism was a modernized infrastructure, including roads, bridges, electric power production, water supply and management, as well as agricultural development and a workable health system. The people of the Philippines also benefited from the establishment of a universal educational system which (although English-speaking) was designed to serve the entire population.

Ruled by Americans, it was natural for American-made household products, music, movies, clothing and popular styling to become enthusiastically accepted by the Filipino people. Indeed, the hunger for consumerism in both countries is virtually identical—there is no difference between an American's or Filipino's joyful acceptance and use of modern technological products like computers and cell phones.

Unfortunately, in the Philippines the abyss between the ultra-rich and those living in abject poverty is unbelievably deep and wide; and this Third World nation has won the dubious honor of being ranked as the most corrupt country in Asia. With a government dominated by rich elites and "compradors"—huge international corporations—the great majority of Filipino presidents have come from powerful, rich families, most of whom acquired their initial wealth as favored tools of the Spanish. After the Spanish defeat, seeking to protect their property and status, they offered their loyalty and support to the new occupiers, and their willingness to be used was gratefully accepted.

During the Japanese occupation in WWII, communist peasant guerrillas known as the Hukabalahap, or "Huks," joined together to fight the Japanese

EPILOGUE

and avoided coordinating or even cooperating with American-led Filipino guerrilla forces. They did so because in their point of view, both the Americans and Japanese were equally unwelcome occupiers. Indeed, infrequent clashes between the Huks and the American-led guerillas occurred, and in 1945, after the Japanese were vanquished, the Huks turned their wrath against the American sponsored, Manila based, Filipino government. Heavily involved in a growing cold war with communist Russia, US aid and military support for the governing elite in the Philippines eventually overwhelmed the Huk movement.

Ironically, it now appears that one thing the Filipino and American people share is a government that ignores the needs of the people in order to serve the ultra-rich and big business.

Where African American Buffalo Soldiers once earned respect and friendship from the Filipino people, the enthusiastic adaptation of American culture and racial attitudes eventually dominated, and in today's Philippines African Americans are, for the most part, disdained.

The centuries-old war for independence from the Catholic-dominated Manila government continues to be fought by the Muslims of Mindanao, including Islamic terrorist groups like the Abu Sayyaf, infamous for kidnapping Americans and other foreigners whose lives are then offered in exchange for ransom.

The American idea that you can forcefully invade, occupy and rule a foreign country for profit, began when the US stole Cuba and dictated that country's Constitution in 1902. The same mistaken belief fueled America's seizure of the Philippines.

During the war that followed, the records indicate that in addition to our own dead (nearly 5,000 men), more than 200,000 Filipino lives were lost. It was during our occupation of the Philippines where, in response to insurgent warfare, we developed the tactic of confining civilian populations to guarded villages, and began the search and destroy missions and patrols which we would later employ in Vietnam, Iraq, and Afghanistan. Making friends was never our true purpose.

As I write this, Rodrigo Duterte, the newest President of the Philippines, says that Donald Trump is his good friend. Indeed, these two enigmatic, unpredictable politicians do have much in common. Both are forced by circumstances to pander to their uneducated, impoverished bases—promising better economic times ahead—while at the same time taking extra care not to lose the support of super rich elites and the larger corporations.

Trump and Duterte are both impulsive and temperamental, but unlike Trump, Duterte's record of supporting extra-judicial killings during his infamous drug war brings him a degree of unparalleled infamy. His Filipino nickname is "Digong" (The Punisher).

As of February 2017, at Duterte's command, approximately 5,800 drug dealer and addict suspects have been gunned down by members of the Philippine National Police and a few vigilante-like paramilitary groups. Despite his outrageous strong-arm tactics, Duterte's actions are generally supported by a majority of the masses, most of whom have suffered one way or another due to the drug-crimes and the terrible addictions this illegal trade produces.

Of the Philippine's population of 130 million, 97 million people are forced to endure a depth of hopelessness and misery that only extreme, unending poverty brings—fertile ground for the purveyors of temporary relief. Accordingly, as it is all over the world, wherever drug use and drug crime is prevalent, they are but the symptoms; the disease is poverty.

Duterte's bloody, ongoing war against drugs is one of the ways he helps maintain the support of his base while ignoring the real problem—the overwhelming economic power and greed of the elites and the compradors. The Filipino oligarchy benefits one and all from American investment, council, and military aid, including money, training and weaponry. The elites get uneasy whenever Duterte threatens to sever American relations. They needn't worry. Duterte knows very well that the Philippines are an American neo-colony. The former three-term mayor of Davao (the largest metropolitan city in Mindanao) is also well aware of the natural distrust of the United States by the peasants of Mindanao, the people with whom he grew up.

In a recent tirade, Duterte railed against American interference, claiming that the people of the Philippines were tired of being treated as "America's little brown brother." It was time, Duterte opined, for America to stop

EPILOGUE

interfering, and it was time, he added, for all American troops to exit the Philippines. Caught up in the emotions of the moment, Duterte even cited the infamous Bud Dajo Massacre, where, early in the 20th century, US soldiers slaughtered 1,000 Filipino Muslims during the Philippine-American War. During the same speech, Duterte claimed that all of the guerrilla fighting and unrest in Mindanao was caused by the Americans and that the conflict would never be resolved as long as they remained.

A few weeks later, to appease the uneasiness and anxiety of the elites, Duterte back-tracked, agreeing to American participation in new military exercises, and even requesting US Naval assistance to fight Islamic terrorist pirates operating in the southern coastal waters. Often, in politics, it isn't what you say, but rather what you do. In fact, under Duterte's presidency, not one of the many military agreements with the US has been violated.

On one hand, Duterte allies himself with the Marcos dynasty, and on the other, with the people of Mindanao, who have been seeking autonomy for decades. Born in Leyte, Duterte lived in Cebu until he was five-years of age, when his father, a popular politician, moved the family to Davao. There, his father's political career blossomed and eventually he was elected as governor of Davao Province.

Rodrigo grew-up with strong nationalistic sentiments, and when he attended university to obtain a law degree, he studied political science under Jose Maria Sison, the founder of the Communist Party of the Philippines. Duterte idolized his mentor. Sison, now seventy-seven, has been living in exile in the Netherlands since 1986, and still refers to Duterte as his old friend. Communicating by messenger and telephone, the two frequently discuss the possibility (yet to be realized) of ending the long civil war being waged by the National People's Army against the Manila government.

Like two ripening peas in a yellowing pod, both Trump and Duterte are adept at saying one thing to this audience, and something else entirely to another.

What's becoming clear in the Philippines is that working brutally to eliminate pushers and addicts has not markedly improved the living conditions of today's impoverished Filipinos.[10]

Being an American who has lived in the Philippines and who married a

229

beautiful Filipina there, I know that most Filipino and American people are basically good and kind, and despite their economic and social problems I remain steadfastly optimistic about their future.

There were two stories that I wanted to tell in this book: the beginnings of American imperialism, and the ongoing saga of our racism. History makes it apparent you seldom get one without the other. In my judgment, except for World War II, the desire for profit, rather than any moralistic or grand principles, has trumped all modern wars in which the United States has been involved.

Back in America, the violent, virulent hatred for African Americans that Fagen's generation faced evolved and moderated. Yet, depending upon which state is being looked at, racism continues to propel the political and economic victimization of selected minorities. Sadly, from time to time the ugliness of savage racial riots still erupts in America's cities. Segregation of US military forces lasted until President Truman changed the policy in 1948. To be sure, there has been progress since then, yet our country continues to wrestle with the same racial conflicts that divided us before we were a nation.

To escape continual victimization at Tampa, Fagen joined the army and fought in Cuba and the Philippines. There he witnessed the oppression and abuse of innocent people by American authorities and soldiers, based entirely upon the color of their skin.

Fagen chose to fight what he could no longer tolerate. In the end, following the primal guerrilla rule that you never attack your enemy until you are sure of winning, Fagen and his extended family retreated forever into the forested mountains of Nueva Ecija.

One cannot help but admire his spirit.

Notes

1. Quote: Boston Post, May 1902 from online: http://www.sfmuseum.net/1906/funston.html.
2. Quote: Letter, Roosevelt to Secretary of War, online Ibid. http://www.sfmuseum.net/1906/funston.html.

3. Quote: Taken from: Professor Gill H. Boehringer, *Imperialist Paranoia and Military Injustice: The Persecution and Redemption of Sergeant Calloway*, http://dialogue21.com/vb/showthread.php?t=7000; 16 pgs. Quote p. 3.
4. Quote extract of Calloway letter from Ibid. p. 4-5.
5. Quote extract from Provost Marshal report, Ibid. p.6.
6. Quote extract from www.ianchadwick.com/essays/cubahistory.html
7. Quote extract 1903, 1905, Ibid.
8. *New York Times,* August 21, 1960, Section III, p.1.
9. Quote extracts from www.rand.org/content/dam/rand/pubs/papers/2008/P2923.pdf; see p. 17, Leland L. Johnson, RAND Corporation, June 1964.
10. See: Online: *An Interview with E. San Juan, jr.* by Andy Piascik, Sri Lanka Guardian, December 17, 2016. http://slguardian.org/2016/12/phillipines-dutertes-killing-fields-peoples-war. Also: *Duterte Always Loved Communists – Except when he was killing them,* by John McBeth, October 19, 2016 Online: http://www.scmp.com/week-asia/geopolitics/article/2038320/duterte-always-loved-communists-except-when-he-was-killing. And *Duterte awaits meeting with Joma Sison,* by Carmela Fonbuena, January 16, 2017; Online: www.rappler.com/nation/135144-jose-maria-sison-home-july.

ACKNOWLEDGMENTS

My heartfelt thanks to the dozens of librarians and research specialists who helped me discover the story of David Fagen. What follows are the names and titles of those whose specialized help and cooperation I will never forget.

Edna Diola-Acena, General Santos City, Philippines, English translations of Filipino documents.

Anne Rosette G. Crelencia, Librarian IV, Filipiniana Division, National Library of the Philippines; also **Ashley Mahiney** and **Manalo Maricel**, NLP.

Rosa Patricia Ospina, Pensacola, English translations of original Spanish language letters and documents from the National Library of the Philippines.

Louise Donahue, my long-time friend and a superbly talented illustrator, graphic artist and designer, for her cover art.

Donna Kinzelman, wife of my dear friend Dr. Matthew Kinzelman, of Destin, Florida, for their encouragement and her editing suggestions.

Paul Harrison, NARA, Washington, D.C., Archives 1 Processing Section. Paul's research into the official records regarding Fagen's military service was foundational to this book. If ever a guy was born to excel at being helpful to pushy writers, Paul is that man.

Sonny San Juan, Jr., Professor Emeritus of Ethnic Studies and Comparative Literature, University of Connecticut; currently professor lecturer, Polytechnic University of the Philippines, and former fellow, W.E.B. Du Bois Institute, Harvard University. Sonny's knowledge of the David Fagen story and Philippine history provided unique and important insights and were a major contribution to the success of this book. A brilliant historian and an outstanding writer in his own right, his many articles and essays on the dynamics of the Philippine-American War are certainly worth a read. I shall always be indebted to Sonny for his gracious encouragement and on-target suggestions. Salamat, my friend.

Rodney Kite-Powell, Saunders Foundation Curator of History, Tampa Bay History Center. A wonderful host who is energetic, friendly, and generous with his time, Rodney is his city's most knowledgeable expert on virtually every aspect of Tampa's development. Many thanks to him and his staff for the many photos they provided from their unique files. Rodney's insights into The Scrub and early Tampa—including a special roof-top tour where he pointed out the boundaries and geography of the young city—helped me understand and feel Fagen's beginnings. For anyone interested in Tampa's history, seeing his interesting and beautiful museum is a must.

Anthony L. Powell, Jr., Historian, Lecturer, Museum Curator. Mr. Powell has the largest collection of photos of Buffalo Soldiers in existence. Many of the photos used in this book, including that of Fagen on the cover, (the only true photo of Fagen that I've found thus far) came from his files. Tony's grandfather was a Buffalo Soldier, so his interest in the history of these black American soldiers comes naturally. On this subject, Anthony Powell's knowledge is unexcelled and his gracious help and encouragement through the course of this work can't be overestimated.

Bill Fletcher Jr., Author, Labor Union activist, former senior staff person of the AFL-CIO, former president of Trans-Africa Forum, a Senior Scholar with the Institute for Policy Studies, and editorial board member of BlackCommentator.com. Bill's friendship and help with the promotion of this book is greatly appreciated.

David Kane and **Franci Ferguson,** my publishers and editors, whose friendship and intellect I value and salute. Their continual encouragement, good humor, and suggestions made writing this book more fun than work. I don't think of these two as partners, or sources, but as family.

Mary Ann Acena-Hoffman, R.N. BSN
The most beautiful, giving, sensitive and loving woman I've ever known. I am one lucky guy. Thanks for putting up with me my love.

Lastly my special thanks to historians **Frank Schubert** and **Michael Robinson**, whose two original articles on Fagen first attracted my attention to his legend.

Phillip W. Hoffman
Pace, Florida

BIBLIOGRAPHY

Principal Sources

The most important sources for this biography were the two historical magazine stories about Fagen written by Michael Robinson and Frank Schubert, General Frederick Funston's book, *Memories of Two Wars, Cuban and Philippine Experiences,* Don Emilio Aguinaldo's *True Version of the Philippine Revolution,* and General Jose Alejandrino's *The Price of Freedom, Episodes and Anecdotes of Our Struggles for Freedom.*

Agoncillo, Teodoro A., Guerrero, Milagros C. *History of the Filipino People,* Fifth Edition, R. P. Garcia Publishing Co., Quezon City, Philippines, 1977.

Aguinaldo, Don Emilio y Famy. *True Version of the Philippine Revolution,* 1899, paperback reprint Valde Books, Lexington, KY, 2012.

Alejandrino, Jose. *The Price of Freedom, Episodes and Anecdotes of Our Struggles for Freedom,* paperback, M. Colcol and Co., Quiappo, Manila, 1999.

Alvarez, General Santiago V. *Recalling the Revolution, Memoirs of a Filipino General,* paperback, Center for Southeast Asian Studies, University of Wisconsin, Monograph Series, 1992.

Caffee, William H., Gavins, Raymond., and Korstad, Robert, editors, *Remembering Jim Crow,* The New Press, New York, N.Y., paperback edition, 2008.

Francia, Luis. *A History of the Philippines,* Overlook Press, Peter Mayer Publishers, New York, N.Y. 2010.

Funston, General Frederick. *Memories of Two Wars, Cuban and Philippine Experiences,* N.Y. Scribners Sons, 1911, paperback reprint, University of Nebraska Press, 2009.

Gatewood, Jr., Willard B. *Negro Troops in Florida, 1898,* Florida Historical Quarterly, Vol XLIX, No. 1, July 1970.

———. *Smoked Yankees, and the Struggle for Empire, 1898-1902,* University of Arkansas Press, Fayetteville, 1987.

Hurley, Vic. *Jungle Patrol, the Story of the Philippine Constabulary, 1901-1936,* paperback reprint, Cerberus Books, Oregon, 2011.

Ingalls, Robert P. *Urban Vigilantes in the New South,* University of Tennessee Press, paperback edition, reprint, University Press of Florida, Gainesville, 1993.

Kramer, Paul A. *The Blood of Government,* University of North Carolina Press, paperback, 2000.

Linn, Brian McAllister. *The Philippine War, 1899-1902,* paperback, University Press of Kansas, 2000.

Morris, Edmund. *The Rise and Fall of Theodore Roosevelt,* Random House Trade Paperback, New York, N. Y., 2010.

Muller, Captain William G. *The Twenty Fourth Infantry, U.S. Army Regimental Record,* 1923, paperback reprint, Old Army Press, Ft. Collins, Colorado, 1972.

Oshinsky, David M. *Worse than Slavery,* Free Press, N.Y., paperback edition 1997.

Pomeroy, William. *The Forest,* Seven Seas Publishers, Berlin, 1965.

Powell, J. C. *The American Siberia, or Fourteen Years' Experience in a Southern Convict Camp,* H. J. Smith and Co., Philadelphia, 1891.

Ramsey, Edwin Price, and Rivele, Stephen J. *Lieutenant Ramsey's War,* 1990, paperback reprint, First Brassey's Five Star Co., 1996.

Robinson, Michael, and Schubert, Frank. *Seeking David Fagen: The Search for a Black Rebel's Florida Roots,* Tampa Bay History, 2008, Vol 22, pp. 19-34.

———. *David Fagen: An Afro-American Rebel in the Philippines, 1899-1901,* Pacific Historical Review, XLIV (Feb. 1975) pp. 68-73.

Schurman, Jacob Gould. *Philippine Affairs, a Retrospect and Outlook,* Charles Scribner's Sons, New York, N.Y. 1902.

Scott, Edward Van Zile. *The Unwept, Black American Soldiers and the Spanish-American War,* Black Belt Press, Montgomery, Alabama, 1996.

Skillen, Don. *Magdolo – The Story of Emilio Aguinaldo: Revolutionary Hero of the Philippines,* Publish America, Baltimore, 2006.

The Spanish American War, a Collection of Documents Related to the Squadron

Operations in the West Indies, Office of Naval Intelligence, Washington, D.C. Government Printing Office, 1899.

Steward, T. G. *The Colored Regulars of the United States Army,* Philadelphia, 1904, paperback reprint, Forgotten Books, Lexington, KY 2012.

Titherington, Richard H. *A History of the Spanish-American War of 1898,* D. Appleton and Co., N.Y., 1900. Paperback reprint, Bibliolife, Charleston, S.C. 2010.

Vivencio, Jose. *Rise and Fall of Antonio Luna,* University of the Philippines, Quezon City, 1972.

Zinn, Howard. *A People's History of the U.S.,* Harper Collins Publishers, N.Y., 1999, reprint paperback Harper Perennial Modern Classics, New York, N.Y. 2005.

Index

10th Cavalry Regiment, 18, 29, 36, 43, 69-70, 111-112, 114
14th Infantry Regiment, 45
1st Cavalry Volunteers (Rough Riders), 63, 69, 111
1st Nebraska Volunteers, 124
20th Kansas Volunteers, 34, 136
23rd Kansas Regiment (U.S.C.T.), 68
24th Infantry Regiment (U.S.C.T.), 2, 18, 26, 36-37, 39-40, 42-44, 47, 50, 59, 71-72, 75, 78, 81-84, 102-103, 107-108, 112, 114, 116, 124, 127, 151, 155, 157, 161, 164, 180, 209, 211, 220, 222-223
24th Infantry Regiment (U.S.C.T.) (p), 82, 100, 154
25th Infantry Regiment (U.S.C.T.), 2, 18, 26, 39, 43-46, 64, 81, 108, 111, 156-157
2nd Georgia Volunteer Infantry, 39
2nd Massachusetts Volunteers, 45
71st New York Infantry Regiment, 114
8th Illinois Regiment, 68
9th Cavalry Regiment (U.S.C.T.), 18, 26-27, 63, 112, 115
9th Cavalry Regiment (U.S.C.T.) (p), 17
A.M.E. Church Review, 132
Abiendo, Sinsorco, 209
Abu Sayyaf, 227
Adams, L.F., 136
African-American deserters join the Philippine forces, 173

Aguinaldo releases political prisoners, 149
Aguinaldo, Baldomero, 180, 182-183
Aguinaldo, Emilio, 117-121, 123, 133, 135, 137, 142, 145-151, 161-164, 172, 180-184, 187, 189, 191, 193-196, 198-200, 203, 218-219
capture of, 196
Aguinaldo, Emilio (p), 185, 197-198
Alamo (steamship), 75
Alejandrino, Jose, 172, 179-180, 183, 196, 203-204, 206, 212-213
Alfonso XII (Spanish cruiser), 24
Alger, Russell Alexander, 90-91, 105-107
Alhambra, Nazario, 195
Almirante Oquendo, 91, 93
Alstaetter, Frederick W., 177-178, 209
American Civil War, 2, 6-7, 11, 30-31, 40, 42
American victory at Santiago, Cuba, 121
An Afro-American Rebel in the Philippines (Robinson, Schubert), 175
Anti-Lynch and Mob Club, 16
anti-war protests in Washington, DC, 121
Apalachicola River, 7
Atchison, Topeka and Santa Fe Railroad, 32

INDEX

Auger, A.A., 104
Baldwin, Frank D., 203
Ball, Robert V., 142
Bancroft (gunboat), 50
Banes Harbor, 54
Barcelona, Santiago, 195-196
Barreto, Alberto, 147
Barry, E.B., 186
Bartolome, Anastacio, 207, 208, 209, 210, 212, 213
Batista, Fulgencio, 225
Bato, Dionisio, 195
Batson, Matthew A., 158
Benevolent Assimilation Decree, 133-134
Bernal, Jose, 150
Beveridge, Albert, 122
Biak-na-bato, pact of, 119
Bilibid Military Prison, 223
Black Codes, Florida, 7-8
Blanco, Ramon, 1st Marquis of Pena Plata, 51, 80, 88-89, 93
Blankart, Magdalene, 175
The Blood of Government: "The heart of the United States' (Kramer), 151
Blue, Ila Jacuth, 6
Bonifacio, Andres, 151
Bonsal, Stephen, 111, 156
Boston Post, 218
Brigada Lacuna,
  see Lacuna Brigade
Brooklyn, 91, 95, 98
Brown, D.T., 84
Brown, Edward, 130
Bryan, William Jennings, 121, 164
Bryant, Dorcas, 37
Bryant, Samuel, 37
Bud Dajo Massacre, 229
Buencamino, Felipe Siojo, 147-149, 151

Buffalo Soldiers, 2, 18, 25, 38, 40, 67-68, 104, 112-113, 124, 130, 151, 214, 221, 223, 227
Buffalo Soldiers (p), 17, 160
Bustamonte, Joaquin, 88
Cabiness, C.N., 209
Cabrera, Rafael, 30
Cadhit, Gregorio, 190, 195
Cailles, Juan Kauppama, 120, 206
Calloway, Juanita, 223
Calloway, John W., 3, 220-222, 224
Calloway, Mamerta de la Rosa, 221, 223
Camp Wikoff, 108
Capron, Allyn, 70
"Captain Emilio", alias of Frederick Funston, 182
Carnegie, Andrew, 121
Carr, Carroll B., 112
Casiguran Bay, 189
Castillo, Demetrio, 57, 60, 64-67, 69
Castro, Fidel, 224-225
  death of, 226
Castro, Raul, 225
Cebreco, Agustin, 60
Cebreco, Jose Candelario, 92
Cervera, Pascual, 51-52, 79-81, 88-89, 91, 93
Cervera, Pascual (p), 93
Chadwick, French E., 94
Churchill, Winston, 25
City of Washington (American liner), 24, 42, 44, 50, 52, 59, 72, 119
Cleveland Gazette, 26, 115, 130, 156
Cleveland, Grover, 24-25
Collins, Joab "Abe", 29
The Colored Regulars (Steward), 43
Conch (Gov't transport No. 14), 45
Conn, John R., 71, 78, 81-83, 86-87, 130

239

INDEX

Constitution of Cuba, 224
Consunji, Don Antonio, 221-222
Consunji, Tomas, 221
Cordin, C.W., 157
Corliss, R.C., 207-210, 212-213
Cornell University, 135
Cowboy Scouts, 173
Creelman, James, 142
Cristobal Colon, 91
Cromwell, Mrs. J.W., 78
Cuba
  Aserrederos, 52, 54, 56-57, 75
  Aserrederos (p), 53
  Baire, 92
  Banes, 54
  Boniato, 87
  Cabanas, 59-60
  Camaguey Province, 30
  Cubitas, 77, 87
  Daiquiri, 59-61, 63-65, 79
  Daiquiri (p), 67
  El Caney, 7, 81, 85, 946
  El Caney (p), 77
  Guantanamo, 52, 54
  Havana, 24, 52, 80, 88, 105
  Havana Harbor, 22
  Holguin, 94
  Las Guasimas, 65-66, 71, 78, 111
  Manzanillo, 77, 79, 92
  Marianaje, 76
  Palma, 92
  Playa Del Este, 93
  Quinta de Doucureau, 87
  Salado, 75
  San Juan, 44, 76-77, 82, 86-87, 89-91, 94
  San Juan Hill, 76-77
  San Luis, 87
  San Vicente, 87
  Santiago, 34, 52, 54, 56-57, 60, 75-77, 80, 84, 86, 88-90, 92, 98-99, 101, 105, 108, 121, 154, 226
  Santiago (p), 53
  Sardinero, 90
  Siboney, 64-66, 71-72, 75-76, 79, 87, 90, 100-103, 105, 107-108, 155
  Siboney (p), 69, 95
Cuban Fair, Madison Square Garden (1896), 29
Cuban soldiers aid Americans in capture of the City of Santiago, 54
Cuban torture of Spanish captives, 68
Dalrymple, John, 173
Davis, Richard Harding, 70, 107
Davis, Varina, 137
Day, Richard C., 174-175
de las Alas, Severino, 148
del Pilar, Gregorio, 147
del Pilar, Gregorio (p), 168
Dewey, George, 52, 117-120, 126, 133
Dingalan Bay, 209
Dodge, Charles, Jr., 107
Domingo, Dionicio, 208
Domingo, Juan, 207
Douglas, Jim
  brother of DF, 5, 12
Du Bois, W.E.B., 2-3
DuBose, Edmond, 173
Duterte, Rodrigo, 227-229
  childhood of, 229
El Caney, battle of, 43, 76-77, 82-83, 111
El Deposito (waterworks), 155, 161, 220
El Pozo Hill, 76, 81, 85, 90, 94, 98, 105
Erb, Frank M., 126

INDEX

escalating conflict between Aguinaldo and Luna, 147
Escario (Garcia), Federico, 92
Estrada, Francisco, 92
Evans, S.T., 130
Fagen, Alice
   sister of DF, 5, 12
Fagen, Charles
   brother of DF, 5
Fagen, David
   $600 bounty for his capture, 207
   aboard *City of Washington*, 119
   arrives in Manila aboard the *Zeelandia*, 151
   as a teenager, 14
   as phosphate miner, 16
   as U.S. Army recruit, 38
   assigned to Fort Douglas, 115
   birth of, 3
   bullied in camp, 161
   conditions onboard *City of Washington*, 52
   considers desertion and defection, 164
   Court-Martials, 161
   death of mother, 12
   decides against staying with Guerilla's after Lacuna surrenders, 206
   description of his alleged capture and murder, 210
   deserts U.S. Army with stolen horse, revolvers & ammunition, 165
   early childhood in "the Scrub", 13
   enlists in U.S. Army, 36
   escapes American soldiers through hut window, 173
   escapes to mountains with his followers, 204
   fights in Battle of El Caney, 81
   guarding San Juan Hill, 85
   has encounter with Funston at the Penaranda River, 180
   illiterate, 29
   inducted into Philippine National Army of Liberation as an officer, 167
   Lacuna determined that if DF will be court martialed if surrendered, 205
   leads ambush, 174
   learns prerequisites of enlistment, 29
   learns Spanish and Tagalog, 168
   lives in camp with a woman, 173
   makes contact with Filipino insurgents, 165
   marches to Intramuros with unit, 154
   marriage to Maggie Washington, 16
   outspoken protester of treatment of Buffalo Soldiers, 114
   physical description of as young man, 16
   physical description of at time of enlistment, 37
   promoted to Captain, 179
   question as to validity of DF's capture and murder, 213
   receives honorable discharge from US Army, 123
   re-enlists in US Army at Fort McPherson, 124
   report of his capture and murder, 208
   returns to burned town of Siboney, 103
   signs enlistment papers with an "X", 37

trained to shoot his weapon, 75
trains guerilla fighters, 171
travels south from UT by rail, 124
travels to the PI, 127
uncertainty of DFs deployment to Cuba, 42
unit receives orders to disembark, 72
unit withdraws from San Juan Ridge to mouth of Santiago Bay, 95

Fagen, George
   brother of DF, 5
Fagen, Joseph
   brother of DF, 5
Fagen, Louisa
   sister of DF, 5, 12
Fagen, Maggie (Washington)
   wife of DF, 16
Fagen, Samuel, 10
   father of DF, 3-6, 8-11
Fagen, Sylvia (Douglas)
   mother of DF, 3-5, 9, 12
Fagen, William
   brother of DF, 5
Fairfield Journal of Maine, 136
Farquhar, Percival, 116
Fernandez, Elisio, 207-209
Filipino National Flag, 119
Filipino psychological warfare toward Buffalo Soldiers, 163
Fish, Hamilton, 70
Florida
   Columbia County, 7
   Dunnellon, 15
   Gainesville, 7
   Hillsborough County, 5
   Jackson County, 7
   Key West, 13-14, 27
   Lakeland, 29, 36
   Live Oak, 11-12
   Miami, 14
   Tampa, 124
   Tampa - "the Scrub", 3-4, 9, 12-14, 16, 18, 29, 35, 38, 47, 114
   Tampa - cigar manufacturing, 13
   Tampa - discovery of phosphate, 13
   Tampa - life for negroes post American Civil War, 7
   Tampa - lynching deaths, 14
   Tampa - military troops in, 21
   Tampa - phosphate mining, 14
   Tampa - population explosion, 13
   Tampa - race riots, 2, 38
   Tampa - racism, 27-28
   Tampa - USCT recruiting operations, 35
   Ybor City, 1, 13-14
Foner, Philip, 116
Forbes Drug Store, 29
The Forest (Pomeroy), 170
Fort Brooke, 1
Fort D.A. Russell, 115
Fort Douglas, 59, 115-116, 124
Fort McPherson, 39, 124
Fortuna, Feliciano, 207-209
The Freeman, 130
Freeman, H.B., 222
frustration over treatment of Buffalo Soldiers, 113
Funston, Edward Hogue, 31
Funston, Eva, 125-126
Funston, Frederick, 29-34, 52, 125, 136-137, 141, 173, 175, 177-183, 185-188, 190-194, 196, 200, 203-204, 206, 211-212, 218-219
Funston, Frederick (p), 30, 185
Furor (destroyer), 91

INDEX

Galloway, John W., 130, 133, 161, 162
Ganzhorn, Jack, 173-175, 178
Garcia, Calixto Ramon de Ineguez, 52-58, 61, 75-78, 86, 89, 91, 98-100, 121, 123
  self-inflicted wound to head, 53
Garcia, Calixto Ramon de Ineguez(p), 53
Gatewood, Willard B., Jr., 27, 38, 155-156
Givens, William, 114
Gomez, Maximo, 57, 64, 99
Gompers, Samuel, 121
Gonzaga, Gracio, 147
Goodrich, Caspar Frederick, 112
Grant (transport ship), 223
Grant, Ulysses S., 42
Gray, Edward, 163, 164
Grayson, William W., 124-125
Greenleaf, Charles R., 101-103
Guaimaro, battle of, 31
Guantanamo Bay, 224
Guasimas, battle of, 106
Habiendo, Sinsorco, 207-208
Hall, John F., 136-137
Hallock, Leroy, 159
Hartley and Graham (firearms dealer), 30
Havana Street Railway, 116
Hay, John, 25, 146
Haya, Ignacio, 13-14
Hazzard, Oliver P.M., 184
Hazzard, Oliver P.M. (p), 185
Hazzard, Russell T., 184
Hazzard, Russell T. (p), 185
Hearst, William Randolph, 70
Hicks, William, 37
Hillsborough River, 14
Holliday, Presley, 43

Hose, Sam, 163-164
Howze, Robert Lee, 113
Hukabalahap "Huks", 226-227
Hull's Phosphate Company, 16, 37
Hunter, Fred, 173
I've Killed Men (Ganzhorn), 174
The Illinois Record, 36
illness among Cuban/American soldiers, 100-101, 103, 105
Ilocano, 209
Ilongot, 191-192
Ilongot (p), 192
Indiana (battleship), 95, 98
Indianapolis Freeman, 211
Indianapolis Recorder, 130
Infanta Maria Teresa (Spanish flagship), 79, 87, 91
Infanta Maria Teresa (Spanish flagship) (p), 93
Iowa, 91
Japan takes control of PI, 226
Jim Crow rules (laws), 5, 18
Johnson, James, 29
Johnson, Leland L., 225
Jose, Vivencio, 147
Katipunan Society, 151
Kawit Company, 150
Kelly, C.D., 62
Kent, Jacob Ford, 83
Kettle Hill, 76, 81, 83, 85-86, 89, 112
Kipling, Rudyard, 131-132
Kirby, C.D., 63
Kirkpatrick, L.J., 36
Knight, Clarke, 10
Kramer, Paul A., 151
Lacuna Brigade, 167, 173, 184, 203
Lacuna, Urbano, 167-168, 172, 174, 176-178, 180-181, 183, 189, 196, 203-206, 210, 212

243

INDEX

LaGarde, Louis Anatole, 102, 107
Las Guasimas, battle of, 65, 71, 114
Lawton, Henry W., 64-65, 81-82, 89, 111, 140, 147, 162
Leavell, B.H., 43-44
Leedy, John W., 33
Lewis, John E., 36, 114
Linares, Arsenio, 52, 79-80, 86
Linn, Brian, 121
Lucas, Willie Ann, 9
Ludlow, William, 75
Luna, Antonio Novicio, 137, 139, 142, 145-151
Luna, Antonio Novicio, assassination of, 150
Mabini, Apolinario, 146-147
Macabebe Scouts, 158-159, 184, 186-187, 190-191, 193-196
Macabebe Scouts (p), 158, 185, 198
MacArthur, Arthur, 141-142, 147, 151, 186, 198, 204, 215
MacArthur, Douglas, 151, 215
USS *Maine*, 22, 24, 32, 46, 109, 115
USS *Maine* (p), 23
Malolos, battle of, 141, 146, 148
Manila Bay, 52, 118-120, 125, 133, 137, 187, 223
Manila, battle of, 126, 133
Manila-Dagupan Railway, 139, 155
Marching to Cuba (ballad), 21-22
Marcos, Ferdinand, 229
Markley, A.C., 103-105, 107-108
Marrow, Anthony A., 37
Marshall, Edward, 70
Martí, José, 14
Mascardo, Tomas Echenique, 148, 183
Mason, Patrick, 130
McClernand, John Alexander, 90
McClure's Magazine, 131

McFarland, Howard, 136
McKay, D.B., 10
McKinley, William, 25, 90, 99, 105-106, 117, 121, 127, 131, 133-135, 137, 218
Memories of Two Wars (Funston), 33, 177, 210
Mercedes (Spanish cruiser) (p), 92
USS *Merrimac*, 94
Merritt, Wesley, 120-121
Metcalf, Wilder, 126, 136
Miles, Nelson A., 35, 43, 54, 98-99, 102, 109
military punishment
  spread eagle, 161
  hanging act, 161
Miller, Orville H., 124-125
Mitchell, Burton I., 174, 184, 194
Mitchell, Burton I. (p), 185
Moore, Preston, 130
Moro Castle (p), 58
Moro Rebellion, 215
Morris, Edmund, 106-107
Mount Arayat, 167
Mount Sinai African Methodist Episcopal Zion Church, 37
Muller, William G., 42
National People's Army, 229
Native American Tribes, 16, 133
Nebraska Avenue Carpenter Shop, 37
negro soldiers bond with Filipino community, 156
Negro Troops in Florida, 1898 (Gatewood), 27
The New Age, 43
New Jersey
  Weehawken, 115
New York, 98
  Brooklyn, 114

244

INDEX

Montauk Point, 108, 109, 114, 115
New York Herald, 70, 107, 111, 179
New York Journal, 70
New York Times, 177, 224
USS *New York*, 52, 57
Newton, Harry W., 184
Newton, Harry W. (p), 185
Nigger War, 133, 151, 164
Nueces (transport ship), 108-109
Obama, Barack, 225
Ohio Volunteers, 1-2, 39
Omaha Daily Bee, 124
Orizaba (steamship), 75
Oshinsky, David M., 11
Otis, Elwell Stephen, 135, 139-141, 146-147, 159, 162
"Pagain", Filipino nickname for DF, 167
Paget, Alfred W., 51
Palanan Bay, 191
Paras, Thomas, 221
Pasig River, 126
Paterno, Pedro, 147-149, 151
Paz, Juan, 150
Penaranda River, 179
pest camp (hospital), 102-105, 107
Philippine National Army of Liberation, 120, 135, 138, 145, 151, 167-168
Philippine Islands
  Albay Province, 173
  Angeles, 149
  Arayat, 164-165, 177, 203
  Bacoor, 140
  Bayambang, 148
  Bongabong, 207, 209-210, 212
  Cabanatuan, 145, 147, 149-150, 165
  Cabiao, 165
  Caloocan, 125, 155
  Calumpit, 148, 158
  Casiguran, 189-190
  Cavite Province, 183
  Cebu, 229
  Davao, 228-229
  Dinundungan, 193-194
  Gapon, 174
  Intramuros, Manila, 154
  Isabela Province, 180
  Leyte, 229
  Liclab, Nueva Ecija, 150
  Luzon, 118, 122, 135, 137, 169, 173, 180, 183, 203, 214
  Macabebe, 158
  Malibay, 145
  Malolos, 139, 141-142
  Manacling, 174
  Manila, 120, 132, 139-140, 145, 147, 155, 162, 207, 220, 223
  Marikina, 145, 155
  Mexico, 164, 220
  Mindanao, 227-229
  Mindoro, 214-215
  Nueva Ecija, 146, 165, 167, 181, 187, 189, 194, 196, 204, 207, 210, 212-213, 221, 224, 230
  Palanan, 180-183, 187, 191, 193-194, 200, 203-204
  Pantabangan, 180-181
  Papaya, 204
  Penaranda, 174
  Prayal Cabiel, 220
  San Fernando, 149, 161-162, 164, 207, 220
  San Isidro, 146, 165, 174, 176, 178-179, 181, 186, 204-205, 220
  Santa Ana, 164, 220

245

INDEX

Santa Cruz, Laguna Province (p), 206
Santa Rosa, 221
Santos Bongabong, Nueva Ecija, 207
Tarlac, 150
Tayug, Pangasinan, 222
Victoria, Laguna, 150
Yrurulong/Yururulong, 208-209
Philippine Islands, annexation of, 116
Philippine Islands, purchase of, 116
Philippine National Police, 228
Philippine Organic Act (1902), 227
Philippine Republic Congressional vote for peace, 147
Philippine-American War, 124, 170, 180-181, 229
phosphate industry in Florida, 13-15
Pioneer Florida, 10
Placido, Hilario Tal, 190-191, 193-195
Plant, Henry B., 13
Platt, Orville, 224
Pluton (destroyer), 91
Pointer, Ann, 10
Pomeroy, William, 170
Port Tampa Bay, 42
Pratt, E. Spencer, 118
President McKinley explains acquisition of Philippine Islands, 122
Price of Freedom (Alejandrino), 203
Prioleau, George W., 27, 115
proclamation to the Filipino people by Aguinaldo, 198
Pullen, Frank W., Jr., 46, 64
Ramon de Las Yaguas Brigade, 57
Remembering Jim Crow (Chafe, Gavins, Korstad), 6, 8-10

Remey, George Collier, 186
Richmond Planet, 130, 162, 220
Rio Chico Pampanga River (stream), 172, 174
Rio Grande de Mindanao, 165
The Rise and Fall of Antonio Luna (Jose), 147
Roberts, W.B., 68
Robinson, Michael C., 160-161, 175, 212
Roman, Francisco, 32, 149-151
Roman, Francisco, death of, 150
Roosevelt, Theodore, Jr., 25, 50, 63-64, 70-71, 101, 105-106, 109, 112, 117, 131, 219, 223
Roque, Roman, 184
Rough Riders, 50, 63, 69, 70-71, 78, 101, 106, 109, 112, 114
Rusca, Eduardo, 150
Russell, Lewis, 173
Sage, Russell, 25
Saguntum, siege of, 83
Sampson, William T., 51-52, 54-58, 62, 76, 94
San Francisco Call, 140
San Juan Hill, battle of, 43-44, 76-77, 82-87, 104, 106, 115
San Juan Hill, battle of (p), 82
San Juan Ridge, 95
San Juan River, 78, 83, 90
San Juan, battle of, 112
Sanchez, Francisco, 87
Sandico, Teodoro, 180
Santiago Bay, 51-52, 54, 59-60, 91, 95
Santiago Harbor, 22, 51, 55-56, 58, 94
Santiago Harbor (p), 58, 93
Santiago, battle of, 57-58, 68, 92, 94-95, 112, 116

INDEX

Santiago, battle of (p), 65, 84
Santos, Don Clemente, 204
Santos, Teodorico, 163
Saragossa, battle of, 83
The Saturday Review, 25
Schubert, Frank N., 14, 37, 49, 160-161, 175, 212
Schurman Commission, 147-148
Schurman, Jacob Gould, 135, 145-147
Scranton Tribune, 211
Seeking David Fagen (Schubert), 14
Segismundo, Cecilio, 181-184, 186-187, 190, 194
Segovia, Lazaro, 182, 184, 186, 190-191, 193-196
Seguranca (ward liner), 50-51
Seneca (steamship), 75
Shafter, William R., 34-35, 39-40, 42, 50-51, 55-58, 64-66, 75-78, 81, 85-90, 94-95, 98-103, 105-107
Shafter, William R. (p), 34
Sherman, John, 121
Sherman, William T., 42
Shores, Garth, 173
Shurman, Jacob Gould, 147
Siboney, burning of, 103
Sickles, Daniel E., 30
Sierra Madre Mountains, 180, 183
Sierra Maestra (mountain range), 54
Sigbee, Charles, 24
Sison, Jose Maria, 229
Smith, E.V., 182
Smith, H.C., 26
Smoked Yankees and the Struggle for Empire (Gatewood), 155
The Souls of Black Folk (Du Bois), 3
South Florida Railroad, 13
Spanish-American War, 16, 21, 113

St. Johns, Lake Eustis and Gulf Railroad Company, 11
Stewart, Rev. T.G., 43, 108
Summit of the Americas (Panama), 225
Sunland Tribune, 10
Suwannee River, 7
Taft, William H., 223
Tagalog, 127, 135, 158-159, 168, 173, 207, 210
Tagalogs, 159
Tampa Bay, 4-5, 15, 17, 50
Tampa Board of Trade, 13
Tampa Harbor, 35
Tampa Harbor (p), 41
Tampa Morning Tribune, 1, 18, 39
Taylor, J.D., 180-182
Tayman, Charles E., 37
Tecson, Pablo, 175, 180, 183
Tillman, Ben, 121
Titherington, Richard H., 49, 83
Toral, Jose, 86, 89-90, 94-95, 98
  will not surrender troops, 90
torture, "water cure", 159-160
Treaty of Paris (1898), 53, 133, 135, 137, 179
Truman, Harry S., 230
Trump, Donald, 227, 229
Turner, James B., 165
Twain, Mark, 121, 179
U.S. executions of Filipinos, 170
U.S. Sovereignty over Cuba, Puerto Rico, Guam & PI, 116
Umiray River, 207-209
United Fruit Company, 224
United States Census (1870), 5
United States Census (1880), 9
United States Colored Troops (U.S.C.T.), 2, 18, 21, 35
Unwelcome homecoming for Buffalo

247

Soldiers, 115
Vara del Rey (y Rubio), Joaquin, 83
Ventus, Manuel, 177-178
Vicksburg (gunboat), 186-189, 191
Vicksburg (gunboat) (p), 187-188, 197-198
Victor, William, 173
Villa, Simon, 150, 193, 195-196
Vizcaya, 91, 93
Washington Bee, 132
Washington Evening Star, 130
Wasp (armed yacht), 50
Wheaton, Loyd, 186, 207, 210
Wheeler, Joseph "Fighting Joe", 66-67, 86
White Man's Burden: The United States and the Philippine Islands (Kipling), 131
Whitman, F.H., 126
Wildman, Edwin, 219
Williams, Arthur, 222
Wilson, Woodrow, 220
Wood, Leonard, 69-70, 224
Worse than Slavery (Oshinsky), 11
Ybor, Vincente Martinez, 13-14
yellow fever in camps, 78, 101-103, 105-106, 109
Young, John, 29
Young, Samuel Baldwin Marks, 66, 69-70, 161-162, 164
Yucatan, 50, 64
Zeelandia (steamer), 127, 130, 151
Zialcita, Lorenzo, 147
Zinn, Howard, 25, 126

ABOUT THE AUTHOR

Phillip W. Hoffman wrote TV shows for *Combat!* and other dramatic TV series during the 1960s. The writer also spent nine years teaching a writing class at the late Jay Silverheel's Indian Actor's Workshop in Los Angeles. His first non-fiction book, *Simon Girty Turncoat Hero*, required eighteen years of research and changed both Canadian and American perspectives on early America's most vilified and notorious frontier character of the Revolutionary War. In addition to his writing merits, Hoffman is an award winning, world renowned cutlery designer whose original Lakota knives were accepted into the Permanent Design Collection of the Museum of Modern Art in New York City. He lives with his RN wife Mary Ann, and three dogs, in Pace, Florida.

www.ingramcontent.com/pod-product-compliance
Lightning Source LLC
Chambersburg PA
CBHW070609170426
43200CB00012B/2638